SHAKESPEARE'S
WINDOW INTO THE SOUL

OTHER BOOKS BY MARTIN LINGS

The Book of Certainty: The Sufi Doctrine of Faith, Vision & Gnosis

A Sufi Saint of the Twentieth Century: Shaikh Aḥmad al-ʿAlawī

Ancient Beliefs and Modern Superstitions

What is Sufism?

The Qur'anic Art of Calligraphy and Illumination

Muhammad: His Life Based on the Earliest Sources

Collected Poems

The Eleventh Hour: The Spiritual Crisis of the Modern World in the Light of Tradition and Prophecy

Symbol and Archetype: A Study of the Meaning of Existence

SHAKESPEARE'S
WINDOW INTO THE SOUL

*The Mystical Wisdom in
Shakespeare's Characters*

MARTIN LINGS

Foreword by
H.R.H. THE PRINCE OF WALES

Inner Traditions
Rochester, Vermont

Inner Traditions
One Park Street
Rochester, Vermont 05767
www.InnerTraditions.com

Originally published in 1966 in the United Kingdom by Allen and Unwin and in the
    United States by Humanities Press, under the title *Shakespeare in the Light of Sacred Art*
Second edition published in 1984 in the United Kingdom by Aquarian Press Limited
    and in the United States by Inner Traditions, under the title *The Secret of Shakespeare*
Third edition, revised and expanded, published in 1996 in the United Kingdom by
    Quinta Essentia
Fourth edition published in 1998 in the United States by Inner Traditions, under the
    title *The Sacred Art of Shakespeare*
Fifth edition published in 2006 in the United States by Inner Traditions, under the title
    Shakespeare's Window into the Soul

The Library of Congress has cataloged a previous edition of this title as follows:
Lings, Martin.
        The sacred art of Shakespeare : to take upon us the mystery of
things / Martin Lings ; with a foreword by H.R.H. The Prince of Wales. —
1st U.S. ed.
            p.   cm.
        Rev. ed. of: The secret of Shakespeare. 3rd ed., rev. and enlarged. 1996
        Includes bibliographical references and index.
        ISBN 0-89281-717-8 (paper)
            1. Shakespeare, William 1564–1616—Criticism and interpretation.
        2. Religious drama, English—History and criticism. 3. Shakespeare, William,
        1564–1616—Religion. 4. Holy, The, in literature. 5. Religion and literature.
        I. Lings, Martin. Secret of Shakespeare. II. Title.
PR2976.L4651998   98-31015
822.3'3—dc21   CIP

ISBN of current title *Shakespeare's Window into the Soul:*
        ISBN-10: 1-59477-120-0
        ISBN-13: 978-1-59477-120-0

Printed and bound in the United States by Lake Book Manufacturing, Inc.

10 9 8 7 6 5 4 3 2 1

This book was typeset in Minion with Trajan and Isadora as the display typefaces

CONTENTS

FOREWORD

BY H.R.H. THE PRINCE OF WALES

I am delighted that it has proved possible to publish a new edition of Dr. Martin Lings's remarkable book. It is a book which seeks to interpret to a wider audience the profound wisdom that is contained within the symbolism of certain plays of Shakespeare. As such it is a book which I found hard to put down as it is clearly written from an intimate, personal awareness of the meaning of the symbols that Shakespeare uses to describe the inner drama of the journey of the soul contained, as it is, within the outer earthly drama of the plays.

The trouble, of course, with writing anything about Shakespeare is that so many other people have done the same, and will continue to do so for generations. Every conceivable theory about the meaning of his plays, about their authenticity, and about their author seems to have been aired at one time or another. Some are more esoteric than others and, I daresay, that Dr. Lings's book has been, and will be, seen as too esoteric for many people's comfort.

Whatever the case, the author's perceptive insight into that other realm of human experience will assuredly strike harmonious chords in *some* people's hearts and may open for them a door hidden in a corner of their being of which they may not have been aware. It may also transform their understanding and appreciation of Shakespeare's plays and of his intuitive genius for comprehending that the true significance of our earthly existence lies within the context of the greater inner odyssey which we are called upon to perform.

THE EARL OF GLOSTER [*blind*]
> The trick of that voice I do well remember.
> Is't not the king . . . O, let me kiss that hand.

KING LEAR [*mad*]
> Let me wipe it first; it smells of mortality.

> *King Lear,* IV, 6, 109–37

PREFACE

Shakespeare has been defined more than once as "the most famous writer in the world." Admittedly, fame does not coincide with excellence; but he is by common consent—we might even say international consent—a dramatist who has never been surpassed, and in addition to his dramatic poetry, parts of which are highly lyrical, he is also supreme as a lyric poet in the double capacity of song-writer and sonneteer, while in a totally different domain he is a by-word as a portrayer of character, achieving by a few brilliant strokes of the pen what most novelists fail to achieve in a full-length novel. But to say all this, if it were merely this, would be to fall far short of his due; for wherever a certain level has been reached in art there are two greatnesses to be considered, not only that of the artist but also that of the man himself.

Shakespeare's greatness as an artist lies above all in the total impact that each of his best plays makes upon us when acted. But being a synthesis, this impact is not easily put into words; and once the curtain is down and we have left the theater, what is said or written tends to do little justice to what we have experienced, and seems unable to account for it.

This book is much concerned with the mystery of the total impact, and this question is not without bearing on Shakespeare's greatness as a man—a greatness that, we maintain, is unmistakably visible through the semi-transparent veil of his plays.

CHAPTER ONE

SACRED ART

In the last few decades there has been a considerable increase of interest in the Middle Ages, which is no doubt partly due to a reaction of the times, but it is also, much more, a case of ignorance giving way to knowledge. In another sense, it is simply a rising to the surface of something that has always been there and is always being rediscovered. Could it not be said that wherever the Middle Ages have not ceased to be accessible, wherever despite the barrier of the Renaissance they have always remained with us, as in the poetry of Dante, for instance, or—to take a more immediately accessible and inescapable example—as in their architecture, their superiority has always been felt at heart? This feeling implies also, if only subconsciously, the acknowledgment of a more general superiority, for it is quite impossible that the great Norman and Gothic cathedrals should have sprung from an age that had no inward excellence to correspond to these superlative outward manifestations.

One of the particular reasons for the present increase of interest in the Middle Ages is in itself highly significant: during the last fifty years Europeans have taken much more interest in the art of other civilizations than ever before, and this has no doubt uprooted many prejudices and opened the door to a certain freshness and objectivity of judgment. Having come to know some of the best examples of Hindu, Chinese, and Japanese art

1

and then as it were returning to their own civilization, many people find that their outlook has irrevocably changed. After looking at a great Chinese landscape, for example, where this world appears like a veil of illusion beyond which, almost visibly, lies the Infinite and Eternal Reality, or after having been given a glimpse of that same Reality through a statue of the Buddha, they find it difficult to take seriously a painting such as Raphael's famous Madonna, or Michelangelo's fresco of the Creation, not to speak of his sculpture, and Leonardo also fails to satisfy them. But they find that they *can* take very seriously, more seriously than before, some of the early Sienese paintings such as Simone Martini's Annunciation, for example, or the statuary and stained glass of Chartres Cathedral, or the twelfth- and thirteenth-century mosaics in St. Mark's at Venice, or the icons of the Orthodox Church.

The reason why medieval art can bear comparison with Oriental art as no other Western art can is undoubtedly because the medieval outlook, like that of the Oriental civilizations, was intellectual. It considered this world above all as the shadow or symbol of the next, man as the shadow or symbol of God; and such an attitude, to be operative, presupposes the presence of intellectuals, for earthly things can only be referred back to their spiritual archetypes through the faculty of intellectual perception, the insight that pierces through the symbol to the transcendent reality that lies beyond. In the theocratic civilizations, if an artist himself was not an intellectual, he nonetheless obeyed the canons of art that had been established on an intellectual basis.

Sacred art in the full sense of the term is art that conforms to canons laid down not by individuals but by the spiritual authority of the civilization in question, as was the case with medieval Christian architecture, Gregorian chant, ancient Greek drama, Japanese No plays, Hindu temple dancing and music—to name only a few examples—and such art is always something of a criterion and also a potential source of inspiration for other less central works of art.

A medieval portrait is above all a portrait of the Spirit shining from behind a human veil. In other words, it is as a window opening from the earthly on to the heavenly, and while being enshrined in its own age and civilization as eminently typical of a particular period and place, it has at the same time, in virtue of this opening, something that is neither of the East nor of the West, nor of any one age more than another.

If Renaissance art lacks an opening onto the transcendent and is altogether imprisoned in its own epoch, this is because its outlook is humanistic; and humanism, which is a revolt of the reason against the intellect, considers man and other earthly objects entirely for their own sakes as if nothing lay behind them. In painting the Creation, for example, Michelangelo treats Adam not as a symbol but as an independent reality; and since he does not paint man in the image of God, the inevitable result is that he paints God in the image of man. There is more divinity underlying Simone Martini's painting of Saint Francis than there is in Michelangelo's representation of the Creator Himself.

Shakespeare was born less than three months after Michelangelo's death, and the two are often spoken of in the same breath as being among "the greatest geniuses of the Renaissance." Yet how does Shakespeare stand in the light of an intellectual approach that enhances, if possible, our respect for Dante, but that greatly diminishes our estimate of several others whose preeminence had long gone unquestioned? The following chapters are an attempt to answer this question in some detail; but a general answer can be given immediately. Let us quote, as touchstone, a masterly summing up of the difference between Renaissance art and medieval art: "When standing in front of a Romanesque or Gothic cathedral, we feel that we are at the center of the world; when standing in front of a Renaissance, Baroque, or Rococo church we are merely conscious of being in Europe."[1] Now without trying to give Shakespeare that central place in the art of Christendom which is held by the medieval cathedrals and by *The Divine Comedy*, could it not be said that to be present at an adequate performance of *King Lear* is not merely to watch a play but to witness, mysteriously, the whole history of mankind?

But this remark could not possibly be made about the majority of Shakespeare's writings, and if we wish to form any estimate of the mature dramatist whose outlook bestowed on him a universality that is a prolongation of the universality of the Middle Ages, the first thing to be done is to set most of the plays on one side for the moment so as not to confuse the issue. Few writers can have developed so much during their period of authorship as Shakespeare did. By the end of the sixteenth century he had written some twenty-two plays; but none of these can be said to represent his maturity, though some of them,[2] in various ways, give an unmistakable foretaste of what was to come.

---

[1]Frithjof Schuon, *The Transcendent Unity of Religions* (New York: Harper and Row, 1984) p. 61, *note*.

[2]For example, *Romeo and Juliet, A Midsummer Night's Dream, Henry IV, As You Like It,* and *Twelfth Night.*

There can no longer be any doubt that already at the age of thirty[3] or before, Shakespeare was familiar with the various doctrines—some truly esoteric, others merely occultist—which so passionately interested the London dramatists and other writers of the day, as well as the aristocrats who sustained, protected, and encouraged them, including two successive patrons[4] of the players for whom Shakespeare wrote his plays and with whom he acted. Needless to say, the mainstream of the mystical legacy of the Middle Ages was Christian; but by the end of the sixteenth century it had been swelled by many tributaries—Pythagorean, Platonic, Cabalistic, Hermetic, Illuminist, Rosicrucian, Alchemical. In the margin of some of these traditional currents were sciences such as astrology and magic, and many minds were captivated and even monopolized by side issues of this kind.

But centrally, the non-Christian traditions coincided with Christian mysticism, despite differences of terminology and perspective. They were concerned first with the means of purifying the soul of its fallen nature, and finally with the fruit of that restoration of the primordial state, the soul's beatific reunion with God. Shakespeare, like Lyly, Spenser, Chapman, and Ben Jonson—to name only a few—was well aware that the result of the chemical marriage of sulphur and quicksilver, or of "the King and the Queen," the *magnum opus* of the Alchemists, is the perfected and resurrected soul, and that the alchemical work is thus an indispensable first stage on the path that leads finally to the mystic union of the perfect soul with the Divine Spirit. This union is in fact the theme of Shakespeare's alchemical poem *The Phoenix and the Turtle*, as Paul Arnold has demonstrated in his detailed commentary;[5] and if it be objected that this poem strikes too profound a note of maturity to be counted as a work of the mid-nineties,[6] the same union, a marriage preceded and conditioned by trial and purification, is nonetheless the theme of more than one of Shakespeare's earlier plays. In this connection the reader has only to glance at Arnold's well-documented chapters on *Love's Labour's Lost* and *The Merchant of Venice*[7] or at Jean Paris's chapter on "the alchemical theatre" in *Shakespeare*.[8]

---

[3]In 1594; it was probably in this year that he wrote *Love's Labour's Lost,* and in the following year *Romeo and Juliet* and *A Midsummer Night's Dream.*

[4]See Paul Arnold, *Esotérisme de Shakespeare,* Mercure de France, 1955, pp. 60–61.

[5]Ibid., pp. 130–39.

[6]It was first published only in 1601.

[7]Paul Arnold, *Esotérisme de Shakespeare,* Chapters II and IV.

[8]Seuil, 1981.

The point to be made here is not that many of the earlier plays trace out symbolically the way of the Mysteries, but that they are too merely theoretical to be fully and "concretely" mysterial. On the esoteric path doctrinal knowledge has to be acquired by the mind before it can be existentially assimilated by the man as a whole; and this process of development is outwardly reflected in the chronological order of the plays. It is one thing to make use of an assemblage of symbols, but it is another thing to enter into that symbolism totally.

Let us suppose, to bring home our meaning, that Shakespeare had not lived to reach his maturity, or, in other words, that we had to build our estimate of his greatness on the basis of *Romeo and Juliet, A Midsummer Night's Dream, The Merchant of Venice, Richard II, Henry IV, Much Ado About Nothing, As You Like It, Julius Caesar,* and *Twelfth Night,* these being probably the best of his earlier plays. The difference between that estimate and the one we are happily able to make would differ considerably from judge to judge, but it could not fail in any case to be vast. For it was only after these plays had been written, that is, just after the turn of the century, that there came a sharp and lasting change, not in orientation but in intensity. It was as if Shakespeare had suddenly come to grips with the universe after having contemplated it for some time with a half-detached serenity. From being in earnest, he had come to be in very deadly earnest. This change is forced on our attention first of all by *Hamlet;* and except for one or two backward glances, mostly in the direction of *Romeo and Juliet* and *Henry IV,* the scope of this book lies inclusively between *Hamlet* and Shakespeare's last complete play, *The Tempest.*

CHAPTER TWO

SHAKESPEARE'S OUTLOOK

It is too often said that the marvelous variety of Shakespeare's characters makes it impossible to divine anything about the author himself. About his temperament this may be true to a certain extent, but as it regards his outlook and ideals it is altogether false. We can learn much about him indirectly even from his villains, and from his heroes we can learn much more, especially toward the end of a play, after he has fully developed them.

But when the hero, in a manifest state of undevelopment, at the beginning or in the middle of a play, gives vent to his ideas about this and that, he is perhaps revealing his own immaturity and may well even be saying the very opposite of what Shakespeare himself thinks. A striking example of this is in *King Lear* when, before Shakespeare has fully developed him, Gloster, who has an important part in the subplot, says:

> As flies to wanton boys, are we to the gods;
> They kill us for their sport.[1] (IV, 1, 222–25)

It is when Edgar hears these words that he decides to set upon his strange

---

[1] Of the many Arden editions of Shakespeare's plays, those published between 1920 and 1930 inclusive are the sources of our quotations almost exclusively. Any significant departures will be noted.

course of action for the purpose of saving his father from despair and suicide. Thanks to his efforts, Gloster is able to say eventually:

> Henceforth I'll bear
> Affliction till it do cry out itself
> 'Enough, enough', and die. (IV, 6, 75–77)

and later still:

> You ever-gentle Gods, take my breath from me:
> Let not my worser spirit tempt me again
> To die before you please! (V, 2, 11)

The great weakness of Gloster, which he eventually overcomes, is lack of faith in Providence. Hamlet also has to make good a certain shortcoming in this respect. The "To be or not to be" soliloquy, from which so much has been deduced about Shakespeare's own views, does not merely not express the maturity of Hamlet but it shows him in the process of discovering his immaturity.

It is always possible that Shakespeare may have drawn on his own past experience for this soliloquy. But we can be certain that it does not represent in any way his settled convictions because its whole tenor is completely contradicted in the last scene of the play by the fully developed, perfectly balanced Hamlet voicing the maturity which Shakespeare has gradually shaped and built up for him. In this scene we find that he has altogether overcome his doubts with which, unlike Gloster, he had never fully identified himself. His now full-grown royalty of nature causes Horatio to exclaim, half in admiration, half in surprise: "Why, what a king is this!" (V, 2, 229–30); and his faith in Providence is unshakable. He says to Horatio:

> There's a divinity that shapes our ends,
> Rough-hew them how we will. (V, 2, 10–11)

Shortly after this in connection with his premonition of his own imminent death, he reminds Horatio, in Gospel terms, of man's obligation to possess the virtue of trust: "There's a special providence in the fall of a sparrow" (V, 2, 229–30). This is no doubt as near as Shakespeare dare come to quoting, on the stage, the well-known passage of St. Matthew:

Are not two sparrows sold for a farthing? And one of them shall not fall on the ground without your Father. But the very hairs of your head are all numbered. Fear ye not therefore, ye are of more value than many sparrows (10:29–31).

The gist of what Hamlet says could be summed up: All that matters is to be ready for death when its moment comes. His actual words "the readiness is all" have their equivalent in any equally significant passage in the last act of *King Lear*. The news of the defeat and capture of Lear and Cordelia plunges Gloster once more into "ill thoughts" as they are called by Edgar, who pulls him out of them by reminding him that just as a man has to submit to Providence as regards the time and manner of his birth, so also he must submit as regards the time and manner of his death and not seek to pluck the fruit before it is ripe.

> Men must endure
> Their going hence, even as their coming hither.
> Ripeness is all. (V, 2, 9–11)

It will be noticed that in these two speeches of Hamlet and Edgar, as also elsewhere, Shakespeare is concentrating on the most universal aspect of religion. He is concerned with man's having the right attitude of soul toward Providence rather than with any particular mode of worship. Nor do we believe that this springs in the main from the extreme religious soreness and sensitivity of his times which made Christianity a dangerous topic. But we will come back shortly to the question of his universality. Meantime there are some other clarifications to be made. Before the end of his period of authorship it was forbidden by law to mention the name of God on the stage. But one could always refer to "the gods"; and if he deliberately chose to set many of his maturer plays in a pre-Christian setting, it is to be noticed nonetheless that his attitude toward Greece and Rome is not typical of the Renaissance. He does not merely borrow the surface of classical antiquity. He places himself at the very center of the ancient world. For him, and for Dante, just as for the ancient priests and priestesses at Delphi, Apollo is not the god of light but the Light of God.

In the form of his drama Shakespeare belongs to his age. Marlowe's *Dr. Faustus* is outwardly in some respects more medieval than anything Shakespeare wrote. But in outlook Marlowe was altogether a man of the

Renaissance, whereas Shakespeare seems in a sense to go back as time goes forward and by the turn of the century he had become, unlike many of his fellow dramatists, the continuer and the summer-up of the past, the last outpost of a quickly vanishing age. To say this is not really to say anything new; it is rather a case of putting two and two together. Bradley says of *King Lear*: "It does not appear to disclose a mode of imagination so very far removed from the mode with which we must remember that Shakespeare was perfectly familiar in the Morality plays and in *The Faerie Queene*." Of *Othello* Wilson Knight says: "Othello, Desdemona and Iago are Man, the Divine and the Devil," and he remarks in general that Shakespeare's heroes are "purgatorial pilgrims." Of *Macbeth* Dover Wilson says: "*Macbeth* is almost a morality play," and he says much the same of the two parts of *Henry IV.* Moreover, in this last connection, and with regard to Shakespeare as a continuer of past tradition, he reminds us: "Before its final secularisation in the first half of the sixteenth century, our drama was concerned with one topic and one topic only: human salvation. It was a topic that could be represented in either of two ways: (i) historically, by means of miracle plays which in the Corpus Christi cycles unrolled before the spectators' eyes the whole scheme of salvation from the Creation to the Last Judgement; or (ii) allegorically, by means of morality plays, which exhibited the process of salvation in the individual soul on its road between birth and death, beset with the snares of the World or the wiles of the Evil One."[2] Dover Wilson does not define the word "salvation" and for the purpose of his book it is not necessary to do so. But as regards medieval art in general it is important to distinguish between what may be called esoteric works, which look beyond salvation to sanctification, and exoteric works, in which sanctification is at best no more than a remote ideal. If Shakespeare is a continuer of the past, which of these two categories does his art belong to, the exoteric or the esoteric?

An example of what may be called an exoteric work which stops short at salvation in the lowest sense is *The Castle of Perseverance*. In this morality play mankind *(humanum genus)* is represented as having led a very questionable life, and he is saved from Hell in the face of justice by operation of the Divine Mercy. A supreme example of an esoteric work is *The Divine Comedy* which presupposes salvation and deals with man's purification and his ultimate sanctification or in other words his regaining of what was lost

---

[2]Dover Wilson, *The Fortunes of Falstaff,* Cambridge University Press, 1964, p. 17.

at the Fall. It may be said that in the Middle Ages the mass of the laity was considered as following the path of salvation, whereas the monastic orders, and the lay orders attached to them, and one or two other brotherhoods such as those of the Freemasons and the Companions, aimed at following the path of sanctification. In other words they aimed at passing through Purgatory in this life. It is now known that Dante belonged to a brotherhood that was affiliated to the Order of the Temple,[3] and that was more or less driven underground when the Order of the Temple was abolished. Some have supposed that Shakespeare was a member of the brotherhood of the Rosie Crosse; others believe him to have been a Freemason. This is a part of his secret that will probably never be known, and in any case it is not within the scope of these pages to dwell on anything that is not obvious from what he wrote. What *is* obvious, however, is that his plays far transcend the idea of salvation in its more limited sense; and it may be remarked in passing that this does suggest that their author was following a spiritual path, which itself implies attachment to an order.

At the beginning of Act V of *The Winter's Tale,* with reference to the long penance done by King Leontes during the sixteen years that elapse between the two parts of the play, the priestlike Cleomenes says:

> Sir, you have done enough, and have perform'd
> A saint-like sorrow: no fault could you make,
> Which you have not redeem'd; indeed, paid down
> More penitence than done trespass: at the last,
> Do as the heavens have done, forget your evil;
> With them forgive yourself. (V, 1, 1–6)

In *King Lear* the blind Gloster, recognizing the King's voice, asks to kiss his hand. Lear replies: "Let me wipe it first; it smells of mortality" (IV, 6, 137). This remark contains not only the very essence of the play but also of most of Shakespeare's other maturer plays; for in the course of them what does Shakespeare do but wipe away mortality, that is, the sin of Adam, from the hand of the hero? The hand must be altogether clean: there is no question of more or less. In *Hamlet* the Prince says of himself in the middle of the play that he is fairly virtuous: "I am myself indifferent honest"; but Shakespeare's purpose goes far beyond such mediocrity. The porter to the

---

[3] See René Guénon, *L'Esotérisme de Dante,* Gallimard, 1957, p. 11.

Gate of Purgatory, that is, the gate of salvation, is by definition of unfathomable mercy. Hamlet could have passed by him at the beginning of the play: so could Leontes at the moment of repentance, sixteen years before the speech just quoted; and so could Lear long before the end of the play. But the porter to the Gate of Paradise, that is, the gate to sanctification, is relentlessly exacting; and for his heroes and heroines, Shakespeare stands as that porter. He will let nothing pass except perfection; and so he makes Hamlet add to the above quoted words: "but yet I could accuse me of such things that it were better my mother had not borne me" (III, 1, 23–26).

Character after character is developed to a state of virtue which is pushed, one feels, to the very limits of human nature, until each could say, with Cleopatra:

> Give me my robe, put on my crown; I have
> Immortal longings in me. (V, 2, 279–80)

Even those who refuse to admit that Shakespeare himself speaks through any of his characters cannot escape from the fact that it is Shakespeare himself, and no one else, who is the architect of his plays. And when, after a certain maturity has been reached, play after play follows the same quest for human perfection, each play in its totality (over and above the marvelous variety of detail) hammering home the same message, we have no alternative but to conclude that Shakespeare was altogether preoccupied, at any rate for the last fifteen years of his life or more, by the same question that preoccupied Dante.

It was, however, Dante's privilege to establish, for Christendom, one of those summits of art that every theocracy is bound to have, and this cannot possibly be said of Shakespeare. Christendom is indeed the nearest traditional civilization to his art, and providentially he was born just in time to be able to endow his plays with a medieval grandeur drawn from that world. But he does not speak in its terms. We have already given two examples of his universal manner of expression: Hamlet's "the readiness is all" and Edgar's "ripeness is all," but these are merely two of a multitude. Again and again throughout his plays we are reminded of what Sophocles has called "the unwritten and unassailable statutes of the Gods . . . not of today nor yesterday but from all time, and none knoweth when they were ordained."[4] These words are often taken as a reference to what is generally

---

[4]*Antigone*, 454–57.

11

known as the Perennial Philosophy or *religio perennis;* and it is in this all-underlying religion and not in any particular religious form that Shakespeare's sacred art is rooted. That does not mean that he was not a devout practicing Christian.[5] Prereligious piety cannot be adopted in exchange for the particular religion of any time and place. Moreover, an essential factor of that piety is the mediation between Heaven and earth, a spontaneous characteristic of primordial man in virtue of his, as it were, organic access to the Spirit. But failing this, mediation can only be by the performance of rites that *religio perennis* does not bestow, and that those who have regained that liberating access still continue to perform for more than one reason.

"This deep-seated heredity [*religio perrenis*] is like the remembrance of the lost Paradise and it can erupt in the soul by a kind of providential atavism."[6] We believe Shakespeare to have been an outstanding example of this possibility. Not that we would deny the same atavism for Dante, but from him it shines through a veil. He was a gift from Heaven to Christianity wherein he had a function to perform, whereas Shakespeare was a gift to the increasingly secularized closing centuries of this cycle of time, that is, to the seventeenth century onwards, and to no period more than to the present. All the different traditions are in agreement that we are nearing the end of a temporal cycle, nor is this old age any longer overlaid, as it was some five hundred years ago with the relative youth of Christianity and Islam, which are already now, especially the former, showing distinct signs of decrepitude—so quickly do developments take place when the end is near. And what is true of the traditions is also true of men: everyone on the earth is now in a sense old, which means that everyone is somehow faced with the question "Is it to be, for me, the wisdom of age or its senility?" We have considered this situation at greater length elsewhere.[7] It is mentioned here because today, although the vast majority have opted without knowing it for the negative alternative, there are inevitably some who have not; and the terminal wisdom that they represent has a close affinity with *religio perennis.* So, be it repeated, has Shakespeare: he is in fact clearly too much in his element in that outlook for it to have been forced

---

[5]Hamlet's reference to the sparrow is one of many indications that the Gospel is often present in Shakespeare's mind.

[6]Frithjof Schuon, *The Essential Writings*, p. 531.

[7] *The Eleventh Hour*, ch. 5. Archetype, 2002.

upon him just by the religious problems of his day. Those problems served to compel him to lift the veil through which Dante was obliged to speak.

If it be asked whether we have the right to place any of Shakespeare's plays, even the mature ones, in the category of sacred art, a powerful plea for *yes* is implicit in the fact that the central theme of these plays is not merely religion, which in itself would be insufficient, but the very essence of religion, namely the Mysteries. Let us add to this a remark from Schuon's masterly chapter on the degrees of art: "The distinction between a sacred and a profane art is inadequate and too precipitate when one wishes to take account of all artistic possibilities; and it is therefore necessary to have recourse to a supplementary distinction, namely that between a liturgical and an extraliturgical art."[8] This has the advantage of safeguarding the already mentioned[9] category of sacred art in the traditional sense, while at the same time not labeling as profane certain extraliturgical manifestations of the Divine Spirit which "bloweth where it listeth."

---

[8] Frithjof Schuon, *Esoterism as Principle and as Way,* Harper Perennial Books, p.186.
[9] Ibid, p. 2.

CHAPTER THREE

HENRY IV

If *Hamlet* is Shakespeare's first really great play, the outlook that dominates it is nonetheless already to be found in several of his earlier plays. Particularly striking in this respect is *Henry IV* which, in its two parts, must have been written within three or four years before *Hamlet,* probably between 1597 and 1599.

Dover Wilson says: "*Henry IV* was certainly intended to convey a moral. It is, in fact, Shakespeare's great morality play."[1] He adds:

> Shakespeare plays no tricks with his audience. . . . Prince Hal is the prodigal, and his repentance is not only to be taken seriously, it is to be admired and commended. Moreover the story of the prodigal, secularized and modernized as it might be, ran the same course as ever and contained the same three principal characters: the tempter, the younker, and the father with property to bequeath and counsel to give.[2]

This is altogether convincing, but it leaves unanswered the question as to whether the play is exoteric or esoteric. Or is it not in fact both? The idea of

---

[1] René Guénon, *L'Esotérisme de Dante* (Gallimard, 1957), p. 14.
[2] Ibid., p. 22.

different meanings existing simultaneously at different levels, however strange it may seem to us, was altogether familiar to men of letters throughout the Middle Ages and even later—witness Spenser's *The Faerie Queene.*

According to Dante, "writings are to be understood and should be expounded chiefly according to four meanings"[3] or in other words the literal meaning should be considered as a veil over three others, which he specifies as "allegorical, moral[4] and anagogical." The same principle is to be found also in other arts: the idea that a true work of architecture should have at least three meanings was certainly familiar to Freemasons as late as the sixteenth century. A cathedral, in addition to its literal meaning as a place of worship, was planned as a symbolic image of the whole universe, and by analogy, as an image of the human being,[5] both body and soul. The symbolism of a building as an image of the human soul, the inner world of man, corresponds to the fourth and highest meaning mentioned by Dante, the one which he calls "anagogical," and which he illustrates by interpreting the Exodus of the Jews from Egypt to the Promised Land to mean, in addition to its literal or historical meaning, the exodus of the soul from the state of original sin to the state of sanctification. Now this is also the highest or deepest meaning of the story of the return of the Prodigal Son, and it could be said to underlie all faithfully told stories of the prodigal, including Shakespeare's *Henry IV,* even without the author's intention. But Shakespeare's intention is undoubtedly there; we do not need to examine his text over-carefully to see that he conceived the newly crowned King Henry V's rejection of Falstaff as representing more than salvation in the ordinary limited sense of the word; for him it is clearly no less than the equivalent of the Red Crosse Knight's victory over the dragon in *The Faerie Queene;* and this victory, whatever else it may mean, clearly signifies above all the soul's final purification, its final complete triumph over the devil.

We must be grateful to Dover Wilson for his timely reminder that "Shakespeare lived in the world of Plato and St. Augustine; since the French Revolution we have been living in the world of Rousseau; and this fact lays many traps of misunderstanding for unsuspecting readers."[6] He also says:

---

[3] *Il Convivio,* II, chap. 1.

[4] This meaning is, as we shall see, of much vaster scope than that of most of the so-called morality plays.

[5] For details of these correspondences see Titus Burckhardt, *Sacred Art in East and West,* Perennial Books, and his *Chartres: And the Birth of the Cathedral,* World Wisdom, 1995, p. 45.

[6] René Guénon, *L'Esotérisme de Dante,* p. 7.

"The main theme of Shakespeare's morality play is the growing up of a madcap prince into the ideal king."[7] Putting two and two together, it must be remembered that in the world of Plato and St. Augustine no man who was less than a saint could possibly pass as "the ideal king."

No limit can be set to the extent of Prince Hal's reform. His world is very remote indeed from the world we live in, the world of mediocrities and relativities in which epic is stifled beyond breathing point, while the psychological novel thrives and grows fat. There is an unmistakable ring of the absolute about the last scenes of *Henry IV*, which makes it difficult, from any point of view, to attribute to the new King, anything that falls short of perfection. Nonetheless this play can be said to have two meanings in relation to the human soul, one exoteric, and the other esoteric; but as elsewhere in Shakespeare, these two meanings are not altogether distinct, for the lower meaning as it were opens on to the higher. *Henry IV* can be considered as a morality play in which the final perfection remains far above the spectators' heads, although it serves as a shrine of orientation for their ideals; and it can be considered as an esoteric or mystical drama, the purpose of which is to draw the spectator into the mesh of the plot, into the very person of the hero.

The meaning of *Henry IV* as a morality play is its literal meaning and needs no comment. As to its deeper meaning, one of the principal keys that the text offers us is the son's identification of himself with his dead father. A strange "alchemy" has taken place by which the spirit of the old King is reborn in the person of the new King whose former faults— "affections" or "wildness" as he calls them—have died and lie buried with the old King.

> My father is gone wild into his grave,
> For in his tomb lie my affections;
> And sadly with his spirit I survive. (Pt. 2, V, 2, 123–25)

The young King also uses the image of the corrupt tide of vanity flowing out into the waters of the ocean so that a new and truly royal tide may flow in. Not far below the surface here, as elsewhere in Shakespeare's plays, lie the words of the Gospel "Except a man be born again he cannot see the Kingdom of God."

---

[7] Ibid, p. 22.

The heir's identification of himself with his father is important because in order to have a full understanding of *Henry IV* it is necessary to understand that "Everyman" or the human soul is represented not merely by the Prince alone and by the King alone, but also, above all, by a synthesis of the Prince and the King. In its static aspect, as a fallen soul that "smells of mortality" and must die before a new soul can be born, the soul is personified by the King; and the symbolism is strengthened by the fact that the King is a usurper to the throne, just as fallen man is a usurper to the throne of earth, which belongs by rights only to man in his original state, man created in the image of God. On the other hand, in its dynamic aspect, inasmuch as it is capable of being purified, and inasmuch as the foundations of the new soul are being laid there, the soul is personified by the Prince who, at any rate according to the logic of the play, will not be a usurper when he becomes King. It is not only the faults of the Prince that die with his father's death but also the stigma of a crown that had been usurped. The dying King says of his own wrongful seizure of the throne:

> All the soil of the achievement goes
> With me into the earth . . .
> How I came by the crown, O God forgive,
> And grant it may with thee in true peace live. (IV, 5, 189–90; 218–19)

The substance of the soul of "Everyman" is also represented by England, which is in a state of discord and which is gradually brought into a state of peace. The two plots of the play, the bringing to order of the Prince and the bringing to order of the country, run parallel to each other and have the same significance. Civil war is a most adequate symbol of the fallen soul, which is by definition at war with itself; and the meaning of this particular internal strife in England is heightened by the King's intention to convert its energies, as soon as possible, into a holy war. The whole play is in fact consecrated by the beginning and ending, as it were, in the shadow of the Holy Land. At the beginning of Part I the King announces his intention of leading a crusade to Jerusalem; and toward the end of Part II he reaffirms this intention, announcing that all preparations have been made to set out for Palestine as soon as the rebels at home have been defeated:

> Now, Lords, if God doth give successful end
> To this debate that bleedeth at our doors

> We will our youth lead on to higher fields
> And draw no swords but what are sanctified.
> Our navy is address'd, our power collected,
> Our substitutes in absence well invested,
> And everything lies level to our wish. (IV, 4, 1–7)

The rebels have in fact already been defeated, but the news has not yet reached him. Symbolically connected with this is another "already" which, though it dawns on him later, he has also not yet grasped: he is already in "Jerusalem"—the Jerusalem Chamber of the Palace of Westminster where this scene takes place; and here, shortly after his just quoted speech, when news comes that the civil war is at an end, he suddenly sinks down in mortal sickness. From this moment the play's deeper meaning wells to the surface as it were and obliterates the other meanings. The only connection between the good news and the King's illness is a spiritual one: the end of the civil war means that the pilgrim's journey is at an end, that the old soul is now ripe for death so that the new soul may be born. If the King is no more than dying and not yet dead, this is simply because the return of his prodigal son has not yet been fulfilled. Once this has taken place the King asks to be carried back into the Jerusalem Chamber, in order that he may die "in Jerusalem."

The Jerusalem chamber has also its meaning for the Prince. We may remember that in *The Faerie Queene* the Red Crosse Knight is only able to overcome the dragon because the fight takes place at the threshold of the Earthly Paradise, within reach of the Waters of Life and the Tree of Life.[8] Now Jerusalem is symbolically equivalent to the Earthly Paradise; and the Prince's real victory over himself, when he speaks of "The noble change that I have purpos'd," (IV, 5, 154) takes place as he stands by his dying father's bed at the threshold of the Jerusalem Chamber, before his final meeting with Falstaff. This symbolism is strengthened by another; for if any particular moment can be assigned to the Prince's victory, it is at his foretaste of royalty when, believing himself to be by rights already King, he places the crown on his own head.

---

[8] Spenser died in 1599, about the time that Shakespeare was writing this play. *The Faerie Queene*, which death prevented him from finishing, is mentioned here and elsewhere as an example of symbolism parallel to Shakespeare's at the end of the sixteenth century, without any claim that Spenser had a more than theoretic understanding of the symbolism that he was using.

The last scenes of *Henry IV* Part II make an undeniably strong spiritual impact. But neither part of *Henry IV,* when taken as a whole, has anything approaching the closely knit intensity of a play like *Hamlet.* In particular we cannot help noticing that there is no real conflict: like the killing of the dragon, the rejection of Falstaff symbolizes the most difficult thing in the world, and yet the Prince has not had, as far as we can see, the slightest difficulty in rejecting him. Secondly—and this weakness is connected with the first—Shakespeare makes the rejection of Falstaff very dramatic, but he has not previously brought home to us dramatically Falstaff's utter villainy. The villainy is there in the text, but we only discover it by analysis; the plot of the play does not depend on it at all, so that at the end we have a certain sense of disproportion that leaves us with a vague feeling of injustice. But it may well be that we partly owe the excellence of some of Shakespeare's later plays to his experience in writing this. Perhaps when conceiving the part of Iago he said to himself, thinking of Falstaff: "This time there shall be no mistake!"; and perhaps when he set Hamlet to kill the dragon he said to himself: "This time it shall *not* be easy!"

CHAPTER FOUR

HAMLET

The basic theme of *Hamlet* is summed up in the Prince's own words: "Virtue cannot so inoculate our old stock but we shall relish of it" (III, 1, 118–20). This means: "It is no use plastering one or two superficial virtues over our old stock, that is, the original sin which permeates our nature, since in spite of all such virtues, we shall still continue to reek of the old stock." But in order to express fully what is in Hamlet's mind here we must add: "There is only one thing which can effectively wipe out the stench of our old stock and that is the complete reversal of the Fall, total liberation from the grip of the enemy of mankind, in other words, the slaying of the dragon, or more simply, in the language of this play, revenge."

As to Hamlet's manner of expression, Shakespeare allows himself here, under cover of the Prince's "madness," to come within close range of divulging esoteric secrets. Initiation into the Mysteries is nothing other than the inoculating or grafting of a scion of man's primordial nature onto the old stock of his fallen nature which will thus be effaced, stench and all, provided that the new primordial scion be duly tended and implacably protected against any suckers that the old stock may put forth in an attempt to reestablish itself. That tending and that protection are the rites and disciplines of the Lesser Mysteries, the path of purification from original sin and the recovery thereby of man's Edenic state. This complete reversal of the

Fall is precisely what is meant according to the play's deepest meaning, not only by "revenge" but also by "honor," the symbolism of which is bound up with that of revenge. No revenge, no honor: for men of understanding, the subhuman plight of fallen man is a state of global dishonor.

In its immediate impact upon us sacred art is like a stone thrown into water. The ever-widening ripples illustrate the limitless repercussions that are made, or can be made, upon the soul by this impact, fraught as it is with several meanings at different levels. One meaning can, as we have seen, open out onto another deeper meaning[1] that lies beyond it. In this way sacred art often conveys far more than it appears to convey, far more sometimes even than the mind in question is conscious of or could take in by way of ordinary didactic teaching.

Needless to say, the initial impact itself must captivate the mind and the emotions. According to the literal meaning of *Hamlet*, we are given many strong and obvious reasons why Hamlet should kill Claudius, enough at any rate even to make us forget for the moment that revenge is un-Christian. Nonetheless, it would be true to say that there is no common measure between the literal meaning of this play and the deep sense of urgency that Shakespeare instills into us. So long as we are in the theater we are not far from feeling that revenge is the most important thing in the world; and we are right, for there *is* nothing more important, and indeed nothing more Christian, than what revenge stands for here.

The allegorical meaning serves to universalize the literal meaning and thus to guarantee its spiritual significance. Both are at the same cosmic level; but though the allegory does not transcend the human plane, it nonetheless expands it, sometimes even to its full extent. The discords of Shakespeare's great plays are often suspended more or less explicitly between two harmonies which in certain cases have to be identified, allegorically speaking, with the Edenic Age and the Millennium. When that is so the Fall of man is to be seen through a deliberately transparent veil, a veil that is never more transparent than it is in *Hamlet*. The Ghost's revelation to the Prince is, as regards its allegorical meaning, like a puzzle with a few missing pieces which it is not difficult for us to supply in the light of those pieces which we are given—the garden with its fruit trees, the serpent, the guilty woman, whose guilt has something mysteriously unfathomable about it. The *Genesis* narrative is undoubtedly here. There is also, explicitly, the first fruit of the Fall,

---

[1] Not that every detail in the text has a deeper meaning. Conversely, there are some details that only make good sense on the deepest plane of all.

the sin of fratricide.² But the Fall itself was in fact a murder also, the slaying or making mortal of Adam by the serpent, and the forbidden fruit was the "poison" through which that murder was effected.

The Queen is not merely Hamlet's mother; she is his whole ancestral line going back to Eve herself; and inasmuch as she is Eve, she represents, in general, the fallen human soul, especially in its passive aspect. In other words, she represents that passivity which in man's primordial state was turned toward Heaven and which after it lost contact with the Spirit has come more or less under the sway of the devil or, in the words of the play, having "sated itself in a celestial bed" has come to "prey on garbage." No doubt in foresight of her repentance the Ghost says to Hamlet:

> Leave her to heaven,
> And to those thorns that in her bosom lodge,
> To prick and sting her. (I, 5, 86–88)

So meantime the Prince takes upon himself to personify those thorns in the hope, we may conclude, of finally waking her conscience that she has lulled to sleep.

According to the letter of the law, the Queen is altogether innocent of the murder of King Hamlet and indeed altogether ignorant of it. But the fact that she was willing to marry a monster of a man almost immediately after having been widowed of his opposite makes her eminently qualified to personify the initial guilt of fallen humanity, for however the Fall may be represented, it amounts essentially to exchanging a "celestial" treasure for earthly "garbage." Moreover, since the Fall, as we have seen, may be considered as a murder, to personify the Fall is to personify its guilt in that respect also, which makes Gertrude in a sense the accomplice of Claudius. Nor can it be denied that her consent to marry him meant that she had stifled within herself the memory of her first husband's outstanding qualities, and to stifle is to kill, which to a certain extent gives Hamlet the right to accuse her of having killed his father, as he does, albeit indirectly and under cover of madness, when he puts into the Player Queen's mouth the lines:

---

²The murderer himself says:
> Oh, my offence is rank, it smells to heaven;
> It hath the primal eldest curse upon't,
> A brother's murder! (III, 3, 36–38)

In second husband let me be accurst!
None wed the second but who kill'd the first. (III, 2, 191–92)

Unlike the writer of epic, the dramatist has a very limited space at his disposal. Consequently, he often chooses to build a house of more than one storey. In *Hamlet* the soul is not only represented by the Prince and by his mother; its state is also reflected in the condition of the country. Not that there is actually a subplot of civil war as in *Henry IV*, but nonetheless "Something is rotten in the state of Denmark" and "The time is out of joint" and needs to be "set right."

Fallen man stands between two perfections, one past and one future, that which was lost and that which is to be gained. In this play it is the dead King Hamlet who stands for the past perfection and its loss, whereas Fortinbras represents the perfection that is to come. It is he whom the dying Hamlet is to name as his heir. The analogy between the symbolism of this play and that of *Henry IV* is by no means exact in every detail; but the dead King Hamlet, at any rate as regards legitimacy, corresponds to the dead King Richard II, whereas Queen Gertrude and her son correspond to King Henry IV and his son, while Fortinbras in a sense corresponds to that son regenerated as King Henry V. It would be a mistake however to seek to establish a precise correspondence here between parent and parent and between son and son. It is true that Gertrude is burdened with guilt toward King Hamlet just as Henry IV is burdened with guilt toward King Richard; but Prince Hamlet, the censurer of self and others, also has much in common with Henry IV, whereas in some respects, as we shall see, Gertrude may be said to come closer, symbolically, to the repentant prodigal Prince Hal.

As a parallel to the whole action of the Danish play, a parallel that powerfully underlines its deepest meaning, the soul of King Hamlet is being purified in Purgatory. But the dead King has also another aspect. Just as Adam was not only the man who fell but also the most perfect of all creatures, made in the image of God, so also King Hamlet, who in a sense corresponds to Adam, is not only a purgatorial pilgrim but also a symbol of man's lost Edenic state. It is in virtue of this that he refers to his own marriage with Gertrude as a "celestial bed," and is spoken of by Hamlet in terms of human perfection:

A combination and a form indeed,
Where every god did seem to set his seal
To give the world assurance of man. (III, 4, 60–62)

It is also in virtue of this aspect that he acts as spiritual guide to his son.

There can be no problem here for any member of the audience, since we are all accustomed to thinking and speaking of Adam in these two different ways. Nor is there any contradiction between the general impression of great majesty made by the Ghost and his having, at cockcrow,

> started like a guilty thing
> Upon a fearful summons (I, 1, 148–49)

For Shakespeare has enough imagination to know that a soul in Purgatory is by definition preoccupied by a sense of the magnitude of his imperfections which, as regards himself, the Ghost describes as "the foul crimes done in my days of nature" (I, 5, 12). The purgatorial aspect of King Hamlet can nonetheless be said to unite in him the two Adams, for his status as a soul in Purgatory means that he is already saved and on his way to Paradise. It is thus that the Catholic Church speaks of souls in Purgatory as *animae sanctae,* holy souls.

The difference between simple piety and mysticism might almost be summed up by saying that the averagely pious man looks at the story of the Garden of Eden for the most part objectively, whether he takes it literally or allegorically. The mystic, on the other hand, looks at it subjectively as something which intensely, directly, and presently concerns himself. Again, the averagely pious man is aware of the existence of the devil, but in fact, if not in theory, he imagines him to be more or less harmless and has little idea of the extent of his own subservience to him. In general he is extremely subject to the illusion of neutrality. But the mystic knows that most of what seems neutral is harmful, and that "one may smile and smile and be a villain" (I, 5, 108). The ghost initiates Hamlet into the Mysteries by conveying to him the truth of the Fall not as a remote historical fact but as an immediate life-permeating reality, an acute pain that will not allow his soul a moment's rest; and every man in fact is in exactly the same situation as the Prince of Denmark, did he but know it, that is, if he were not

> Duller . . . than the fat weed
> That roots itself at ease on Lethe wharf. (I, 5, 32–33)

What the Ghost says to Hamlet could almost be paraphrased: "Latterly you have been feeling that 'all is not well.' I come to confirm your worst suspicions and to show you the remedy. Since man has been robbed by the devil of his birthright, there is only one way for him to regain what is lost and that is by taking revenge upon the robber."

With all the ardor of the novice, in answer to his father's last injunction "Remember me!" the Prince replies:

> Remember thee?
> Yea, from the table of my memory
> I'll wipe away all trivial fond records,
> All saws of books, all forms, all pressures past,
> That youth and observation copied there;
> And thy commandment all alone shall live
> Within the book and volume of my brain,
> Unmix'd with baser matter. (I, 5, 95–104)

He is true to his word in the sense that from now on the thought of the task that has been laid upon him remains uppermost in his mind. But that does not make any the less ironical his earlier words when the Ghost first told him the bare fact that he had been murdered without yet having told him who the murderer was:

> Haste me to know it, that I, with wings as swift
> As meditation or the thoughts of love
> May sweep to my revenge (I, 5, 29–31)

Yet Hamlet, unlike Othello and Lear, is a supreme psychologist, and knows himself as well as he knows others. Moreover if he is slow to act he is quick to think, and it does not take him long to replace the momentary impulse of sweeping to his revenge with the consciousness that the mandate laid on him by Heaven constitutes an almost unbearably difficult task. The scene ends with his couplet:

> The time is out of joint; O cursed spite
> That ever I was born to set it right! (I, 5, 189–90)

We have, however, been promised that he will succeed, for at the end of the preceding scene, when Marcellus says: "Something is rotten in the state of Denmark," Horatio immediately adds: "Heaven will direct it" (I, 4, 90–91).

Dante mentions the different meanings of a work of art, literal, allegorical, moral, anagogical, in an order that rightly suggests a hierarchy, leading up to the anagogical or esoteric meaning that is the highest. As to that which comes second to it, the ethical aspect of dramatic art may be said to concern the spectators insofar as they are drawn to identify themselves, in varying degrees, with whatever increase of beauty of soul is set before them on the stage, and to dissociate themselves from all movements in the opposite direction. The simile used earlier of the widening ripples caused by a stone cast into water may serve to illustrate not only the opening out of the literal meaning onto the further meanings but also, subjectively, the gradual heightening and deepening of the receptivity of spectator and reader insofar as they are capable of spiritual growth. The same simile is also apt for the moral message as a whole, since unlike the three others this message is present at every level. In its highest reaches it is absorbed into the supreme message: to portray, as Shakespeare constantly does in his maturer plays, the dazzling plenitude of virtue, without which there can be no perfection and therefore no passage through the Mysteries, is to trace out a dimension that is truly anagogical, a necessary aspect of the steep ascent of the mysterial way. Otherwise expressed, this message, like virtue itself, is as it were suspended between human goodnesses and their supreme archetypes, that is, the Divine Qualities. "Be ye perfect, even as your Father in Heaven is perfect." The phrase "to excel oneself," if properly used, indicates that the virtue in question partakes in some degree of the transcendent. Shakespeare is explicit in this respect, for example, as regards the virtues of Duncan in *Macbeth* that have power to "plead like angels, trumpet-tongued" (I, 7, 19). Another outstanding example is Cordelia's self-sacrifice in *King Lear,* a sacrifice upon which "the Gods themselves pour incense" (V, 3, 20–21).

It must be remembered that the closely knit brevity of the dramatic form calls for simplicity and speed; and when the theme of a play is the Mysteries, something can be gained by making it begin not too far from the threshold of fulfillment. Shakespeare by no means always avails himself of this possibility, but when he chooses to do so, as in this play and in certain others, he makes his audience conscious, sometimes even from the very start, of a virtual perfection of moral substance in his heroes and heroines, a virtuality that is almost already an actuality except for what the drama itself is destined to actualize. Upon our first contact with Hamlet and Othello, for example, we are immediately aware of a magnanimity that has a touch of the absolute, a grandeur of soul that enthralls and edifies. From his first entry Othello confronts us with a majesty that is maintained throughout; and Hamlet, in his own very different way, is a no less striking example. In this latter case the initial effect is strengthened by contrast: against the foil of the extreme hypocrisy of Claudius and of the flatterers who pander to him, the profound sincerity of Hamlet is overwhelming. It is all the more so, when seen on the stage, for being visual, with the prince himself in black and everyone else dressed for festive merrymaking, a contrast that is held at considerable length before our eyes and doubled in its effect by the mourner's prolonged unbroken silence matched by the unchanging solemn sadness of his face, all leading up to his words, when he finally does speak in answer to his mother's query as to why, since death is a common occurrence, it should seem so particular to him in the case of his father:

> Seems, madam! Nay, it is; I know not 'seems.'
> 'Tis not alone my inky cloak, good mother . . .
> Together with all forms, modes, shows of grief,
> That can denote me truly; these indeed 'seem,'
> For they are actions that a man might play;
> But I have that within which passeth show;
> These but the trappings and the suits of woe. (I, 2, 76–82)

Then when he is left alone, and in scenes that closely follow, other aspects of perfection become manifest. We have before us a brilliantly gifted and highly sensitive prince, brought up to be King, a youth endowed with a vast and probing intelligence that is implacably objective, the severest of critics but without a trace of arrogance, being himself his first object of criticism, a man dedicated to truth and allergic to falsity in any form, a soul that reverberates with love of good and abhorrence of evil.

> Fie on't! O fie! 'Tis an unweeded garden
> That grows to seed; things rank and gross in nature
> Possess it merely. (I, 2, 135–37)

This heartfelt disgust at the corruption of the Danish court under Claudius is balanced by the heartfelt joy that radiates from him at any manifestation of the opposite. It is remarkable how impressive Hamlet's gratitude is for the existence, despite this corruption, of one or two individuals whom he can trust, in particular Horatio and Marcellus. It is they who witnessed the appearance of the Ghost and have sworn to keep that, and all things connected with it, a secret; and these lines, which immediately follow their oath, are intensely moving for the depth and nobility of soul from which they spring:

> So, gentlemen,
> With all my love I do commend me to you;
> And what so poor a man as Hamlet is
> may do, to express his love and friending to you,
> God willing, shall not lack. (I, 5, 183–87)

We may quote also, from Hamlet's praise of Horatio in another scene:

> Give me that man
> That is not passion's slave, and I will wear him
> In my heart's core, ay, in my heart of heart,
> As I do thee. (III, 2, 79–82)

Hamlet is also quick to recognize, in others, a virtue that he himself needs to perfect. The example that first comes to mind is that of Fortinbras, who is the theme of Hamlet's soliloquy that begins: "How all occasions do inform against me!" (IV, 4, 32). But this reflection might also have been made on another somewhat later "occasion" which much more directly "informs" against Hamlet; and though he himself is not present to take note of it, the audience can do so for themselves. This "occasion" concerns Laertes, who is also, like the Prince of Norway, an object of Hamlet's esteem: "That is Laertes, a very noble youth," (V, 1, 24–26) he says to Horatio as the mourners enter for the funeral of Ophelia; and later in the scene he protests to Laertes himself:

> What is the reason that you use me thus?
> I loved you ever.

Now both Hamlet and Laertes were absent from Denmark at their fathers' respective deaths; and Laertes was given to understand, through various rumors, that his father had died at the hand of Claudius. Immediately he goes back to Denmark, gathers around himself a multitude of supporters, overcomes the royal guards, and to the accompaniment of shouts "Laertes shall be king, Laertes king!" (IV, 5, 107) he breaks into the palace, confronts Claudius, and says to him:

> O though vile king,
> Give me my father! (IV, 5, 114–15)

Hamlet, for his part, is also given, together with the news of his father's death, an imperative reason for taking action against Claudius, namely that he has usurped the throne, or, to use the Prince's own words, that he has shown himself to be a thief, a "cut-purse,"

> That from a shelf the precious diadem stole
> And put it in his pocket! (III, 4, 100–101)

If Hamlet had set about doing what Laertes did, he would no doubt have found himself very soon at the head of a powerful host that would almost certainly have been joined by rapidly increasing sections of the army itself; and if, in preference to Claudius, there had been cries of "Laertes shall be king," how much more would the people have shouted for their beloved Prince! It is true that Hamlet's failure to take action can be partly attributed to one of his virtues, that he is totally devoid of worldly ambition. But that does not excuse him for neglecting his responsibilities and leaving his country in the hands of a man whom he knows to be utterly debased, even though he does not yet know him to be a regicide. The weakness that Hamlet has to overcome, and does overcome in the end, is shown up very clearly in the light of Laertes' strength in that particular respect. Nor is Hamlet deceived, as we shall see, in judging him to be "a very noble youth."

In accordance with worldwide tradition it could be said that to regain what was lost at the Fall is to become once more in all fullness a priest-king, which is what man was created to be, king because he was placed at the center of this earthly state to be there the viceregent of God, priest because his centrality has also a vertical aspect, that of being mediator between Heaven and earth. This definition is relevant to many of Shakespeare's greater plays, and it is nearly always the priestly dimension which most needs to be developed and perfected. At the outset of *Hamlet* however the Prince is more priest than king. Not that he has not already also a wealth of royalty in his nature, but it falls short of fullness in one direction, and his growth to adequacy in that respect is the main theme of the drama.

The texture of many of the plays, and none more than *Hamlet*, provides a favorable setting for the simultaneous presence of more than one meaning. On the one hand, to go back to Shakespeare's mastery of his art, he partly achieves his extraordinary dramatic concentration by not wasting words. He never fails to tell us explicitly everything that we really need to know; but apart from the essential, he not infrequently challenges us to open, with the keys of what he has given us in the way of implications, the doors that he has not opened himself. His economy in leaving many things unsaid thus serves not only to increase the tension but to introduce an enigmatic element that can have a subtly galvanizing effect upon the audience. This is akin to the use of paradox in aphorisms: if we say, for example, that divinity is the most truly human feature of man, the barbed shaft of what seems like a contradiction in terms can spur the intelligence to abandon the habitual channels of thought and to transcend itself. In this connection it should also be remembered that perplexity is universally recognized in mysticism as a possible stepping-stone to intellection; nor can it be denied, with regard to enigma, that the mysterious may open out onto the mysterial—to use this latter word in the sense of that which is related to the Mysteries.

If the play is somewhat haunted by enigma, it is also haunted by madness, first of all the feigned madness of Hamlet, then the unfeigned madness of Ophelia; and madness is, like the use of paradox, yet another example of escape from the rut of ordinary mental processes. The fact that madness is in most actual cases an escape in a downward direction is altogether irrel-evant to what we are considering here. As to the feigned madness of the Prince, one of the play's lesser enigmas is that Shakespeare, despite his lavish use of soliloquy, never lets his protagonist explain why he has come so immediately to the decision that it is an imperative necessity for him to pretend to be mad. But in this case we can easily take up the Bard's challenge and fill the gap ourselves. The pretense might seem at first a contradiction of Hamlet's sincerity, of his "I know not 'seems,'" whereas in fact it finds in these very words part of its explanation. His newfound knowledge of how his father died makes it impossible to continue as before. His words, "I do not set my life at a pin's fee," (I, 4, 65) are no longer true, for his life has now a purpose to it and must therefore be protected from the danger that besets it. How much easier it would be for Claudius to kill him than it is for him to kill Claudius! Perhaps he is already under a secret sentence of death. If not, he will be under sentence as soon as the suspicions of Claudius are aroused; and he knows that his sincerity, combined with his ultra-sensitivity, would make it impossible, if he continues to behave normally, for him to hide his loathing for his uncle. Moreover a regicide is bound to be suspicious of others and always on his guard. So is a usurper, and Claudius is both of these at once. But madness, at any rate of the kind that Hamlet would feign, might serve to disarm him somewhat, as far as the madman was concerned; and the mad are usually humored, which would give him more liberty and perhaps more opportunity of fulfilling the task imposed on him. Another reason for the pretense, albeit a secondary one, is that it would relieve the tension for himself. He said, at the end of his first scene: "But break, my heart, for I must hold my tongue!" (I, 2, 159) He will now be able to talk, and even to say many pertinent things. So much for the literal meaning.

As to what lies above it, since spiritual wisdom, from a worldly point of view, is a kind of madness, madness can be made to serve, in certain contexts, as a symbol of spiritual wisdom. Shakespeare avails himself of this possibility more than once in his plays; and in *Hamlet*, in addition to its more outward meaning as a stratagem and a blind, the "antic disposition" which the Prince puts on serves above all to underline the drastic change that has taken place in his life. In his soliloquies he shows no trace of madness; but as soon as he has to face the world, that is, when Horatio and Marcellus enter, shortly after the exit of the Ghost, the newfound spiritual outlook that fills his soul almost to bursting point has to find an outlet in what Horatio describes as "wild and whirling words." It is under cover of this "wildness" that Shakespeare momentarily allows the deeper meaning of the play to come to the surface, for what Hamlet says is:

And so without more circumstance at all,
I hold it fit that we shake hands and part;
You, as your business and desire shall point you;
For every man hath business and desire,
Such as it is; and, for mine own poor part,
Look you, I'll go pray. (I, 5, 127–32)

And prayer, which in the widest sense of the word may be said to comprise all forms of worship, is in fact man's chief weapon of "revenge."

In connection with madness, it may be recalled that the already quoted line: "Let me wipe it [my hand] first; it smells of mortality," which brings the deeper meaning of *King Lear* to the surface, is spoken by Lear when he is mad. The fact that Hamlet's madness is feigned whereas Lear's is not makes no difference to its symbolism. Another kind of "madness" which has the same significance is the "folly" of the professional fool, and it may in fact be wondered whether the Prince has not partly taken his cue, for his own play of madness, from his memories of Yorick. Many of the darts that he throws are more akin to the sallies of a jester than to the ineptitudes of a lunatic, as when, for example, Claudius says to him after Polonius's death: "Where's Polonius?" and he replies: "In heaven; send thither to see; if your messenger find him not there, seek him i' the other place yourself" (IV, 3, 35–38). Hamlet almost immediately takes Horatio and Marcellus into his confidence as to his intention to feign madness, and later he takes Horatio altogether into his confidence. Later still he confides everything to his mother. There is yet another person on whom, in the nature of things, he would like to unburden his heavily laden soul, and that is Ophelia. But when in his first scene, summing up his mother's guilt, he says: "Frailty, thy name is woman!" (I, 2, 146) the generality of this remark not only serves to clinch still further the allegorical equation of Gertrude with Eve, but it may also be taken, as regards the literal meaning of the play, to indicate that in addition to his mother Ophelia has likewise come into his mind, if only in the form of the question, "Is she perhaps equally frail?" And when later he comes and gazes into her face, is he not trying to find with his eyes the answer to the question: "If I tell her everything as a secret, would she be capable of not telling her father?" We, wise after all the events, might be inclined to say, "Yes." But "No" is evidently the answer his eyes must have given him. Moreover he had no right to take any risks; and she had already shown evidence of the considerable degree of her subjection to her father by repelling the Prince's letters and refusing to give him access to her. So he leaves her without a word, for the only utterance he could have made to her at that moment would have been to tell her the whole truth.

Hamlet is not a drama of love, but of spiritual warfare, of renunciation, and of death and rebirth. The task laid upon the Prince by his father is something of a death sentence. It is not easy to kill a king, especially when that king is of the nature of Claudius. It is less easy still to kill a king and to escape with one's own life, and Hamlet, far from being an optimist, is an implacable realist. He therefore cannot help wondering what will happen to Ophelia after he is gone. As to the present, despite his love for her, it is clearly no time for marriage; and it is in any case clear to the priestlike Hamlet that everything must be sacrificed to "the one thing necessary." For Ophelia, therefore, the best solution would no doubt be to enter a convent, which would protect her, after his almost certainly imminent death, from the "things rank and gross in nature" which are all that is left in the "unweeded garden" that the world has now become.

In the "nunnery scene," where we first see them together, Shakespeare once more allows the deeper meaning of the play to rise to the surface under cover of Hamlet's "madness." The first part of the spiritual path is "the descent into Hell." The deeper meaning of Dante's *Inferno*[3] is the descent of Dante into the hidden depths of his own soul. The novice has first to learn the meaning of "original sin"; he must come to know the evil possibilities that lie, almost unsuspected, beneath the surface illusion of being "indifferent honest." But in "The Divine Comedy" the discovery of the soul's worst possibilities and purification from them are treated separately. The *Inferno* and the *Purgatorio* correspond to an altogether exhaustive Confession followed by a full Absolution. The "architecture" of Dante's poem demands this separate treatment, as also the fact that it has an eschatological as well as a mystical meaning. Occasionally, as we shall see, Shakespeare also treats the two phases separately, but more often, as in *Hamlet*, he represents them as taking place simultaneously. The killing of Claudius will mean reaching not only the bottom of Hell but also the top of the Mountain of Purgatory, for revenge means purification.

Hell and Purgatory together constitute what Greco-Roman antiquity knew as the Lesser Mysteries *(mysteria parva)*. Hamlet has now fully entered into these Mysteries and is thus in a situation parallel to that of his father— hence his preoccupation with sin. Very significant are the words he says to himself when he sees Ophelia approaching:

> Nymph, in thy orisons
> Be all my sins remember'd. (III, 1, 88–89)

And the gist of all that he says to her is in the following speech:

> Get thee to a nunnery; why wouldst thou be a breeder of sinners? I
> am myself indifferent honest; but yet I could accuse me of such
> things that it were better my mother had not borne me. I am very
> proud, revengeful, ambitious; with more offenses at my beck than I
> have thoughts to put them in, imagination to give them shape, or
> time to act them in. What should such fellows as I do crawling be-
> tween heaven and earth? We are arrant knaves all; believe none of
> us. Go thy ways to a nunnery. (III, 1, 122–32)

---

[3] The references here and elsewhere to Dante do not mean to suggest that Shakespeare owes anything to him directly. Of this we know nothing. *The Divine Comedy* can nonetheless help to throw light on certain aspects of these plays because it is based on principles with which no intellectual of Shakespeare's time could fail to be familiar.

What mysticism terms "the descent into Hell," that is, the discovery of sinful propensities in the soul which were hitherto unknown, sometimes takes the form of actually committing the sins in question, as happens, for example, with Angelo in *Measure for Measure* and with Leontes in *The Winter's Tale*. The case of Macbeth is, as we shall see, quite different, for that is a descent without return, unrelated to the Mysteries.

When Hamlet, on his way to speak with his mother, suddenly comes upon Claudius praying and is about to kill him, he refrains from doing so on the grounds that to kill him while at prayer would amount to sending him to Heaven, which would be "hire and salary, not revenge." To be truly revenged he must send him to Hell. We have here a perfect example of how action of great importance can be paralyzed by too much mental business, as he has said in the most famous of his soliloquies:

> And thus the native hue of resolution
> Is sicklied o'er with the pale cast[4] of thought,
> And enterprises of great pitch and moment
> With this regard their currents turn awry
> And lose the name of action. (III, 1, 84–88)

His words are, as he enters upon his uncle:

> Now might I do it pat, now he is praying;
> And now I'll do't; and so he goes to heaven;
> And so am I revenged. (III, 3, 73–75)

His "now I'll do it" shows "the native hue of resolution" which immediately, in what follows, "Is sicklied o'er with the pale cast of thought" (I, 5, 83). The "cast" is indeed "pale," for the given pretext is pitifully unconvincing. It is not to be imagined that a man of Hamlet's spiritual intelligence could sincerely believe that it is so easy to go to Heaven and that a man as wicked as Claudius could do so simply for having died when his knees were bent in prayer; nor, in all justice, did the regicide wish to send his victim to Hell, nor did he do so; and worst of all, the pretext throws to the winds one of the chief reasons for killing Claudius:

---

[4]Vomit.

Let not the royal bed of Denmark be
A couch for luxury[5] and damned incest. (I, 5, 82–83)

Thus, from the literal point of view, that is, according to *Hamlet* as a morality play, the Prince's inability to take decisive action makes him ready to snatch at any pretext for procrastination. A blind eye has therefore to be turned to the actual pretext given, the more so in that if taken seriously, to represent weighed thoughts, it would be in flagrant contradiction with the character of its speaker. What sin can compare with the implacable determination to send a soul to Hell?[6] And how is such appalling malevolence, worse than anything that Claudius the man is guilty of, to be reconciled with Hamlet's nobility of character? These considerations do not however apply to the pretext if we bear in mind the mystical significance of revenge.

To be more explicit, the different levels of interpretation are in agreement that it is Hamlet's spiritual immaturity that prevents him from taking action. But whereas at the lower level the pretext he gives has to be rejected by the audience as nonsense, that is, as the proverbial "straw" at which a drowning man will clutch, at the highest level the pretext makes profound sense that is perfectly compatible with the Prince's goodness. To see this we have only to consider the significance of Claudius at the different levels.

According to the literal meaning, Claudius is an evil man on his way to Hell. Allegorically, as the killer of King Hamlet, he is the "Serpent" who was responsible for the making mortal of Adam and who thereby gained a hold over the entire human race. Anagogically Claudius is that very hold itself, and to kill him is to set oneself free from it and so eliminate "original sin" which results from the satanic grip. Now in Claudius the man, to go back to the literal meaning, the evil fluctuates somewhat—as Iago's evil never does in *Othello*—and it is only in the last two acts of the play that it has become a fixation. Until then there are moments when the regicide's allegorical significance is, as it were, suspended. The prayer scene is one of these brief

---

[5] *Luxuria*, the Latin term for the deadly sin of lust.

[6] As answer to this question we may quote from *Measure for Measure* (written about the same time as *Hamlet*) what the Duke says about sending a soul to Hell. He has been trying to prepare Barnardine for death, a criminal justly sentenced to be executed for murder. When asked if Barnardine is ready to die, the Duke replies:

> A creature unprepar'd, unmeet for death;
> And to transport him in the mind he is
> Were damnable . . . (IV, 3, 66–68)

respites, and on such rare occasions, Satan's manifestation of himself in Claudius recedes. To kill him then would only constitute a perfect revenge in the literal sense. It would also root out the rottenness from Denmark and "set right" what is "out of joint"; but it could not bear the weight of allegory, let alone that of anagogy, and this is just what the words of the pretext must be interpreted as saying.

Revenge on the devil must be absolute. It requires no apologies. There must be no scruples and no compromise. But the time is not yet ripe. There would be no revenge, and therefore no self-purification, in killing Claudius at that moment because Claudius is not himself. Sometimes the soul's worst possibilities may manifest themselves only partially, in such a way that it would be quite easy to overcome them. But nothing final could be hoped for from resisting them on such an occasion; it is only when those possibilities really show themselves for what they are, when they are rampant in all their iniquity, only then is it possible, by stifling them, to give them the death-blow or mortally wound them. As Hamlet says:

> When he is drunk asleep, or in his rage,
> Or in the incestuous pleasure of his bed,
> At gaming, swearing, or about some act
> That has no relish of salvation in't;
> Then trip him, that his heels may kick at heaven
> And that his soul may be as damn'd and black
> As hell, whereto it goes. (III, 3, 89–95)

In this scene the devil is far from manifesting himself fully in Claudius. The dragon has not yet come out into the open. Or in other words, Hamlet has not nearly reached the bottom of Hell. His father has transmitted to him the knowledge of the full villainy of Claudius but he has not yet had direct experience of it. All that he has learnt so far is relatively indirect compared, for example, with what he finds when he opens the letter to the King of England and reads Claudius's instructions to have him beheaded immediately on arrival; but the very bottom of Hell is only reached when the Queen lies dead and Hamlet's own body has tasted the poison. Meantime, before he can kill the great devil he has first of all to account for the lesser devils, Rosencrantz and Guildenstern, for whose death in England, "No shriving time allowed" (V, 2, 47), he is responsible; and like Dante's "cruelty" toward some of the sufferers he sees in Hell, who are really elements in his own soul, Hamlet's attitude becomes immediately understandable and acceptable and reconcilable with his nobility of nature if we realize that all the victims of his revenge are in a sense part of himself.

Rosencrantz and Guildenstern are indeed nothing but prolongations of Claudius. They would not be there at all if they had not been expressly sent for by him, to act as his spies; and Shakespeare makes it clear, in the last speeches of any length that he puts into their mouths (III, 3), that they have found their true element in the regicide's corrupt court, where they have quickly developed into monsters of flattery and hypocrisy. As to Polonius, despite his extreme subservience to Claudius, the worst we can do is to reserve our judgment and leave his case undecided as Hamlet appears to leave it in his recently quoted gibe at Claudius. But Hamlet also says, this time in all seriousness, pointing to the old man's body:

> For this same lord,
> I do repent ...
> and will answer well
> The death I gave him. (III, 4, 172–77)

Nor is it permissible to forget the last line that we hear Ophelia sing before she makes her final exit: "God ha' mercy on his soul" (IV, 6, 198), which may no doubt be said to outweigh all other considerations.

The great bedroom scene that follows the prayer scene is as it were the center of the play. The Queen instinctively equates her son with her conscience, and she has been holding him at a certain distance. Even now, when the two are to be alone together at last, she has contrived, or rather let us say willingly consented, to have a third party present, hiding behind the arras. The presence of Polonius at the beginning of this scene means the presence, in the soul, of the determination to brazen things out. The Queen's first words to Hamlet referring to Claudius as his "father," are shameless in their effrontery: "Hamlet, thou has thy father much offended" (III, 4, 9). But when Hamlet's sword pierces the body of Polonius, the way is opened for conscience to pierce through the soul's mask of self-justification. The sword itself may be said to represent the truth that pierces through the foolish blindness of which Polonius is the embodiment; and it is immediately after his death that Gertrude comes to know at last the truth about Claudius.

The word "immediately" is by no means pointless. The audience, ever since the first appearance of Hamlet and his mother, have had an increasing desire to see them alone together on the stage. Shakespeare has kept them waiting; but now that longed-for moment has come. What they want above all is the satisfaction of hearing the Prince tell the Queen how his father died, and of seeing how far it will change her attitude to her second husband. Now it is true that she as well as Claudius has witnessed the poisoner's crime re-enacted in some detail by the players under Hamlet's guidance, and she has also witnessed the overwhelming impact of that episode upon Claudius. This experience serves the purpose of enabling her to grasp the whole truth in an instant when the time comes for her to be told, but meantime it amounts to no more than a subconscious preparation. Her brazen words to Hamlet as he joins her make it clear both to him and to the audience that she has not yet drawn any conclusions either from the play itself or from the King's reaction to it. She therefore needs to be informed; nor is it nearly enough, from the point of view of dramatic art, that Hamlet, in listing his uncle's vices, should simply include the word "murderer," as he does later in the scene. That merely implies that he has already conveyed to her the facts of the murder; and so indeed he has, but with such marvelous economy that in the performances of *Hamlet* that we are accustomed to seeing on the stage or on the screen it does not come across to the audience, and they are denied the satisfaction they have been waiting for.

This shortcoming is too great a violation of the unwritten laws of drama to be blamed on Shakespeare. It is not possible that the consummate dramatist could have made such a blunder at so vital a moment in the play. But editors can easily go astray, and that is what has happened here, initially through some editor's clumsy insertion of a stage direction which is lacking in both the Quarto and Folio editions of *Hamlet*. At what point precisely does the Prince lift the arras and reveal the body of Polonius? As we shall see, the text itself makes it clear when this should take place; but the editor in question has timed it four lines too late; and unfortunately he has been followed, with one exception,[7] by all subsequent editors—at least, all whose work I have seen—including Edward Dowden, the editor of the 1928 Arden edition. The apparent reason for the general acceptance of this delay is that it makes the lifting of the arras, when it comes, more "dramatic"; and so, for the sake of a somewhat paltry effect, one of the most truly dramatic moments in Shakespeare has been sacrificed, a moment that any actors would be glad to exploit for the display of their talent, and, what is more, the very moment that the audience have been waiting for with such expectation.

Let us briefly consider the action as it takes place from the entry of the

---

[7] The editor of the current Arden edition, Harold Jenkins, times it right. His interpretation of the spoken words, however, does not seem to differ from that of the other editors.

Prince. The Queen, seeing almost at once that she can no longer control her son in virtue of her parental authority, makes a move as if to go in search of others. Hamlet, no doubt taking her by the arm, says:

> Come, come and sit you down; you shall not budge;
> You go not till I set you up a glass
> Where you may see the inmost part of you. (III, 4, 18–20)

Still thinking him to be mad, the Queen is not unnaturally afraid, and cries for help. Polonius echoes her, presumably as loud as possible in the vain hope that there might be someone within earshot. A shout can disguise a voice; and who indeed could be expected to be, at night, behind the arras in the Queen's closet, except the King? Hamlet assumes that it must be him, and making a pass through the arras he kills Polonius who with his last breath, groans or sighs: "Oh, I am slain!" (III, 4, 25). Admittedly, a dying utterance will also tend to disguise the voice, but probably less than a shout. At any rate it seems to be at this moment that Hamlet begins to doubt the identity of his victim; and when the Queen exclaims: "Oh me, what hast thou done?" he replies: "Nay, I know not; is it the king?" Having put this urgent question, it would be unnatural if he did not then and there give himself the answer by lifting the arras. It is moreover necessary that he should do so precisely then as a cue for the Queen's cry of dismay when she sees the dead and bleeding body of Polonius: "Oh, what a rash and bloody deed is this!" (III, 4, 2, 5–7). It is the crucial passage that immediately ensues; and if it be played more or less as follows, all problems vanish, no loose thread is left hanging and the audience is more than satisfied.

At first Hamlet is appalled: for anyone of his sensitivity, it is not nothing to have killed a relatively innocent man by mistake, a man who is more-over his beloved Ophelia's father whom, whatever his limitations, she dearly loves, as the Prince knows. He slowly and solemnly echoes the Queen's words: "A bloody deed!" He is for the moment disconcerted: altogether contrary to his purpose, he has put himself instead of his mother in the wrong. Then he proceeds to redress the balance; and since it is imperative that she should take him seriously and not continue to think him mad, he must seek to convince her of his perfect sanity both by the way he looks at her and by his slow recollected and impressive manner of speech as he adds:

> almost as bad, good mother,
> As kill a king, and marry with his brother. (III, 4, 28–29)

There must be a pause at "king," since the two halves of the line have to be taken separately in that they concern two different persons. Admittedly by reason of its syntax, the whole line might seem at first sight to concern the Queen and to accuse her of murder as well as of incest; and we have already seen that her subservience to the regicide makes her in a sense his accomplice. Nonetheless the line cannot be passed over lightly as a mere echo of the Player Queen's "None wed the second but who killed the first." There are overwhelming reasons for us to take "as kill a king" to be nothing other than an accusation against Claudius alone. First, the context demands mention of a killing in the ordinary sense such as can serve as a parallel to the Prince's killing of Polonius. "Almost as bad" is a typically Hamlettian ironic equivalent of "nothing like so bad." Second, the context also demands that Hamlet shall not speak to his mother, at this juncture, in anything but clear terms. Such indeed is his express purpose, "I will speak daggers to her but use none" (III, 2, 415) and the daggers must not be blunted by anything enigmatic. Moreover, in order to convince her of her guilt, he would have been on his guard against including in his accusations any blame that she could easily deny. Third, for his "daggers" to make their full impact, that is, for her to be fully vulnerable to their thrust, it is necessary for her to know that the man to whom she has given herself, body and soul, is the murderer of her first husband; and if in those four words "as kill a king" and his subsequent corroboration of them Hamlet is not telling her exactly how his father died, then he never does tell her, and that would be, we repeat, too great a violation of dramatic art to be attributed to Shakespeare. But in fact Shakespeare is here displaying his art of the stage to its full.

The slow emphatic delivery of the four key words with a pause at "king" not only gives time for Hamlet to speak with his eyes as well as his tongue, but also for the truth to dawn on the Queen. We may suppose that she scarcely hears "and marry with his brother," which Hamlet throws in so as not to leave her for a moment without blame. She too must let her eyes speak and perhaps draw closer to him, looking into his face as she queries his words with her own "As kill a king?", at first half incredulous, but then convinced by the certitude conveyed to her from Hamlet and, in retrospect, by the guilty reaction of Claudius to the players' enactment of the poisoning in the garden. Her questioning echo of his words means: "Was the king your father in fact killed, not by a snake as we were told, but by a man?" Yet she herself knows the answer almost as she puts the question, and Hamlet sees that she knows it and that there is no need for him even to name the man, so he simply caps her query with his implacable "Ay, lady, 'twas my word" (III, 4, 30). Seldom can a dramatist have portrayed such intimacy between characters as Shakespeare does here between mother and son; and intimacy, telepathic almost by definition, has power to replace the spoken thought by the unspoken thought. In fact, such is the verbal thrift at this point that Hamlet is able to convince his mother of the whole iniquitous truth in less than one line.

He now speaks to Polonius:

> Thou wretched, rash, intruding fool, farewell!
> I took thee for thy better; take thy fortune;
> Thou find'st to be too busy is some danger. (III, 4, 31–33)

When the play is acted in obedience to the printed text, that is, to the editors, Hamlet does not raise the arras until just before he utters these words. We are accustomed to hearing them declaimed as an outburst of savage exaspera-tion; and this violence is often kept up long enough to be turned against his mother and to set a feverish temperature for the dialogue that follows. But in fact, when the Prince addresses the dead man, he has already had time to adjust himself to the shock of the unforeseen accident. He has moreover already achieved something with his mother, enough to give him a presen-timent of his mastery of the situation. Violence is therefore not called for. He can well afford to bid farewell to his victim with solemnity, stern no doubt, but not without a touch of pity. Then, all the more terrible for his calm weighing of words, he makes ready to speak his "daggers" to the Queen:

> Leave wringing of your hands. Peace! sit you down,
> And let me wring your heart; for so I shall
> If it be made of penetrable stuff,
> If damned custom have not braz'd it so
> That it is proof and bulwark against sense. (III, 4, 34–38)

She makes a last vain effort to resist her conscience by taking refuge in her innocence of the murder and her ignorance of it. There should be a stress on "I" in the line which follows:

> What have I done that thou dar'st wag thy tongue
> In noise so rude against me? (III, 4, 39–40)

But this serves to give Hamlet the best possible cue for overwhelming her with what she inescapably knows to be true, and she is eventually driven to say:

> O Hamlet, speak no more;
> Thou turn'st mine eyes into my very soul,
> And there I see such black and grained spots
> As will not leave their tint.[8] (III, 4, 88–91)

It is often the case in Shakespeare's greater plays that there should be more than one "purgatorial pilgrim," more than one "Everyman"; and although the part of Gertrude is short in words, from her first appearance she holds the audience in the grip of an intense interest that is only second to their interest in Hamlet. Her repentance signifies her qualification to follow her son and enter upon the path of purification. It is at this moment that the ghost, unseen by her, reappears to Hamlet and delegates him to be the spiritual guide of his mother; and under the inspiration of his father's words:

> Oh, step between her and her fighting soul . . .
> Speak to her, Hamlet. (III, 4, 113–15)

he tells his mother what she must do. In this scene the literal meaning itself is drawn up to the mysterial level. The Prince speaks to his new disciple with an exalted penetration worthy of a master who has years of practical experience of the mystic path behind him. The spiritual dialogue ends with her solemn oath:

> Be thou assured, if words be made of breath,
> And breath of life, I have no life to breathe
> What thou hast said to me. (III, 4, 197–99)

The two lines which immediately follow have in themselves no direct spiritual significance, but they are spiritually most moving as expressive of a profound norm of human relationship that had been torn asunder and is now perfectly restored. This is the first time that we have seen the mother and the son at ease together, and the extraordinary effect of their words

---

[8]Nothing I can say to myself will make them leave their black tint to take on a lighter color.

upon us is enhanced by the very ordinariness of his question and her answer:

> I must to England; you know that?
>> Alack,
> I had forgot; 'tis so concluded on. (III, 4, 200–201)

To judge from the cuts in the First folio edition of *Hamlet,* published only seven years after Shakespeare's death, we may assume that the full text of this play was considered then, as now, too long for the requirements of theatrical performance. Unfortunately, one of the passages nearly always sacrificed today is Act IV, scene 4, without which the balance of the play as a whole is seriously upset. In this scene Hamlet, on his way to the Danish coast to set sail for England, has a glimpse of Fortinbras, the young Prince of Norway, who is leading his army through Denmark to fight against the Poles; and this glimpse reveals to Hamlet a hero endowed with the virtue that he himself most needs to develop. The scene where Fortinbras first appears is needed above all in that it marks a stage in the development of Hamlet, who drinks a new strength into his soul from his vision of Fortinbras. In the soliloquy that is prompted by his foretaste of his own true self there is a ring of confidence and resolution that we have not heard before:

> From this time forth,
> My thoughts be bloody, or be nothing worth! (IV, 4, 65–66)

Objectively of course the world "bloody" must be taken to mean "concerned with slaughter," that is with the killing of Claudius. But subjectively it means "from the heart," that is, penetrated by resolution. No longer shall "the native hue of resolution" be "sicklied o'er with the pale cast of thought." He promises us, and convinces us, that from now on the process will be reversed: instead of imposing its own pallor on other faculties, thought shall borrow resolution's own natural color, which is blood-red inasmuch as it springs from the heart. It must be remembered in this connection that the word "heart," which in its ordinary sense refers to the central organ of the body, has universally also the mystical sense of center of the soul; witness such terms as "Eye of the Heart"[9] that are common to all traditions. And

---

[9] The capitals here denote the transcendent sense of the organs in question.

Shakespeare is in line with the whole ancient world in assigning resolution to the Heart. Intellect and resolution, the crowns of intelligence and will respectively, are both, according to the esoterisms of West as well as East, enthroned in the Heart, the gateway to the Spirit, the "narrow gate" which alone allows passage from this world to the Beyond. It is significant that one of the great Sufi poets terms the path of the Mysteries as "the way of resolution."[10]

The spirituality of the mystic is magnetic for all other souls that are of the right metal; and the Prince draws in his wake not only his mother but also Ophelia. Her madness takes us by surprise; it is not difficult however to imagine the reasons for it—Hamlet's supposed loss of his sanity, her own supposed loss of his love, his madly precipitate departure, her father's sudden unaccountable disappearance, then (we do not know how long afterwards) news of his death and burial, *all without any explanation whatsoever,* and all in the absence of her brother on whom she might have leaned for support. But at a higher level of meaning her gains are far greater than her losses. She can be said in a sense to have followed Hamlet's behest "Get thee to a nunnery" inasmuch as her madness is indeed a retreat in which she has renounced all worldliness. For her there are only two categories of persons, the dead and the dying:

> And will he not come again?
> And will he not come again?
> No, no, he is dead,
> Go to thy death bed.
> He never will come again. (IV, 5, 189–93)

Her great supports are hope and patience: "I hope all will be well. We must be patient" (IV, 5, 177). Lear's madness is likewise a spiritual retreat, and he too preaches patience. There is also a sharp discernment in both madnesses, an insight that enables Ophelia, with regard to others, to know *what* they are, even if she fails to know *who* they are.

In her last scene, when she distributes her flowers, it is natural that she

---

[10]Umar ibn al-Farid in his poem *al-Khamriyyah* (the Winesong). See my annotated translation in the anthology *Sufi Poems,* Islamic Texts Society, 2004. The term in question is there rendered "the path of firm resolve."

should go first to Laertes as the nearest and dearest of those present. But she does not know who he is and speaks to him rather as if he were her beloved Hamlet. Rosemary for remembrance, and pansies for loving thoughts, are the flowers she gives him. His comment, "A document in madness," that is instruction in the guise of madness, is a clear indication that her distribution is not without significance. To Claudius, who is standing next to Laertes, she gives fennel, the symbol of insincerity and flattery, together with columbines which are a sign of cuckoldom, and which are apt in the sense that his wife has been "seduced" from him by the Spirit. The Queen she recognizes as a fellow traveler upon the path of repentance and purification that leads, in good time, to grace: "There's rue for you; and here's some for me; We may call it herb of grace o'Sundays" (IV, 5, 177). To the unnamed gentleman, no doubt typical of the new Danish court, she gives a daisy, which is associated with dissembling and with being an upstart; and to Horatio she says: "I would give you some violets but they withered all when my father died." The violet is the flower of fidelity (IV, 5, 180–81).

Also authoritative is Ophelia's serenity: she has found peace in her retreat, without a trace of bitterness; and her last words, in which she extends to "all Christian souls" (IV, 5, 199) her already quoted prayer for mercy on her father, are in perfect keeping with her "nunnery," for to renounce worldly life is to renounce particularity and to take on a more universal responsibility. In the same way her final "God be wi' you" must be pronounced, not as a mere formality, but as a solemn blessing. It anticipates the words of Laertes at her burial: "A ministering angel shall my sister be" (V, 1, 263).

In that same churchyard scene, before the funeral procession enters, Hamlet, who is himself to die the next day, has the inevitable certainty of death brought home to him with a concrete realism that makes his bones ache, and those of the audience too. He is made to hear death in the knocking together of dead men's bones as the gravedigger throws down one against another; he sees, touches and smells death as he takes the jester's skull in his hands; he even almost tastes death as he remembers how often as a child he had put his lips against what is now no more than two rows of teeth set in two jawbones: "Here hung those lips that I have kissed I know not how oft" (V, 1, 201–8).

There is yet another sign that his days are numbered, for it comes out that the gravedigger had taken up his profession on the day that Hamlet was born, thirty years previously; and for him the Prince is already almost a thing of the past, one who has not only come but gone. A strange and sudden chill emanates from the words, spoken with the objectivity of a chronicle: "It was the very day that young Hamlet was born; he that is mad, and sent into England" (V, 2, 160–62). Moreover the scene is to end with the actual burial of everything that had represented, for Hamlet, the possibility of earthly happiness, and he himself finally leaps into the grave, where the convulsive violence of his outburst is indeed suggestive of a death agony.

We learn from hagiographies that more than one mystic has sought before now to familiarize himself with death by laying himself out in a coffin; and this scene amounts to that for Hamlet. It leads up to his speech in the final scene where he expresses his readiness to die at any time. What does it matter if a man die young, since no man really ever possesses any of the things he leaves behind him at death? "Since no man has aught of what he leaves, what is't to leave betimes?" (V, 2, 233–34). We have come a long way from the attitude toward death that is expressed in the most famous of his soliloquies.

The Mysteries are a pact between the Divine and the human, and they lay on man the obligation of perseverance, that is, resolution faithfully maintained. Hamlet's fulfillment of his pact lies in his perpetual preoccupation with "honor" and "revenge." As to the Divine part of the pact, Horatio's already quoted promise, "Heaven will direct it," may be said to have its fulfillment in various ways, most of them no doubt hidden, but some of them manifest, like the appearance of the Ghost in the Queen's closet immediately after the Prince has won over his mother to repentance. A subsequent example is his glimpse of Fortinbras, which was nothing other than a grace, for there was no human intention behind the encounter. Next, and most direct of all, there is the inspiration that saves him from Claudius's plot to have him killed in England. This is inextricably identified, as far as his spiritual development is concerned, with the clearly providential church-yard episode, which comes after the inspiration but which precedes it for the reader and the spectator. It is only in the last scene of the play that we hear of Hamlet's inspired activity on board the boat and that we see the effect of that grace upon him, interwoven with the effect of his foretaste of death. He ascribes, with considerable insistence, every detail of his escape to Divine intervention, and his account of what happened enables trust in Providence to take its place as cornerstone in the remarkable image of kingliness that Shakespeare gives us in Hamlet at the beginning of this scene. His now full-grown royalty of nature causes Horatio to exclaim: "Why, what a king is this!" (V, 2, 62). It is significant also that only here, for the very first time, does Hamlet mention, among Claudius's other iniquities that he has robbed him of the crown that he himself had hoped to wear; and when Horatio implies that there is no time to be lost because news of what has happened will shortly come from England, and when Hamlet replies:

> It will be short; the interim is mine;
> And a man's life's no more than to say 'One'. (V, 2, 73–74)

we are certain that Claudius has not long to live.

"Everyman" now knows that he has almost come to the end of his journey and that the end will be victory but also, necessarily, death. The spiritual station of Hamlet at this moment is comparable to that of Henry IV who on hearing of his victory against the rebels sinks down in mortal sickness with the words: "And wherefore should these good news make me sick?" (Pt 2: IV, 4, 102). As to Hamlet's foreboding of death, it is just before the entry of the King and Queen and Laertes for the fencing match that he intimates to Horatio his premonition that he is going to die. Horatio begs to be allowed to postpone the match, but Hamlet will not hear of it. His refusal is perhaps the greatest speech of the play, and we have already quoted the essence of it:[11]

> Not a whit; we defy augury; there's a special providence in the fall of
> a sparrow. If it be now, 'tis not to come; if it be not to come, it will be
> now; if it be not now, yet it will come; the readiness is all; since no
> man has aught of what he leaves, what is't to leave betimes? Let be.
> (V, 2, 229–35)

To be ready for death when it comes is all that matters; and in telling us this, Hamlet tells us that he himself is ready. As such, he is spiritually even more magnetic than before; and in addition to the souls of the Queen and Ophelia, there is yet another soul that is destined to be drawn in his wake. In speaking to Horatio about the fate of Rosencrantz and Guildenstern he remarks that it is dangerous for men of "baser nature" to insinuate themselves between two "mighty opposites," that is, in this case, between Claudius

---

[11] See pp. 7–8 and 46.

and himself. Claudius is mighty because he is on the throne albeit as a usurper, but Hamlet himself is mighty with the Divine right of kings which is his in virtue of his now fulfilled kingliness of nature or, in other words, in virtue of his now being up to the mandate laid on him, or yet again because, since all Heaven is on his side as he now knows beyond doubt, the clash is ultimately between Michael and Lucifer. It is his serenely objective application of the word "mighty" to himself that in fact prompts Horatio's already quoted exclamation "Why, what a king is this!" but Rosencrantz and Guildenstern are not the only ones whose destiny brings them into this zone of danger. Claudius also maneuvers Laertes into the same fatal situation, and at first it seems that the son of Polonius will prove to be the perfect tool for the end toward which he is being manipulated. He has merely to be told whose hand it was that struck his father down; and the madness of Ophelia followed by her death adds timely fuel to the fire of Laertes' anger.

It is in a state of raging hatred of Hamlet that Laertes, having invoked curses on his head, jumps into Ophelia's grave; and he adds, when the Prince jumps in after him: "The devil take thy soul!" (V, 1, 280). Yet within less than twenty-four hours it is Claudius who is the object of Laertes' hatred, whereas Hamlet is the object of his esteem almost to the point of brotherly love, without there being any direct explanation in the text or indeed any indication that a change is taking place, except for the "aside" of Laertes shortly before he wounds Hamlet: "And yet 'tis almost gainst my conscience" (V, 2, 307). This is yet another example of enigma resulting from the extreme concentration of Shakespeare's art. But here again, as always, he has given us the keys to open the doors he has not opened for us expressly.

He has however explicitly affirmed Laertes' nobility of nature through the mouth of Hamlet himself; and that weighty judgment cannot but mean that Laertes is qualified for the way of the Mysteries since, in the eyes of a man like the Prince, the fact of being "very noble" could not possibly mean anything less. This estimate is moreover confirmed when Hamlet avows his regret for his share of the clash in the graveyard:

> But I am very sorry, good Horatio
> That to Laertes I forgot myself;
> For by the image of my cause, I see
> The portraiture of his; I'll court his favours. (V, 2, 75–78)

Literally this means: we are both sons of slain fathers whose deaths make us in honor bound to avenge them. But beyond that it places Laertes side by side with Hamlet also as regards the supreme significance of honor and revenge.

The outset of Laertes' spiritual path is when he starts out from France to Elsinore to wreak his vengeance upon Claudius and we may assume that it is for this purpose that he bought the poison from the mountebank. By nature he would shrink from being a poisoner, but with regard to the enemy of mankind such scruples are out of place; witness the words of Hamlet, when he finally uses this very same poison against that enemy: "Then venom to thy work" (V, 2, 333). Nor has Laertes set off on the wrong track, as he is later led to believe, since the regicidal act of Claudius is truly responsible for both of Laertes' bereavements, his father's death and his sister's madness leading to her death. If King Hamlet had not been murdered there could have been no question of Polonius hiding behind the arras in the Queen's closet, and the loves of Hamlet and Ophelia would presumably have flowered into a harmonious marriage. It is thus clear that Claudius is in a sense doubly qualified for his allegorical significance. The main theme of the tragedy equates him at that level, as we have seen, with the serpent who "poisoned" our first ancestor, and he retains this significance throughout. But as the action proceeds there is a piling up of wrong; and toward the end, in what we might call the Laertes theme, the stress is rather on the global responsibility of Claudius, his quantitative guilt, which qualifies him to bear, allegorically, the guilt for all the evil that exists herebelow. Laertes himself never in fact learns the full extent of the iniquity in question; but in his final summing up to Hamlet there is nonetheless a ring of totality in his denunciation of Claudius: "The king, the king's to blame" (V, 2, 331).

As to what lies above and beyond allegory, let it be said once again that whereas Claudius must be seen allegorically as the contriver of man's fall and as the gainer thereby of a hold over all mankind, anagogically or mysterially he personifies that hold itself; and the path of Laertes, like that of Gertrude, affords us a very direct image of the Lesser Mysteries. In the purgatorial process of which these Mysteries are woven, it is always initially a question of loosening, with a view to finally throwing off, the grip of Satan who, for his part, will seek to tighten his hold, as Claudius succeeds in doing at first when he persuades Laertes to turn his revengeful animosity in another direction on the grounds that he, Claudius, is not to blame. At first the bare fact that it was Hamlet and not Claudius who killed Polonius seems on the surface to support Claudius' claim; but other facts subsequently come to light, as we shall see, and these enable the better nature of Laertes, momentarily overcome by the deceiver, to reassert itself. Claudius, not being able to see in depth, is blind to his nobility; but he can see his surface, the plane of temperament; and given the circumstances, Laertes' temperament suits to perfection the plot of Claudius, who rightly senses that once the young man has been set in impetuous motion upon a course, it will indeed be difficult for anything to turn him aside. That difficulty was nonetheless to be overcome by his nobility, too late to save Hamlet's life, but in time to reverse, for himself, the process of the fall of man.

As to the way toward that end, it seems probable that even before they all leave the graveyard, Claudius has begun to lose something of his hold over Laertes, whose mistaken attitude toward the Prince may well have begun to waver, having reached its climax in his already quoted curse "the devil take thy soul!" At any rate, for the rest of the scene, Laertes remains totally silent, which in itself is not conclusive either way. But during that silence two facts, hitherto unknown to him, are impressed upon him. We may assume that Claudius, in seeking to augment Laertes' thirst for revenge against the killer of his father, had taken care to say nothing about Hamlet's madness lest it should seem to exonerate him and thus take the edge off Laertes' hostility. But in the graveyard Claudius is, despite himself, obliged by circumstances to beg Laertes to excuse Hamlet's behavior there on the ground of his madness. The Queen likewise strenuously affirms her son's madness. Thus doubts of Hamlet's full responsibility for Polonius's death will at least have crossed Laertes' mind even before the Prince himself pleads his innocence, as he does so disarmingly the next day. The other unknown fact that is suddenly and powerfully brought to light in the graveyard is the depth and sincerity of Hamlet's love for Ophelia, and Laertes may well have suffered some stabs of conscience, remembering how he had so emphatically warned his sister against taking Hamlet's professions of love seriously. Was he altogether innocent, he may have wondered, of having sowed seeds which might have contributed to the madness of both these lovers?

Enough has perhaps been said to explain the already quoted aside of Laertes: "But yet 'tis almost gainst my conscience." That aside however is merely a milestone on a way that leads far beyond the domain of "almost." That the violent collision on Ophelia's grave should come to be transformed into harmonious union can no doubt best be explained, as has already been intimated, by the powerful magnetism of spirituality on Hamlet's side and, on the side of Laertes, his being of just the right metal to be drawn by the magnet in question. Nor is it to be doubted that when the King and Queen and their courtiers enter, together with Laertes, for the fencing match, the spiritual maturity of Hamlet, which has just evoked Horatio's exclamation of wonderment, would be found to have at least some effect upon any other sensitive man. Moreover the Mysteries are always fraught with a choice, which in the case of Gertrude was put explicitly before her; but Laertes does not have to be told: "Look here upon this picture, and on this," (III, 4, 53) for the two "mighty opposites" are there, standing before him in the flesh. Birds of a feather flock together; and when Laertes sees his "enemy," the kingly Hamlet, side by side with his "ally," the depraved usurper, it is scarcely possible that he should not be assailed by discomforting thoughts of being on the wrong side. Unlike Rosencrantz and Guildenstern, he himself is very definitely not of the feather of Claudius.

The actor who plays Laertes must therefore make it clear, almost from his entry in this final scene, that he is a man divided against himself, that is, until his dissociation from Claudius and his union with Hamlet have been completed. Meantime, by a meager residue of his initial impetus, he continues to move on in the course in which he is set, and mechanically picks out, according to plan, an unbated foil from among the bated ones. But his dividedness robs his fencing of all its brilliance, as we may gather from remarks made by both Hamlet and Claudius.

As soon as Hamlet's wound tells him that his adversary's weapon is unbated, he closes with him and snatches from him the misdirected blood-stained blade. In doing so he pulls the man himself altogether free from the grip of their common enemy. Then he confirms this freedom by handing him his own innocence in the form of the bated foil. Laertes' last links with Claudius are snapped. That sudden reversal of the weapons and with it his own sudden vulnerability, like a dazzling manifestation of Divine justice, completely overwhelm him with a sense of his need to atone for his blindness; and his brief but full purgatory may be said to take place while he desperately fences for his life with no more than the bated foil in his hand against the now fatally armed Prince. When he in his turn is wounded he says to Osric: "I am justly killed with mine own treachery" (V, 2, 318) and then to Hamlet:

> The treacherous instrument is in thy hand,
> Unbated and envenom'd; the foul practice
> Hath turned itself on me; lo, here I lie,
> Never to rise again; thy mother's poison'd;
> I can no more. (V, 2, 327–31)

51

But he is to die victorious, having had his share in Hamlet's slaying of the Dragon, for which he now gives the signal: "The king, the king's to blame" (V, 2, 331). And when Hamlet thereupon kills Claudius by stabbing him and pouring the deadly drink down his throat, Laertes applauds the justice of the deed, for which he himself had supplied the blade and indicated the poisoned cup. His victory is sealed by his dying words:

> Exchange forgiveness with me, noble Hamlet:
> Mine and my father's death come not upon thee,
> Nor thine on me! (V, 2, 339–42)

And it is above all sealed by the Prince's answering absolution: "Heaven make thee free of it! I follow thee" (V, 2, 343).

Laertes' participation in Hamlet's victory is also apparent from another angle. We have already seen in *Henry IV*, as we shall also see in considering some of the later plays, that as regards the deepest meaning there are two harmoniously coexisting and mutually corroborating modes of interpretation, one of which might be called analytical and the other synthetic. According to the first of these there is, in *Henry IV*, more than one Everyman, each with his own individual way, the King and the Prince; according to the second, Everyman is a synthesis of father and son taken together. But the synthesis may consist of more than two elements, as in fact it does in other plays: a varying number of subordinate characters may be taken to personify different aspects of the central character, and Everyman will then consist of the protagonist together with the subordinates in question. To interpret *Hamlet* in this way, with the Prince as the sole Everyman, and to revert now to Laertes, we have already seen that, like Fortinbras, he personifies precisely those qualities that are as yet only virtual in Hamlet and of which the development is an essential aspect of the main theme. The absence of Laertes for most of the play is thus very significant, and so is his return just at the moment when all that he represents has been brought to life in the Prince by his vision of Fortinbras. Also significant is Ophelia's already mentioned confusing of Laertes with Hamlet—we might say her fusion of Laertes into Hamlet—when she says to him: "There's rosemary, that's for remembrance; pray you, love, remember" (IV, 5, 174–75). A phase of the same fusion is their grappling with each other in her grave, an antagonism destined to become a union and perhaps furthered in that direction by her angelic presence. The union is also prefigured by the interpenetration of their weapons as they fence, and then, even more, by their interchange of weapons. Laertes' rapier can be said, symbolically, to sum up all that the Prince has needed to develop in himself. His having already developed it gives him the right to that mortally effective blade and empowers him to take possession of it. When he does so, it is as if he had absorbed Laertes into himself and taken him with him upon his own victorious way.

From the same synthetic standpoint Ophelia personifies all the love and happiness that Hamlet has sacrificed in this life with a view to the next life whither she herself has already been transferred before the end of the play; and we have also seen that Gertrude is in a sense the fallen soul of Hamlet, a significance that is confirmed by her allegorical equation with Eve, he himself being its faculties of intelligence, conscience, and will. But this synthetic mode of interpretation is less called for here than it is in some other plays. Rather to the contrary, the vast canvas upon which the tragedy of the Prince of Denmark is woven has almost epic dimensions that favor a recognition of more than one Everyman, each with his or her own individual way; and it remains for us to complete what has already been said about the way of the Queen.

Here again we are compelled to use our imaginations, along the definite lines laid down for us by the dramatist. If the great bedroom scene is the first time we see her alone with her son, it is also the last. That scene is prolonged and confirmed in a brief aside (IV, 5, 17–20) in which she simply expresses her consciousness of her guilt, thus showing a preoccupation that is characteristic of a novice upon the way. But apart from this we never again see her in circumstances that enable her to speak freely. Claudius is nearly always there and when he is not, his place is taken by Ophelia, whose presence is also inhibiting, albeit in a different way. In this respect, what is generally accepted today as the final text is almost certainly more elliptical than Shakespeare originally intended it to be when he conceived the play. After the King and Laertes withdraw together at the end of Act IV, scene 5, the First Quarto has a scene in which Horatio tells the Queen of Claudius's unsuccessful attempt to have Hamlet killed in England and Hamlet's return. When the Queen learns that her son is back in Denmark, she tells Horatio:

> Bid him awhile
> Be wary of his presence, lest he fail
> In that he goes about

which means, freely paraphrased: "Tell him to make quite sure that Claudius does not kill him before he kills Claudius." But although this scene is left out in all the later editions of the play, according to the final text a letter is brought from Hamlet to his mother, presumably telling her everything. Moreover, on the basis of Claudius's remark at the end of the church-yard scene: "Good Gertrude, set some watch upon your son," (V, 1, 318) we may imagine that mother and son have ample time to discuss the whole situation.

As to the last scene, because she knows that Claudius is determined to kill her son and that he has spent much time talking to Laertes who is determined to avenge his father's death, it is more than probable that she has fears of a plot between them, whence perhaps her message to Hamlet that he should speak to Laertes in a friendly way before the fencing match. Certainly—and the playing of her part should be based on this—she knows her son's life to be in the very greatest danger. She therefore watches Claudius's every move; nor can there be any doubt that when he calls for a glass of wine, drinks from it to the sound of trumpets and cannon, then offers it to Hamlet, having thrown the priceless pearl he speaks of into it, she suspects or even assumes that he has at the same time surreptitiously inserted something else besides, or that the "pearl" itself is not what it appears to be. Hamlet refuses the drink, but only for the moment, whereupon she herself decides to put it to the test, and suddenly takes up the cup to drink her son's health. The King forbids her to drink, but she is not to be stopped: "I will, my lord, I pray you pardon me" (V, 2, 302). Nor when she realizes that her fears were altogether justified, will she allow her sacrifice to be in vain, and when Claudius seeks to make light of her collapse: "She swounds to see them bleed," (V, 2, 319) she finds the strength to protest:

> No, no, the drink, the drink,—O my dear Hamlet—
> The drink, the drink!—I am poison'd. (V, 2, 320–21)

These farewell words, and especially their most moving interjection, must be taken as an expression of her total gift of soul to Spirit. As such they may assure us that her death, like that of Laertes, is a dying into life.

As to Hamlet's last words, it is significant that they are a message to Fortinbras. This, together with the entry of Fortinbras immediately after Hamlet's death marks a certain continuity between the dead prince and the living one. There is a suggestion—nothing more—that Hamlet is mysteriously reborn in Fortinbras, though Shakespeare does not indicate this "alchemy" explicitly here as he does in *Henry IV.* At the end of *Hamlet* the stress lies rather on the fruit of rebirth, that is, not on an earthly horizontal succession, but on an upward celestial continuity. If the play as a whole corresponds to an interpenetration of Dante's *Inferno* and *Purgatorio,* the *Paradiso* is nonetheless not merely implicit. It is expressly anticipated in Horatio's farewell prayer for Hamlet:

> Good night, sweet prince,
> And flights of angels sing thee to thy rest! (V, 2, 37)

CHAPTER FIVE

OTHELLO

The essential feature of man's primordial state was the union of his soul with the Spirit; and one of the most universal symbols of the regaining of that state is marriage, the union of lovers. The prototype of this symbolism in Christianity lies in Christ's own references to himself as "the Bridegroom"; and the Middle Ages were dominated by the conception of the Church or, microcosmically, the soul as the bride of Christ. Let us quote from the beginning of Ruysbroek's *The Adornment of the Spiritual Marriage:*

> This Bridegroom is Christ, and human nature is the bride; which God has made in His own image and after His likeness. And in the beginning He had set her in the highest and most beautiful, the richest and most fertile place in all the earth; that is, in Paradise. And He had given her dominion over all Creatures; and He had adorned her with graces; and had given her a commandment, so that by obedience she might have merited to be confirmed and established with her Bridegroom in an eternal troth, and never to fall into any grief, or any sin.
>
> Then came a beguiler, the hellish fiend, full of envy, in the shape of a subtle serpent. . . . And the fiend seduced the bride of God with false counsel; and she was driven into a strange country, poor and miserable and captive and oppressed, and beset by her enemies; so that it seemed

as though she might never attain reconciliation and return again to her native land.

But when God thought the time had come, and had mercy on the suffering of His beloved, He sent His only Begotten Son to earth, in a fair chamber, in a glorious temple; that is, in the body of the Virgin Mary. There he was married to his bride, our nature.[1]

Medieval art was continually expressing this union, in various ways, as for example in pictures of the mystical marriage of St. Catharine of Alexandria with Christ, she representing the perfect soul and he the Spirit. But the Virgin Mary, in virtue of her Assumption and Coronation and her function as Co-Redemptress, also stands for the Spirit, and so by extension may be a perfect woman. In *The Divine Comedy*, when Dante reaches the Garden of Eden on the top of the Mountain of Purgatory, Beatrice his beloved, personifying spiritual wisdom, descends from Heaven and the two meet in the terrestrial Paradise; and in *The Faerie Queene*, the sequel to the Red Crosse Knight's victory over the dragon is his marriage to the Lady Una.

In *Othello* the black Moor and his white lady are soul and Spirit. Like Cordelia, Desdemona is "the pearl of great price" that was wantonly thrown away. Othello describes himself as:

> One whose hand,
> Like the base Judean,[2] threw a pearl away
> Richer than all his tribe. (V, 2, 344–46)

As for Iago, Othello says of him, after his iniquity has been revealed: "I look down toward his feet; but that's a fable," meaning: I look down to see the devil's cloven hooves; but since I see that Iago, who is unquestionably the devil, has ordinary human feet, I now learn that the current idea about the devil's feet is a mere fable. Then he strikes at Iago with his sword saying: "If that thou be'st a devil, I cannot kill thee." And in fact he cannot kill him; Iago remarks to Lodovico: "I bleed sir, but not kill'd" (V, 2, 284–86).

The sudden and secret marriage of Othello and Desdemona at the beginning of the play has taken Iago by surprise. But this union of soul and

---

[1] Translated by C. A. Wynschenk Dom, 2005.
[2] We retain the First Folio's "Judean" in preference to "Indian" of the later Folios and of the Arden edition. The metrically called-for stress on the first syllable helps to confirm the reference to Judas.

Spirit is only virtual; it marks the outset of the spiritual path, not the end, and symbolizes initiation rather than realization; and the first scene opens upon the devil preparing to do all in his power to wreck the marriage before it can come to fullness. To start with he can do little, for although husband and wife are temporarily separated, the Senate agrees that Desdemona shall follow Othello to Cyprus; but their first night there together is disturbed by the drunken brawl that Iago has staged; and the next morning he begins to imbue Othello with the suspicion that Desdemona is unfaithful to him, so that the two lovers are never really in peace together until at the end they are lying dead side by side upon the marriage bed. Only then, after it has passed through the "narrow gate" of death, is the soul truly united with the Spirit.

But it has a foretaste of Paradise, when the Moor arrives in Cyprus to find that Desdemona is already there before him. Her speedy coming has been almost miraculous, for as Cassio says:

> Tempests themselves, high seas and howling winds,
> The gutter'd rocks, and congregated sands,
> Traitors ensteep'd to clog the guiltless keel,
> As having sense of beauty, do omit
> Their mortal natures, letting go safely by
> The divine Desdemona. (II, 1, 68–73)

When Othello enters he says:

> It gives me wonder great as my content
> To see you here before me. O my soul's joy!
> If after every tempest come such calms,
> Let the winds blow till they have waken'd death!
> And let the labouring bark climb hills of seas
> Olympus-high, and duck again as low
> As hell's from heaven! (II, 1, 184–90)

We have here an anticipation of the terrible "storm" that is to follow, but also, in a sense, a guarantee of the final peace.

It may be asked: If Desdemona symbolizes the Spirit, why does she not see through Iago, as Cordelia would undoubtedly have done? But apart from the fact that Desdemona's proneness to think well of people unless given good reasons for not doing so is an aspect of her generosity and childlikeness and therefore part of her perfection, it must be remembered that a symbol can never account for every aspect of the higher reality that it symbolizes. One has the impression that no one was more critical of Shakespeare's symbols than the author himself and that he was continually striving to make them fuller and more all-embracing. We have already suggested that Claudius in *Hamlet* may be partly the result of Shakespeare's consciousness of the inadequacy of Falstaff as a personification of the devil; but although we might be tempted to say that Iago is an "improvement" on Claudius, it no doubt would be a mistake to suppose that Shakespeare was dissatisfied with his portrayal of the Danish regicide and usurper, who is perfectly adequate to represent the devil allegorically. In this same context of comparisons, whatever we may say about Cordelia and Desdemona, each of the two is exactly right for the play she belongs to, at every level of meaning. Nor can we fail to mention here, as an essential aspect of this adequacy, that Desdemona is the ideal complement to Othello. The ancient world and the Middle Ages held that every human being is perfectly matched by another human being of the opposite sex. The two may be separated by time and space and may never meet in this life, but if they do, no ordinary earthly passion can compare with the love that each feels for the other. Consequently, since a true symbol must be perfect of its kind, we may say that where the symbolism of sexual love is used, only such total and "absolute" love as this is fully worthy to represent the primordial relationship between soul and Spirit, and it is clear that Shakespeare had no less than such love in mind when he drew the characters of Romeo and Juliet, for example, of Othello and Desdemona, and of Antony and Cleopatra. In *Othello*, as in these other plays, we are made to feel that there is something cosmic and universal in the intense mutual attraction between the lovers; and our thoughts leap to identify themselves with Othello's when he says in the last scene, with reference to his wife's death:

> Methinks it should be now a huge eclipse
> Of Sun and moon, and that the affrighted globe
> Should yawn at alteration. (V, 2, 98–100)

After Iago, by far the most villainous of Shakespeare's villains, there is no other single character of whom it can be said that allegorically he stands for the devil. In his subsequent plays, as we shall see, it suits his purpose better to let his villains represent certain aspects of evil, without actually personifying evil's root. Edmund, in *King Lear,* is indeed villainous, but there is no common measure between him and Iago as regards what motivates their crimes. Edmund's chief motive is worldly ambition, whereas Iago's villainy is ultimately determined by love of evil and hatred of good. They have nonetheless much in common as regards outlook, and this outlook serves, incidentally, as a clear indication of where Shakespeare stands in the transition from Middle Ages to Renaissance which was still not quite complete in the England of his day. More than once his drama is a meeting place, almost a battleground, for the two points of view; and it is significant that Iago and Edmund are both out and out humanists, that is, typically representative of the Renaissance, and typical rebels against medieval tradition. Iago even goes so far as to deny the existence of virtue as an ideal since that implies, most unhumanistically, that there is some power above man which sets a standard for man to conform to.

> Virtue! a fig! 'tis in ourselves that we are thus or thus. Our bodies are
> our gardens to the which our wills are gardeners . . . If the balance of
> our lives had not one scale of reason to poise another of sensuality, the
> blood and baseness of our natures would conduct us to most prepos-
> terous conclusions; but we have reason to cool our raging motions,
> our carnal stings, our unbitted lusts. (I, 3, 322–25)

Iago might almost have said: "Thou, reason, art my goddess," just as Edmund does in fact say "Thou, nature, art my goddess" (I, 2, 1). Either remark is centrally humanist, for according to humanism, humanity is the highest thing in existence, and humanity as such is limited to reason and to nature. Beyond reason, which marks nature's upper boundary, the supernatural begins. Under the flag of Renaissance humanism, naturalism in art and rationalism in thought march together side by side. It is clearly humanism, the rationalistic denial of all that is superhuman and supernatural that the medieval Hamlet means by the word "philosophy" when he says:

> There are more things in heaven and earth, Horatio,
> Than are dreamt of in your philosophy.[3] (I, 5, 166–67)

---

[3] These lines are certainly not directed against Horatio. The possessive "your" is here general and impersonal. The Arden editors quote as a parallel Hamlet's "Your worm is your only emperor for diet."

Nor can there be any doubt that Hamlet is here voicing Shakespeare's own view. The same may be said of the equally medieval Duke of Vienna in *Measure for Measure* when he sums up Barnardine's badness:

Sirrah, thou art said to have a stubborn soul
That apprehends no further than this world. (V, 1, 478–79)

It is in the nature of things that lovers of Shakespeare should have drawn up different hierarchies of excellence for his plays according to their own individual preferences. By some, *Hamlet* is placed at the summit, by others, perhaps the majority, *King Lear,* by others the play we are now considering, and so on. Nor is it ever difficult, though we may not agree, to sympathize with the enthusiasm in question and to see the reasons for it. By way of relevant example, there is no problem for us even in Macauley's verdict: "*Othello* is perhaps the greatest work in the world." The appeal of this play is indeed overwhelming, and it involves us irresistibly almost from the start. The immediacy of its grip is no doubt due in part to its simplicity. Not that *King Lear* and *Hamlet* fail in any sense to grip us also, but they do so in a somewhat different way. In both we are confronted with situations of a fascinating complexity, whereas in *Othello* we find ourselves face-to-face with a mutual love of immense magnitude, a fiendish hatred on the part of a third person, the devotional fidelity of a fourth, and relatively nothing else. We rejoice at the Moor's marriage with Desdemona as a union of perfect complements, and we are filled with apprehensive hatred for the man who is bent on ruining this great happiness which, as we are soon drawn to feel, is mysteriously part of ourselves. The suspense quickly becomes tremendous, maintained as it is by the rapid sequence of Iago's diabolically clever schemes for obtaining the effects that he needs, one by one, in order to make Othello believe that white is black and black is white, that truth is falsehood and falsehood truth.

Literally speaking, Iago is an altogether self-centered, hardened, unprincipled skeptic, a soul compounded of deceit, envy, suspicion, hatred, bitterness, and revengefulness, so devoid of virtue as to be blind to its existence in others, a blindness that ultimately proves to be the cause of his downfall. His envious disposition nonetheless opens his eyes to the fact that despite his persistent consummate acting of the part of a faithful, kindly, honest, and trustworthy man, an outward show which deceives everybody, he is inevitably bound, being what he actually is, to be somewhat unattractive. Fairly well-liked by everybody, he is greatly liked by nobody.

Very significant is his remark about Cassio just before the final scene:

He has a daily beauty in his life
which makes me ugly . . .
No, he must die. (V, 1, 19–22)

He no doubt senses that there is a faint element of patronage in Othello's reiterated praise of him, "honest Iago," a refrain of typical Shakespearean irony that runs throughout the play. He is, for the Moor, a most loyal and reliable supporter, but one who is to be kept at a certain distance as warrant officer and not brought into the closer relationship of lieutenant. That is the pretext Iago gives for his hatred of the Moor; and it is a short and easy step from this literal meaning, wherein Iago is the enemy of Everyman, to his allegorical significance as the enemy of man.

The devil is by definition preoccupied with undermining man's belief in the Spirit, in the Transcendent, in the Hereafter, in religion, in everything that Desdemona personifies. But here—and this fits in with the relative simplicity of the play—the allegory does not take us far back into the past and forward into the future as it does in *Hamlet, Macbeth,* and *King Lear.* Rather to the contrary, it brings the past and the future into the present in the sense that Iago represents a perpetual characteristic of this world, namely that the devil is always at man's elbow, bent on leading him astray. There is in fact even something literally "perpetual" about Iago, in that he is so often present on the stage, if not in the foreground at least in the background, or with an off-stage control of the on-stage march of events.

In the frequent short dialogues between Iago and Roderigo, the literal meaning and the allegory sometimes coincide. Roderigo can be said to represent fallen man as such, impotently and unescapably caught as he is in the devil's clutches. The already dwelt-on antitraditional rationalistic humanism that Iago preaches to Roderigo is precisely what the devil seeks to instill into the minds of men when a sacred civilization has reached the stage of decadence to which Christendom had already declined in the time of Shakespeare. The situation was not yet quite ripe for the new faith of "enlightenment" that was to come in the next century followed by the evolutionism and progression of the last hundred and fifty years.

It has been not unreasonably said, I forget by whom, that if Othello and Hamlet could have changed places there would have been no tragedy in either case. Hamlet would have seen through Iago and Othello would have had no difficulty in accomplishing the act of royal justice that would have avenged his father's death and rid his country's throne of the profligate regicide usurper. However that may be, we can safely say, somewhat along the same lines, that if human perfection is the ideal of being a priest-king, and if the theme of *Hamlet* is, as we have seen, the Prince's fulfillment in himself of the royal aspect of that ideal, the theme of *Othello* is concerned with its other aspect, that is, with the Moor's addition of priestly wisdom to the royalty that his nature already possesses. In his farewell speech, now wise, he tells the Venetians that they must speak of him as

> Of one that loved not wisely but too well;
> Of one not easily jealous but, being wrought,
> Perplex'd in the extreme. (V, 2, 342–44)

He does not mean here that he had loved Desdemona too much, but on the contrary, that he had not loved her enough. The wisdom in question is certainly not worldly wisdom such as might limit the extent of passion, but wisdom in the higher sense that would have added its light to the heat of passion and made him see that Desdemona was, in fact, goodness itself. Then he would have been proof against "being wrought" by Iago's deceptions, whereas a blind love that had too much passion in proportion to its wisdom made him a relatively easy victim. This brings us to another consideration of some importance.

Despite the play's simplicity, the Moor is not the only purgatorial pilgrim, nor will it be without interest to dwell here on a close analogy between two Shakespearean characters who have perhaps never yet been spoken of in the same breath. When Othello is married, Iago's wife becomes companion-servant to Desdemona. Emilia is thus a soul who is constantly in the presence of a Saint and who is soon overwhelmed with devotion to that Saint. Like Laertes in *Hamlet,* she falls far short of the protagonist in other respects; but just as Laertes possesses from the start that aspect of resolution which in the Prince flowers to fullness only in the last act, so Emilia's love for her mistress is quick to acquire precisely that element which the Moor's love lacks. She loves her "wisely," with a love penetrated by the certitude of her goodness. She, like others, is deceived by Iago again and again, but he cannot deceive her about this.

Another striking parallel between Laertes and Emilia is that each is tricked by the devil into serving his cause, she a reluctant accomplice from the start, he at first a willing one, but with a growing reluctance that becomes as great as hers; and there is likewise a remarkable analogy between the ultimate expiatory atonement of both these tragic figures.

As to what calls for expiation, it is true that Emilia, like Laertes, has certain excuses: her desire to please her husband is natural and her fear of him is understandable. Nonetheless, the incident of the handkerchief that Desdemona accidentally drops shows in Emilia a lack of principles and of scruples that needs to be overcome. She well knows how upset Desdemona will be when in vain she searches high and low for her missing treasure, and she knows that she herself will presumably have to make a show of joining in the search. But instead of immediately giving it back to her, she says:

> I am glad I have found this napkin:
> This was her first remembrance from the Moor
> My wayward husband hath a hundred times
> Woo'd me to steal it; but she so loves the token,
> For he conjured her she should ever keep it,
> That she reserves it evermore about her
> To kiss and talk to. (III, 3, 291–97)

Then when Iago comes in and takes it from her she says:

> If it be not for some purpose of import,
> Give't me again; poor lady, she'll run mad
> When she shall lack it.

He replies:

> Be not acknown on't[4]; I have use for it.
> Go, leave me.

She goes out and he continues:

> I will in Cassio's lodging lose this napkin,
> And let him find it. Trifles light as air
> Are, to the jealous, confirmations strong
> As proofs of holy writ: this may do something.
> The Moor already changes with my poison . . .

---

[4] Do not admit to knowing anything about it.

> Look where he comes! Not poppy, nor mandragora,
> Nor all the drowsy syrops of the world,
> Shall ever medicine thee to that sweet sleep
> Which thou owedst[5] yesterday. (III, 317–34)

We are told by Othello that the fatal handkerchief has certain powers, and it may be wondered whether these include the safeguard that it cannot be mishandled with impunity. To this we shall never know the answer, but it is certainly not without irony that Iago should gloat over it as he holds it in his hand, for it is precisely this trifle "light as air" that is destined, when the time comes, to unmask his villainy totally and in an instant, with confirmation "strong as proofs of holy writ."

A fundamental aspect of dramatic art is the creation of imperative needs in the spellbound souls of the audience, and then the marvelous fulfillment of those needs. The imperative need for truth and light which dominates the last half of *Othello* reaches its climax in the last scene but one, which is set in the streets of Cyprus shortly after midnight. This scene has been led up to that afternoon by Iago's success in finally making the Moor determined that both Desdemona and Cassio shall die. He says:

> Get me some poison, Iago; this night.

But Iago replies:

> Do it not with poison, strangle her in her
> bed, even the bed she has contaminated ...
> And for Cassio, let me be his undertaker:
> You shall hear more by midnight. (IV, 1, 208–11)

The midnight scene is often played in total darkness save for occasional torches, and it is entirely dominated by Iago who is present almost throughout. He has persuaded Roderigo to kill Cassio and has stationed him at a point of vantage that Cassio is bound to pass on his way back from the lodging of Bianca where he has been supping. Iago will stand nearby, to help if need be as he has given Roderigo to understand, but in reality to make sure that neither man escapes death, for he needs to be rid of both: to Roderigo he is enormously in debt, and so long as Cassio lives there is always the

---

[5] Ownedst.

danger that the Moor may accuse him directly of having seduced Desdemona. But Cassio is wearing a coat of mail, which Roderigo fails to pierce, and he retaliates, badly wounding Roderigo, while Iago, having given Cassio from behind a severe wound in the leg, slips out briefly to don a nightgown and so seem to have come straight from bed in answer to the cries for help which now break the silence of the night. But even in his absence he dominates the stage, for Othello now enters and says:

The voice of Cassio: Iago keeps his word . . .

and at another desperate cry from Cassio he says:

'Tis he. O brave Iago, honest and just,
That hast such noble sense of thy friend's wrong!
Thou teachest me. (V, 1, 28–33)

and assuming that Cassio is at the point of death he goes off to keep his own promise with regard to the death of Desdemona.

Iago no doubt believes that he has cut through the main artery of Cassio's leg, and that he will already have lost too much blood to live, so when he reappears in his nightgown he makes a show of binding the wound. But first, when Roderigo cries for help and Cassio says "That's one of them," that is, one of those who had attacked him, Iago turns on Roderigo with the words "O murderous slave! O villain!" and stabs him, as he thinks, to death. Roderigo, at last knowing what Iago is, exclaims with what we take to be his last breath:

O damned Iago! O inhuman dog! (V, 1, 6)

Meanwhile others have come to help; Cassio and the apparently dead Roderigo are carried off; Emilia, the last to arrive, is sent to the citadel to give Othello the news; and Iago, left alone in the darkness, ends the scene with the words:

This is the night
That either makes me or fordoes me quite. (V, 1, 128–29)

Despite its negative ending, the remark is clearly triumphant, since everything has moved according to plan; and as in the scene where Cassio is drunk, an episode also engineered by Iago down to the smallest detail, so now yet again he has made the harm he does to others a means of establishing himself as an exceptionally good reliable man who is ever ready to help those in distress. But for all his cunning he had momentarily slipped off his guard earlier that evening in the scene with Desdemona when Emilia was giving vent to her suspicions as to why Othello has so insulted his wife. When she says:

> I will be hanged if some eternal villain . . .
> Have not devised this slander; I'll be hanged else.

He has the presence of mind to say:

> Fie, there is no such man; it is impossible.

But she still continues with vehemence:

> The Moor's abused by some most villainous knave,
> Some base notorious knave, some scurvy fellow.
> O heaven, that such companions thou 'ldst unfold,
> And put in every honest hand a whip
> To lash the rascals naked through the world
> Even from the east to the west! (IV, 2, 130–44)

At these words Iago allows himself to manifest his exasperation, to the point that the thought occurs to Emilia: Can it possibly be that he is displeased because he himself is the very villain I am speaking of? She immediately banishes the thought, but it remains in the back of her mind.

In the scene of darkness that soon follows, all the chief characters are present except Desdemona, and this serves to underline the immense distinction between her and the others. Unlike them, her element is "day," the domain that is lit by the sun of the Spirit; and it is from her, in the next and final scene, as a result of her dying words, that the longed-for light begins to dawn. Othello thinks he has put an end to her life, but when Emilia enters and speaks to him, Desdemona is heard to say:

> O falsely, falsely murdered!

Then, when Emilia runs to her bedside, she adds:

A guiltless death I die.

Emilia exclaims,

O, who hath done this deed?

And Desdemona replies:

Nobody; I myself. Farewell:
Commend me to my kind Lord: O, farewell. (V, 2, 114–23)

This last line must be taken, not as a vague message of affection, but to mean urgently what it says: "Speak well of me to Othello. May you be successful!" We can easily imagine that without this incident, that is, if Desdemona had remained silent, the sequence of events would still have been much the same, thanks to the nature of Emilia. But since the words are there, we cannot ignore them; and they tell us that from now on the light of Desdemona, that is, allegorically and anagogically, the Light of the Spirit, is shining through Emilia; and even literally it means the same, in as much as Desdemona is now beyond the limitations of this world.

Emilia's "commendation" of Desdemona does not take long to begin:

OTHELLO. She's like a liar gone to burning hell:
     T'was I that kill'd her.
EMILIA.   O, the more angel she,
     And you the blacker devil!
OTHELLO. She turn'd to folly, and she was a whore.
EMILIA.   Thou dost belie her, and thou art a devil.
OTHELLO. She was false as water.
EMILIA.   Thou art rash as fire
     To say that she was false: O, she was heavenly true!
OTHELLO. Cassio did top her; ask thy husband else.
     O, I were damned beneath all depth in hell,
     But that I did proceed upon just grounds
     To this extremity. Thy husband knew it all.
EMILIA.   My husband!
OTHELLO. Thy husband.
EMILIA.   That she was false to wedlock?

OTHELLO. Ay, with Cassio . . .
EMILIA.   My husband!
OTHELLO. Ay, 'twas he that told me first:
          An honest man he is, and hates the slime
          That sticks on filthy deeds.
EMILIA.   My husband! (V, 2, 127–47)

The iteration continues and we are indeed tempted to quote every word of this scene which in the history of drama can seldom have been equaled and never surpassed for its power to maintain a total grip on the audience. But suffice it to say that Emilia is beside herself for grief at the death of her mistress, yet still hoping against hope that Iago is not implicated or, more truly, still trying desperately to dismiss the question that had come to her momentarily that same evening to be banished then and there, as we have already seen, the question: "Is it possible that Iago is the villain who has calumniated her?" Should the answer be yes, she herself shares the guilt of the murder for not having saved Desdemona's life by challenging Iago when the suspicion first came to her—an unbearable responsibility. She takes refuge in "if":

If he say so (that she was false to you) . . . he lies to the heart.
She was too fond of her most filthy bargain.

Othello draws his sword at this insult, but she says:

Thou hast not half the power to do me harm
As I have to be hurt . . .
I care not for thy sword; I'll make thee known
Though I lost twenty lives. Help! Help, ho! Help!
The Moor has killed my mistress! Murder! Murder! (V, 2, 163–67)

Montano, Gratiano, Iago, and others enter, and Montano speaks to Othello. But he has no time to answer, for it is Emilia who now totally dominates the scene and who is interested for the moment in no one but her husband whom she immediately accosts. Nor is it anything short of marvelous, we might almost say apocalyptic, after all that the audience has been through, for them to see Iago for the first time at a complete loss, face to face with an implacable judge:

O, are you come, Iago? You have done well,
That men must lay their murders on your neck...
Disprove this villain, if thou be'st a man:
He says thou told'st him that his wife was false:
I know thou didst not, thou'st not such a villain.
Speak, for my heart is full.

IAGO.   I told him what I thought, and told no more
           Than what he found himself was apt and true.
EMILIA.   But did you ever tell him that she was false?
IAGO.   I did.
EMILIA.   You told a lie, an odious damned lie;
           Upon my soul a lie, a wicked lie!
           She false with Cassio! Did you say with Cassio?
IAGO.   With Cassio, mistress. Go to, charm your tongue.
EMILIA.   I will not charm my tongue; I am bound to speak:
           My mistress here lies murdered in her bed...
           And your reports have set the murder on...
           I thought so then: I'll kill myself for grief:
           O villany, villany!
IAGO.   What, are you mad? I charge you, get you home.
EMILIA.   Good gentlemen, let me have leave to speak:
           'Tis proper I obey him but not now.
           Perchance, Iago, I will ne'er go home...
OTHELLO.   'Tis pitiful; but yet Iago knows
           That she with Cassio hath the act of shame
           A thousand times committed; Cassio confess'd it:
           And she did gratify his amorous works
           With that recognizance and pledge of love
           Which I first gave her; I saw it in his hand;
           It was a handkerchief, an antique token
           My father gave my mother.
EMILIA.   O heaven! O heavenly powers!
IAGO.   Come, hold your peace.
EMILIA.   'Twill out, 'twill out. I peace!
           No, I will speak as liberal as the north:
           Let heaven and men and devils, let them all,
           All, all, cry shame against me, yet I'll speak.

70

IAGO.   Be wise, and get you home.
EMILIA.   I will not.

Iago draws his sword in order to silence Emilia forever, but Gratiano stops him.

EMILIA. O thou dull Moor, that handkerchief thou speak'st of
         I found by fortune and did give my husband,
         For often with a solemn earnestness,
         More than indeed belonged to such a trifle,
         He begg'd of me to steal it.
IAGO.   Villanous whore!
EMILIA. She give it Cassio? No alas, I found it,
         And I did give't my husband.
IAGO.   Filth, thou liest!
EMILIA. By heaven, I do not, I do not, gentlemen.
         O murderous coxcomb what should such a fool
         Do with so good a wife?
OTHELLO.   Are there no stones in heaven
         But what serve for the thunder?[6]

He draws his sword to kill Iago, but Iago is too quick for him and runs out, stabbing Emilia on the way. She falls to the ground, and asks them to lay her on the bed beside her mistress, which they do. Then they go out, Gratiano to stand guard at the door, and Montano with the others to arrest Iago. Emilia, left alone with Othello, speaks her last words:

Moor, she was chaste; she loved thee, cruel Moor,
So come my soul to bliss, as I speak true;
So speaking as I think, I die, I die. (V, 2, 167–249)

To be gripped by a work of sacred art does not mean concentration on the literal meaning to the exclusion of everything else, for that meaning is already well on its way to all that transcends it, and it takes us with it in the same direction. Otherwise expressed, if the surface theme, both here and in certain other plays, could be summed up as deception (by self or another),

---

[6] How is it possible that Heaven should not have already struck down anyone so evil as this man instead of letting him continue to live out his span?

blindness, tragic error, enlightenment, contrition, atonement, the impact of a powerful performance will not only compel us to experience this same succession of the phases or states, but it will enable some of us to do so simultaneously at different levels. We will come back to the question of impact in our final chapter; as to the different levels, we have already seen that with regard to the villain of this play, the literal meaning tends to be submerged in the allegory. Is Iago more man than devil for the spectator and the reader, or is he more devil than man? And where the devil is, there is his hold over mankind and also, ultimately, the way of extrication from that hold, the Lesser Mysteries, which always imply, beyond themselves, the Greater Mysteries.

In *Othello,* unlike *Hamlet* and *King Lear,* Hell and Purgatory are treated separately and successively, at least as far as the protagonist is concerned. Almost the whole play is taken up with his descent into Hell: the soul, personified by the Moor, gradually plumbs the very depth of error, that is, of thinking that black is white, and white is black, that falsehood is truth and truth falsehood. But although the descent is gradual, there is no correspondingly gradual development of soul. The first stage of the journey only becomes spiritually effective when, at the bottom of Hell, the truth suddenly breaks in upon Othello like a flash of lightning that lights up in retrospect the whole descent that he had made in darkness, and he is transformed in an instant from a dupe to a wise man. Then follows Purgatory, with an equally concentrated brevity. Although compressed into only a few lines, its anguish is so intense that it altogether convinces us of expiation and purification. He anticipates, and thus wears out to nothing, all that would have separated him from Desdemona, "this heavenly sight," on the Day of Judgement:

> Now how dost thou look now? O ill-starr'd wench,[7]
> Pale as thy smock, when we shall meet at compt,
> This look of thine will hurl my soul from heaven
> And fiends will snatch at it. Cold, cold, my girl,
> Even like thy chastity.
> O cursed, cursed slave! Whip me, ye devils,
> From the possession of this heavenly sight!
> Blow me about in winds! Roast me in sulphur!

---

[7] Often used affectionately by Shakespeare without any derogatory implication.

Wash me in steep-down gulfs of liquid fire!
O Desdemona! Desdemona! Dead! (V, 2, 270–79)

Then, as it were in token that his expiation is complete, a deep calm settles upon his sadness.

The everlasting union of soul and spirit after death is indicated by his dying "upon a kiss" and also by the "marriage sheets" on the bed of his death,[8] a detail that Shakespeare stresses just as much as he stresses the fact of Henry IV's death in the Jerusalem Chamber.

The bed is thus the gate of entry from the Lesser Mysteries to the Greater Mysteries, and through this gate Emilia likewise enters. But the truth dawns more gradually on her than on Othello, and this allows her a certain purgatorial development during the descent. There are three stages in her perception of the truth: first, her brushed-aside suspicion; second, Iago's admission that he had in fact spoken ill of Desdemona to Othello, presumably, as she then no doubt supposes, by way of repeating what others had said or because he was himself of a monstrously suspicious nature; third and finally, the knowledge that he had deliberately devised the whole slander himself from start to finish, knowing it to be totally untrue. As to her purgatory, it could be said to begin with her grief at the death of her mistress, for sorrow can be a deep-reaching purifier, and there is a wonderful expression of a newfound sensitivity in her already quoted words to the Moor:

Thou hast not half the power to do me harm
As I have to be hurt.

Then comes her realization that she might have saved her mistress's life in the light of her own too easily extinguished suspicion:

I thought so then: I'll kill myself for grief.

Lastly there is her realization that the handkerchief, supplied by her, had been the only tangible evidence for Othello that his wife had been unfaithful

---

[8] Anthony says in what is mysterially the same situation as Othello's:
    I will be
    A bridegroom in my death, and run into't
    As to a lover's bed. (IV, 14, 99–101)

to him. She herself, Emilia, had thus been Iago's accomplice, whence her cry of inexpressible anguish:

> O heaven! O heavenly powers!

Her confession of everything, for which she dies, is her expiation.

Othello's farewell must rank as one of the summits of Shakespeare's art in more than one respect. It is certainly one of the most endearing speeches that he has given to any of his characters, to say which is praise indeed. Above all, it reveals the perfection that is the criterion of man's primordial state. We see the Moor as we have never seen him before, with the dimension of priestly wisdom added to his royalty of nature. A solemn dignity is interwoven with his regal majesty, nor do the tears he sheds diminish the overall serenity and restraint of one who has altogether, within himself, relinquished this world. He has already prepared us, by saying earlier to Gratiano who was guarding the door against his escape:

> Be not afraid though you do see me weapen'd
> Here is my journey's end. (V, 2, 264–65)

to which he adds "Where should Othello go?", clearly in the sense that there is no place on earth for him to go to; and now, when Lodovico says to him:

> You must forsake this room and go with us:

his determination that they shall go without him is expressed with subtle eloquence:

> Soft you; a word or two before you go.

He continues:

> I have done the state some service, and they know't.
> No more of that. I pray you, in your letters,
> When you shall these unlucky deeds relate,
> Speak of me as I am; nothing extenuate,
> Nor set down aught in malice; then must you speak
> Of one that loved not wisely but too well;
> Of one not easily jealous but, being wrought,

> Perplex'd in the extreme; of one whose hand,
> Like the base Judean, threw a pearl away
> Richer than all his tribe; of one whose eyes,
> Albeit unused to the melting mood,
> Drop tears as fast as the Arabian trees
> Their medicinal gum. Set you down this;
> And say besides that in Aleppo once . . .

and he goes on to tell them how he had killed a Turk there for striking a Venetian and speaking ill of Venice, fatally stabbing himself at the words

> I smote him thus.

Then he staggers to Desdemona's bed:

> I kiss'd thee ere I kill'd thee: no way but this,
> Killing myself, to die upon a kiss. (V, 2, 328–57)

In this play it is blindness above all that characterizes fallen man, leaving a loophole for him to be "wrought," that is, worked on by the devil, until he is so "perplexed" that he comes to believe the exact opposite of the truth. As we have already pointed out, the Moor is almost perfect even at the outset, and this partly helps to make the quickness of his passage through Purgatory so convincing. It is as if only one element were lacking to complete his perfection, an element of wisdom or vision. Now the descent into Hell for the discovery of the soul's worst possiblities is only necessary because these possibilities are an integral part of the psychic substance and need to be recovered, purified, and reintegrated, for in order to be perfect the soul must be complete. This question will have to be considered more fully in connection with *Measure for Measure*. For the moment it is enough to bear in mind that the lost and perverted elements have first to be found and then redeemed, and that the interval between finding and redemption is likely to be fraught with danger. The case of Othello might be described by saying that when he reaches the bottom of Hell he finds a hitherto unknown blind eye, namely the lost element of vision, lying in the depths of his soul. *Corruptio optimi pessima,*[9] and since this eye, as well as being virtually the

---

[9] Corruption of the best is corruption at its worst.

most precious, is also the most powerful of the psychic elements, it is able to transmit its blindness to the rest of the soul, and he throws away "the pearl of great price." Then dawns the truth. Shakespeare achieves here an overwhelming impact of a kind that drama alone, of all the arts, makes possible. Emilia's revelation of the innocence of Desdemona and the villainy of Iago, her instantaneous and dazzlingly clear proof that white is white and black is black, comes as a *fiat lux,* an irresistible Divine command: "Let there be light." The blind eye is filled with light and takes its rightful place at the summit of the soul. "The stone which the builders rejected is become the head of the corner" (Mark 12:10).

CHAPTER SIX

Measure for Measure

It had become almost a "tradition" until about thirty years ago that *Measure for Measure,* the "bitter comedy," should leave an unpleasant taste in the mouth. It was liable to do so because a superficial first glance at the play is liable to set a director's imagination flowing in the wrong channels. It is immediately obvious which parts are dramatically the most effective, whence the temptation to subordinate everything to these two parts, as if the play were entitled *Angelo and Isabella* on the lines of Shakespeare's double-titled tragedies. If such an idea is allowed to govern the production, and if everything is done to make the audience feel that the essence of the play lies in the clash between these two characters, then the whole balance of one of Shakespeare's masterpieces will be in danger of being upset from the very start.

What is not obvious at first is the basic resemblance between *Measure for Measure* and two other plays that are practically never mentioned with it in the same breath, namely *A Midsummer Night's Dream* and *The Tempest.* It is true that as regards setting they are as remote from it as the supernatural is from the subnatural. What indeed could be more remote from an enchanted wood and an enchanted island than a corrupt city centered around its prison? But this difference is far outweighed by the fact that in all three plays the events can be viewed from a heavenly as well as from an earthly angle, and the audience are permitted to take the higher standpoint not merely at the end as in other Shakespearean plays, but also to a certain extent throughout. In *Measure for Measure* the skylight that makes this possible is the Duke of Vienna; and if it be admitted, as it readily will be, that no parts can be considered more important in *A Midsummer Night's Dream* and *The Tempest* than those of Oberon and Prospero, it must be admitted that the part of the Duke is equally important in the third play.

During the last few decades more than one director has taken this into consideration, allowing the Duke to dominate the play as Shakespeare clearly intended that he should; and these productions have demonstrated that far from deserving the epithet "bitter," *Measure for Measure* is penetrated by a deep serenity that makes it, despite its setting, a herald of the plays of the poet's final period.

Measure for Measure was written about the same time as *Hamlet* and *Othello*, either between the two[1] or shortly after them. In *Hamlet* and *Othello* the devil is represented by a separate character as if he were entirely outside the human soul whose spiritual journey is the deeper theme of the play. Such a manner of representation makes it possible to paint the devil in his true colors and to portray the hero in such a way as to give a definite foretaste of the perfection toward which he is being developed. But in actual fact the first part of the spiritual journey is strictly concerned with the devil's inward presence, which can best be conveyed by foregoing any separate representation of him and by revealing diabolical elements in the soul of the hero; and if the dramatist sets out to do this, he immediately finds himself in something of a dilemma. If the diabolical is not painted sufficiently black, the meaning will be lost; but if it is painted black enough, there is a risk that the audience's sympathies will be alienated from the hero, and this will be fatal to the "alchemy" of the play, for they will not be able to identify themselves with the Everyman that he represents.

In *Measure for Measure* Shakespeare ventures to represent the devil as being inside the soul and at the same time avoids spoiling the effect of his play through the device of portraying Everyman three times, in three closely interwoven plots. These are, to name each after its central character, the plots of Isabella, Angelo, and Claudio. In the second of these Everyman has an unmistakably satanic devil inside him; but although we are in consequence

---

[1] But for this possible exception, the chapters are arranged according to the order in which the plays are generally agreed to have been written. For a more complete list of the later plays, *All's Well That Ends Well* and *Troilus and Cressida* must be added between *Hamlet* and *Othello*, and *Coriolanus*, *Timon of Athens* and *Pericles* between *Antony and Cleopatra* and *Cymbeline*.

alienated from Angelo, and although we are scarcely given time at the end to become fully reconciled to him—though it is up to a good actor to achieve a reconciliation with the audience—this does not spoil the effect of the play, because there are two other souls for us to identify ourselves with, while at the same time the three plots are so inextricable that the clearly established inwardness of the devil in one may serve, as it were by refraction, for his inwardness in the others.

Psychologically, the two characters Othello and Angelo are so different that they are scarcely ever thought of in the same context; but the two spiritual paths traced out by these two characters are "rhythmically" almost identical. In both cases the slow descent into Hell, which takes up almost the whole play, terminates with a sudden dazzling flash of truth and is followed by a Purgatory which is compressed into only a few lines but which in each case is altogether convincing in virtue of its intensity.

One of the keys to understanding in general the descent into Hell, and in particular the part of Angelo as well as corresponding parts in other plays of Shakespeare, is Mariana's speech in the final scene:

> They say best men are moulded out of faults,
> And, for the most, become much more the better
> For being a little bad. So may my husband. (V, 1, 437–39)

As we have seen in the case of Othello, the soul cannot be made perfect until it is complete. In order to reverse the process of the Fall by which part of man's soul came under the domination of the devil, it is necessary first of all to regain consciousness of the lost psychic elements that lie in dormant or semidormant perversion in the nethermost depths of the soul. Thus it is that in some traditional stories the descent into Hell is represented by a journey into the depths of the earth in search of hidden treasure: the lost psychic elements are symbolized by precious stones that have been stolen and hidden by diabolically cunning dwarfs. The second part of the spiritual path is concerned with the winning back of the lost jewels, that is, the freeing of the rediscovered psychic substance from the devil's domination.

If in Othello the fallenness of fallen man is represented as blindness, in *Measure for Measure* the stress is on incompleteness, at any rate as far as Angelo is concerned. At the beginning of the play Angelo appears to be by certain standards almost perfect, but as yet he is merely a human fragment. The Duke is well aware of this; he is also aware that beneath Angelo's limitations there lies a deep sincerity of purpose coupled with a sincere desire for perfection. Certainly, it is not from any intent to harm him but rather to help him to know himself that the Duke confers on him the vice-regency. It is this "initiation" that marks for Angelo the beginning of the descent into the hidden depths of his own soul.

What is traditionally known as "the descent into Hell" is termed so because through it the lower possibilities of the soul are revealed. But the modern development of psychoanalysis makes it necessary to explain that this first phase of the mystic path is radically different from any psycho-analytical descent into the subconscious. Psychoanalysis is largely a case of the blind leading the blind, for it is simply one soul working upon another without the help of any transcendent power. But initiation, followed up by the devotional and ascetic practices that are implicit in it, opens the door to contact with the perfecting and unifying power of the Spirit, whose presence demands that the psychic substance shall become once again a single whole. The more or less scattered elements of this substance are thus compelled to come together; and some of them come in anger, from dark and remote hiding-places, with the infernal powers still attached to them. From this point of view it is truer to say that Hell rises than that the mystic descends; and the result of this rising is a battle between the "mighty opposites," with the soul as battleground. The mystic fights, by definition, on the side of Heaven; but the enemy will spare no stratagem to seduce him into fighting on the wrong side.

In no play does Shakespeare represent more clearly than in *Measure for Measure* the dangers of the spiritual path. At the outset of the path the perverted psychic elements are more or less dormant and remote from the center of consciousness. They must first of all be woken and then redeemed, for they cannot be purified in their sleep; and it is when they wake in a state of raging perversion that there is always the risk that they will overpower the whole soul. This is what happens with Angelo: in his zeal to purify Vienna he has sentenced Claudio to death for fornication. Claudio's sister, Isabella, about to take her vows as a nun, comes to Angelo to plead for her brother's life; and Angelo is suddenly overpowered by irresistible lust. In an aside, he exclaims to the devil:

> O cunning enemy, that, to catch a saint,
> With saints dost bait thy hook! (II, 2, 179–80)

It is necessary that Angelo should be overcome for a while by his lower self in order that his pride may be broken; and in the end he is saved by his basic sincerity which calls down a Divine Grace personified by the Duke.

The chaos in Angelo's soul is instantly reduced to order in the final scene by the flash of truth that is brought about by the sudden appearance of the Duke from beneath his disguise as the Friar. Then begins Purgatory, and Angelo dies as it were ten thousand deaths in the space of a few minutes. But by the beginning of the last scene, even before the appearance of the Duke, Angelo was no longer merely a human fragment: his soul was a chaos of warring virtue and vice, with vice momentarily in the ascendant, but it was at least a complete soul; and it is because the fallen soul in quest of perfection has first of all to be made complete by the addition of faults, which are only subsequently purified and transformed into virtues, that Mariana says: "They say best men are moulded out of faults."

In Shakespeare's maturer plays there are many echoes of his earlier plays, sometimes as if the author felt that he had failed to do justice to a good idea, and wished to try his hand again. There can be little doubt that *The Taming of the Shrew* was in his mind when he conceived the central theme of *Measure for Measure,* but his treatment of the Duke and Isabella is as subtle as his treatment of Petruchio and Katharina is crude. Perhaps if he could have foreseen the fate of *Measure for Measure* in the hands of posterity, he would have made the "taming" of Isabella a little less subtle, or at any rate made his intention more explicitly unmistakable. But we must remember that he wrote on the understanding that he would produce his own plays, or at least be present at the production.

Whenever Isabella jars on us, she was certainly intended to jar. At the beginning of the play she appears, like Angelo, to have a certain perfection, but like him she is no more than a human fragment. Nor could she ever have become fully herself by following the spiritual path that she has already chosen. On the contrary, one feels that the very sacrifices she plans to make would have merely increased the one-sidedness of her development. It is significant that the first words we hear her speak are an expression of disappointment that the nuns of St. Clare—one of whom she hopes to become—are not bound by stricter rules. She is prepared to throw herself wholeheartedly into a life of celibacy, fasting and prayer; but Providence refuses the sacrifices she is prepared to make, which would no doubt have been relatively easy for her, and demands in their place sacrifices of an altogether different nature. Isabella's shortcoming that she has to make good is shown up very clearly in the prison scene when her brother asks her to save his life at the price of her chastity. Shakespeare clearly intends us to think that she is right in refusing; but he does not intend us to think that she is right in saying to her brother:

> Die, perish! Might but my bending down
> Reprieve thee from thy fate, it should proceed,
> I'll pray a thousand prayers for thy death,
> No word to save thee. (III, 1, 143-46)

We know that the Duke is listening to this speech; and though he never comments on the hard and self-righteous streak in Isabella's character, what he arranges for her to do in the last act of the play is such a perfect "measure for measure" that there can be no doubt that it is based on a full knowledge of her particular fault. For first of all she is called upon to make a false declaration in public that she did sacrifice her chastity; and secondly she is called upon to go on her knees and beg for the life of the man who, as she believes, has most terribly wronged both her and her brother, and on whom, with her all too human sense of justice, she is thirsting to have her revenge. Let us recall the situation. Angelo had promised Isabella that he would spare Claudio's life. Instead he sent an order to the prison to hasten on the man's execution, and Isabella hears that her brother is dead. Neither she nor Angelo know that the Duke has contrived to save Claudio's life; and now, in the final scene, the Duke sentences Angelo to marry Mariana and then to be put to death for the death of Claudio. Mariana goes on her knees to beg pardon for her newly married husband. Isabella stands in silence beside her. The Duke refuses Mariana's request; again she asks, and again he refuses. We must imagine that he is longing for Isabella to intervene, but the intervention must come unprompted by him. She still stands there in silence. Then Mariana turns to Isabella and says:

> Sweet Isabel, take my part;
> Lend me your knees, and all my life to come,
> I'll lend you all my life to do you service.

Isabella makes no movement, and the Duke says:

> Against all sense you do importune her.
> Should she kneel down in mercy of this fact,

> Her brother's ghost his paved bed would break,
> And take her hence in horror.

Mariana is not to be silenced, but continues:

> Isabel!
> Sweet Isabel, do yet but kneel by me:

Isabella still stands like a figure of stone: "Hold up your hands, say nothing, I'll speak all," says Mariana, but Isabella's hands remain at her sides. Mariana goes on:

> They say best men are moulded out of faults,
> And, for the most, become much more the better
> For being a little bad. So may my husband.
> O, Isabel! will you not lend a knee?

To which the Duke replies:

> He dies for Claudio's death, (V, 1, 428–40)

Then at last Isabella steps forward, kneels beside Mariana and pleads for Angelo's life with an eloquent objectivity that reveals a dimension in her soul that we have not seen before and that we feel to be most fitting for the future Duchess of Vienna. The Duke has created this situation, deliberately making things as difficult as possible for her, so that her intervention, when it finally comes, may be a real triumph over herself. The victory that is symbolized in *Hamlet* by revenge is symbolized in *Measure for Measure* by the foregoing of revenge.

The part of Claudio runs parallel to those of Angelo and Isabella. For him the most difficult thing in the world is to become resigned to the idea of death. The Duke, although determined to prevent his execution, holds out no hope of life to him until he has attained and made firm the necessary resignation. When Claudio says to him: "I have hope to live and am prepared to die," he replies:

> Be absolute for death: either death or life
> Shall thereby be the sweeter (III, 1, 4–6)

At the end of the Duke's speech, Claudio says:

> I humbly thank you.
> To sue to live, I find I seek to die,
> And seeking death, find life. Let it come on. (III, 1, 42–44)

Later, however, he becomes unsettled again, and the Duke says to him: "Prepare yourself to death. Do not satisfy your resolution with hopes that are fallible: tomorrow you must die; go to your knees and make ready" (III, 1, 166–69), and when Claudio replies that he is "out of love with life," the Duke insists: "Hold you there!"

This third theme of the play, far simpler yet no less profound than the other two, sums up the spiritual path as a "dying into life."

Outwardly *Measure for Measure* represents, in Shakespeare's art, a more direct continuity with the Middle Ages than is to be found in any of his other plays. Consequently, it is not too much to assume that to its earliest audiences, who still had much of the Middle Ages in them, this play would have presented no problems. They would not, for example, with a purely psychological interpretation, have pitied Mariana for being married to such a man as Angelo, for they would have sensed that by the end Angelo had been washed as white as snow. Nor would they have disliked Isabella for taking so long to be merciful, for they would have realized that at the moment of her going down on her knees, the last flaw in an otherwise perfect soul had been forever effaced.

It is by no means impossible to make this clear to a modern audience also; but to no audience can the play be wholly acceptable unless they are made to feel, as unremittingly as possible, that all spiritual wisdom is embodied in the Duke, who personifies the transcendence of the claims of the next world over this world and whose presence in this world is, to use Angelo's words, "like power Divine." The Duke is trebly a symbol of the Spirit. First, he is the spiritual guide of the three souls in quest of perfection. Second, Isabella's marriage with him at the end means no less than the perfected soul's union with the Spirit; for everybody in a sense, but for her in particular, the beginning of the last scene recalls the words of the Gospel: "Behold, the Bridegroom cometh, go ye out to meet him." It is in virtue of being in a sense a prolongation of the Duke that the faithful

Mariana may be said to stand for the Spirit[2] in relation to Angelo, to whom the Duke says:

> Love her, Angelo!
> I have confess'd her and I know her virtue. (V, 1, 523–24)

Third, when the Duke takes his seat on the throne to pronounce the final verdicts, there is an unmistakable impression—certainly intended by Shakespeare—of the Last Judgment, an impression which is made all the stronger because although, literally speaking, the Duke was merely disguised as a priest, we have nonetheless come to look on him as an incarnation of the two functions of spiritual authority and temporal power merged into one. Moreover we cannot help noticing, in retrospect, another resemblance between him and Doomsday's Judge: although he is supposed to be "absent," he has in fact been present all the time.

---

[2]There is nothing transcendent about Juliet, whom Claudio marries. But there is no need to analyze this last marriage, since it may be said to bask in the sun of the other two marriages and to borrow its symbolism from theirs.

CHAPTER SEVEN

MACBETH

Macbeth is the only play of Shakespeare's in which the powers of darkness are shown on the stage, distinct and separate from the human characters. Of the three levels in the hierarchy of the universe, the subhuman witches personify Hell, and they have been drawn up to the human plane by the evil in Macbeth's soul. It is made abundantly clear at the end of the scene of their first encounter with him that before they sought him out he had already formed the intention to kill the King; and it becomes evident from a later scene that he and his wife had already plotted the murder together. Upbraiding him for a momentary hesitation she says:

> Nor time, nor place
> Did then adhere, and yet you would make both:
> They have made themselves, and that their fitness now
> Does unmake you. (I, 7, 51–54)

This means, freely paraphrased: "It is not easy to kill a king; our chief problem—a very formidable one—was to make a when and a where. Yet you were determined to make both. They have made themselves, by the King's decision, without any invitation from us, to come and spend the night in our castle. Is it not ironical that his presence here, which gives us the perfect opportunity we longed for, should at the same time 'unmake you' by generating scruples in your soul?"

Nor is it only the lowest level of existence that is particularly clear cut in this play. Without introducing any divine characters as he does into his last plays, Shakespeare is here at pains to counterbalance the powers of darkness by sharply defined "powers of light." In *Hamlet*, as we have seen, the murdered king has a double aspect like Adam himself, one fallen and the other unfallen. But in *Macbeth* Duncan represents nothing if not sanctity. Too little care is taken in many productions to ensure that the representatives of Heaven are sufficiently impressive. The short but beautifully written part of Duncan calls for an actor who will, from the start, make convincing what Macduff says of him to Malcolm toward the end of the play:

> Thy royal father
> Was a most sainted king (IV, 3, 108–9)

The same applies no less urgently to the actor who plays Malcolm, the prolongation of Duncan.

There can be little doubt that the totally unnecessary Act 1 scene 2— badly written from more than one angle—is a later interpolation, not by Shakespeare. The omission of this scene makes our first sight of the King all the more royal for being in the Palace of Fores. Duncan is an elderly man, of whom it can be said, as we are clearly intended to think, that he has "one foot already in Paradise"; and having confronted us with this personification of the highest of the three levels of possibility for man, Shakespeare loses no time in setting before us the intermediary degree, that of Purgatory, which is implicit in the description of the death of the former Thane of Cawdor who has just been executed for treason, the very sin that, as we know, is being hatched in the soul of the new Thane of Cawdor, Macbeth. It is Malcolm who speaks:

> I have spoke
> With one who saw him die: who did report
> That very frankly he confess'd his treasons,
> Implor'd your highness' pardon, and set forth
> A deep repentance. Nothing in his life
> Became him like the leaving it . . .

Duncan comments:

> There's no art
> To find the mind's construction in the face:
> He was a gentleman on whom I built
> An absolute trust. (I, 4, 3–14)

The equally inscrutable, equally trusted and even more treacherous Macbeth enters at this moment—generally recognized as one of the greatest moments of irony in all drama; and it is soon followed by another comparable moment when the King announces his intention of spending the night at Macbeth's castle and when his host-to-be takes leave to go ahead of him to see that due preparations are made:

> I'll be myself the harbinger, and make joyful
> The hearing of my wife with your approach. (I, 4, 45–46)

Duncan has just proclaimed:

> Sons, kinsmen, thanes,
> And you whose places are the nearest, know
> We will establish our estate upon
> Our eldest, Malcolm; whom we name hereafter
> The Prince of Cumberland: which honour must
> Not, unaccompanied, invest him only,
> But signs of nobleness, like stars, shall shine
> On all deservers. (I, 4, 35–42)

It is significant that he should express himself in terms of light. Macbeth is no doubt meant here as the chief of those on whom secondary honors "like stars shall shine." If he had been made Prince of Cumberland,[1] this might have deflected him from his criminal purpose; but the investiture of a much younger man precipitates the irrevocable crystallization of his worst intent. Lucifer-like, he disdains being the brightest of secondary brilliances.

---

[1] As a near kinsman, he could have hoped for this. The throne of Scotland was not then strictly hereditary; Prince of Cumberland was the title of the heir designate.

In his aside to the audience as he leaves the stage, his words "Stars, hide your fires" have thus a double sense, for they take up the words of the King, and are a proud rejection of all the secondary honors,[2] as well as marking the choice of darkness in preference to light. The aside as a whole is:

> The Prince of Cumberland!—That is a step
> On which I must fall down, or else o'erleap,
> For in my way it lies. Stars, hide your fires!
> Let not light see my black and deep desires;
> The eye wink at the hand; yet let that be,
> Which the eye fears, when it is done, to see. (I, 4, 48–53)

"The eye" is here the light of the conscience; Macbeth's willful suppression of that light is paralleled in the next scene by Lady Macbeth:

> Come, thick night,
> And pall thee in the dunnest smoke of hell,
> That my keen knife see not the wound it makes,
> Nor heaven peep through the blanket of the dark,
> To cry, "Hold, hold!" (I, 5, 50–54)

Both protagonists resolve to be deaf henceforth to all promptings of their better natures, and Lady Macbeth keeps to this implacably until she finally breaks, towards the end of the play, beneath the strain of the murder's terrible aftermath which she had refused to foresee. The further-sighted Macbeth, who does not break, also differs from his wife in having certain initial hesitations. At one point he even decides to forego the murder or at least to postpone it; but the reason he gives when he announces his decision amounts to nothing more creditable than the reaction of one kind of egoism against another:

> We will proceed no further in this business:
> He hath honoured me of late; and I have bought
> Golden opinions from all sorts of people,
> Which would be worn now in their newest gloss,
> Not cast aside so soon. (I, 7, 31–35)

---

[2] Later he goes back on this attitude, but only for a brief moment.

Most of the other reasons given are equally untranscendent, such as the fear of suffering retribution in this life—he says explicitly that he is prepared to "jump[3] the life to come"—and the fear that they may fail in their attempt; and the ease with which Lady Macbeth wins him back to his criminal intention betrays the extreme superficiality of the few moral scruples that he has left. These scruples, the faint residue of light that still remains in his soul, are reflected in the following arguments that he adds to those we have just given. In themselves they are good, but they serve to eliminate all possibility of excuse, for once the murder has been committed they reveal in retrospect the cold-blooded deliberation of Macbeth's choice of evil:

> He's here in double trust:
> First, as I am his kinsman and his subject,
> Strong both against the deed; then, as his host,
> Who should against his murderer shut the door,
> Not bear the knife myself. Besides, this Duncan
> Hath borne his faculties[4] so meek, hath been
> So clear[5] in his great office, that his virtues
> Will plead like angels, trumpet-tongued, against
> The deep damnation of his taking-off.[6] (I, 7, 12–20)

The cause of the Fall of man is traditionally represented as the choice of a forbidden thing loved for its own sake in preference to the whole treasury of Paradisal blessings that are lovable above all for the sake of God whose presence they manifest. We have already seen from *Hamlet* that this choice constitutes a murder.[7] Primordial man was possessed of two natures; and it is not possible for man to choose evil rather than good unless his human nature discards his spiritual nature. Otherwise expressed, his lower nature has to do away with his higher nature. Throughout the first act of *Macbeth* the protagonists are literally preoccupied with the stifling of their better selves; and as a parallel to this psychological process by which they reenact the Fall, it is the victim of their intended outward crime who symbolizes the higher nature they are seeking to eliminate. This symbolism is, moreover, subtly implicit in the above quoted passage, for each of man's two

---

[3] Risk.
[4] Prerogatives of kingship.
[5] Innocent, spotless.
[6] Against the deeply damnable act of killing him.
[7] See pp. 21–22.

natures is "kinsman" to the other, and the lower is "subject" to the higher in addition to being its "host." The Spirit can never be at home on earth, and insofar as it is present, it is always the guest of the soul.

What has been said so far amounts to saying that the audience can identify themselves with neither of the chief characters. In this respect *Macbeth* differs from all the plays we have so far considered as well as those which are the themes of the chapters to come. The presence of an Everyman on the stage serves to draw the audience into this drama. His absence makes it all the more imperative that they should be assimilated by other means; and the result of this challenge is a masterpiece in which Shakespeare the playwright achieves an unsurpassable intensity of dramatic dialogue and dramatic situation, while Shakespeare the poet amazes us with an art that he equals elsewhere but never excels.

To affirm that *Macbeth* is a superbly poetic morality play on the theme of ambition, deadly sin, worldly ruin, death, and damnation is to speak the truth, but it is at the same time a simplification and an understatement. In scene after scene a perfection of writing is reached that makes the term "fiction" totally inadequate. To say what one is tempted to say, that it is "more real than life," might seem to be a pointless contradiction in terms. But we will go so far as to claim that it reveals something of the basic skeleton of reality that "ordinary life" tends to hide; and in so doing it opens up a magnitude of vista that transcends the plane of morality. Or it could simply be said that *Macbeth* is the fruit of manifest inspiration, and that the presence of the Spirit will not be confined within the narrowness of a purely exoteric outlook, and that it refuses to be deprived of the mystical dimension of height and of depth that is its element.

Let us consider a significant section of the drama, beginning with Macbeth's words to his servant just before the dagger soliloquy that immediately precedes the murder:

> Go bid thy mistress, when my drink is ready,
> She strike upon the bell. Get thee to bed. (II, 1, 31–32)

He knows that his wife will understand what he means, namely that the bell is to be the signal that everything is ready for the murder. When it rings, he says:

> I go, and it is done: the bell invites me.
> Hear it not, Duncan; for it is a knell
> That summons thee to heaven, or to hell. (II, 1, 62–64)

91

These words are a powerful reminder, preceded by other reminders, that this world is suspended between Heaven and Hell. But the mention of Hell does not concern Duncan, as Macbeth well knows, for he has already told us that Duncan is so excellent a man

> that his virtues
> Will plead like angels, trumpet-tongued, against
> The deep damnation of his taking-off. (I, 7, 18–20)

We must not, however, suppose that it is merely the word "knell" in the preceding line that compels the speaker to add the words "or to hell." The compulsion of the rhyme is powerfully symbolic. It is not for Macbeth to be speaking of Heaven, for its gates are closed to him. He is compelled to complete the rhyme for exactly the same reason that prevents him, a few moments later, from saying "Amen" when he hears one of the King's guards say "God bless us" and the other "Amen":

> But wherefore could I not pronounce "Amen"?
> I had most need of blessing, and "Amen"
> Stuck in my throat. (II, 2, 30–32)

Macbeth utters the words "or to hell" with reference to himself. An actor could make this clear. It is, moreover, significant that the bell purports to be the signal that Macbeth's "drink is ready," for this cannot be disconnected from something he has previously said, in another of his arguments against the murder:

> This even-handed justice
> Commends th' ingredients of our poisoned chalice
> To our own lips. (I, 7, 10–12)

By "even-handed justice" he means the unbiased law of actions followed by reactions that operates in this world. He tells himself that his own killing of Duncan would inevitably mean someone else's killing of him. To use his actual metaphor, Duncan's draught of death is Macbeth's draught of death. It is therefore yet another grim piece of irony—the play is full of them—that the bell, which is in fact the signal that Duncan's "drink" is ready, should be given out by Macbeth as being the signal that his own drink is ready; and it is the double nature of the drink that makes the bell a double summons, "to heaven, or to hell"—to Heaven for Duncan, and to Hell for Macbeth.

The bell's fatal significance for Macbeth is also subtly confirmed by its juxtaposition with another stage effect of sound—one of the most powerful in all drama. After the servant has been sent to bed, the first uninhibited sound in the dark silence of the night is the bell, for soliloquies are thoughts not sounds, and the thought in question is largely concerned with silence:

> Thou sure and firm-set earth,
> Hear not my steps, which way they walk, for fear
> Thy very stones prate of my whereabout. (II, 1, 56–58)

After the bell, apart from whatever undercurrent there may be from wind and owl and other voices of nature, there is again the silence of soliloquy or the half silence of the hushed dialogue between the murderer and his accomplice. The next full sound which follows that of the bell is the sudden knocking on the gate at the castle's south entry, a sound inexorably uninhibited and, unlike the bell, totally beyond the control of Macbeth and his wife. It is the signal, but this time in fact, not merely in pretense, that Macbeth's "drink" is ready, or virtually so; for the knocker is Macduff, the man not "of woman born," who is destined to administer the draught of death to Macbeth. But although the knocking—relentlessly louder and louder—is beyond Macbeth's control, he is himself in one sense the knocker, for he has brought his doom upon his own head. The knocking is his, and the gate he knocks on is the gate of Hell, as we learn from the Porter.

As far as known crimes are concerned, it would seem that the bottom of Hell is reached with the murder of Lady Macduff and her children. This scene is immediately followed by the scene in England where Malcolm enlarges Everyman's vision of Hell, even beyond the guilt of Macbeth, by imputing all possible sins to himself. Once this point has been reached, there takes place a kind of purification where Malcolm solemnly disowns all the iniquities he has laid upon himself. It is also significant that the true repentance is the theme of Malcolm's already quoted first speech in the play, when he tells his father, with regard to the treacherous Thane of Cawdor,

> That very frankly he confessed his treasons,
> Implored your highness' pardon, and set forth
> A deep repentance . . . (I, 4, 5–7)

These indications would be too slight in themselves to warrant the claim that there is in *Macbeth* a substantial layer of meaning that corresponds to the second part of Dante's epic. The account of the repentance of the Thane of Cawdor does, however, serve to make the audience's thoughts dwell for a moment on the idea of atonement, and that is important, for it is from the auditorium that this play needs to borrow its purgatorial pilgrim. The above speech also serves to set up a standard of measurement from which it can be seen, by stark contrast, that the bitter regrets of the protagonists, however intense they may be, are very remote from "deep repentance," without which there can be no question of Purgatory.

A distinction is to be made between the deliberate descent into Hell with a view to Purgatory, and the doomed descent of the damned. It is to these alone that the closing words of the inscription on Dante's gate apply: *Lasciate ogni speranza, voi ch'entrate.*[8] The terrible truth of these words is enacted in this tragedy. From the first knock onward, the scenes that concern Macbeth and his wife are like the *Inferno* without Dante himself. He, the author-spectator, who is privileged to enter Hell and then to leave it for Purgatory, corresponds to our play's spectator, who is invited—or compelled as the case may be—to build his own Purgatory on the basis of the two protagonists' Hell.

The audience can identify themselves, not with the actual crimes that Macbeth perpetrates, but with his sense of guilt, for it must be remembered that Christendom is by very definition a world of sinners acutely aware of standing in need of a Redeemer, a world avowedly steeped in such guilt as can only be outweighed by the Passion of the Divine Savior. Moreover, the horror of the actual deed of murder suddenly and briefly restores to Macbeth something of his better nature. He is never so sympathetic throughout the play as he is at this moment of uncontrolled self-abhorrence. It does not last, being no more than a drawn-out lightning flash in a pitch-dark night, but it is long enough for the audience to identify themselves wholeheartedly with his sense of guilt, and to drink it into their souls. The intensity of his feeling thus enriches their own consciousness of sin and neediness. But they come together only to separate almost at once, for Macbeth's situation is so unbearable that they are impelled to dissociate themselves from it through the only possible outlet, which he is unable to take. However fierce his regrets, he cannot repent, whereas they can; and that "can" has now become, thanks to these moments of anguish, an imperative "must."

---

[8] Give up every hope, ye who enter.

They part company, he for the path of despair, and they for the path of atonement. By this means the dimension of Purgatory is surreptitiously added to the play.

There is also a second guilt in the state of original sin. The choice that caused the Fall was only possible because the soul had deliberately violated, and thereby partially paralyzed, its own sense of proportion; and by reason of this paralysis, fallen man tends to turn a blind eye to the enormity of his betrayal. In the first half of the play it is the temptress herself who voices this willful blindness. The consciousness of sin is thus galvanized into life, for the best of the audience, not only by Macbeth's positive example but also, negatively, by the appalling example of its opposite in Lady Macbeth. A supreme instance is when she says, just after the murder: "A little water clears us of this deed" (II, 2, 66). As the pendulum of dialogue swings between husband and wife, the audience is "accused" now of one guilt, now of the other, the guilt of sin and the guilt of "innocence"; and in the murder scene they undergo this double onslaught to the accompaniment of the knocking that, as we have seen, sounds the alarm of retribution and of doom.

It may be argued that these considerations no longer hold good, seeing that many members of a modern audience refuse to accept the notion of original sin and are not conscious of being fallen men. Perhaps the best answer to this would be the question: "Are they not *subconscious* of being fallen men?" However that may be, sacred art, to be operative, presupposes the full concept of human perfection, that is, the concept of sanctity, and thereby the awareness of falling short of that ideal. This awareness may be acknowledged by many of those who disown, by automatic modernist reaction, the term "original sin." Yet the imperfection in question is one and the same.

Shakespeare achieves his effect by what must be amongst the most powerful expressions of guilt in all literature. Their power lies not only in their poetry but also in their relevance, each to its moment in the drama. There is never any slackening of dramatic tension. The following extract may serve to recall the perfection of the whole.

As Lady Macbeth goes out with the daggers that Macbeth has forgotten to leave beside the sleeping guards, the silence is suddenly broken by the first knocking upon the gate. Macbeth is instantly shattered in soul:

> Whence is that knocking?
> How is't with me, when every noise appals me?

We may assume that he lifts his hands to clutch his head and sees again that they are covered with blood.

> What hands are here? Ha! they pluck out mine eyes.
> Will all great Neptune's ocean wash this blood
> Clean from my hand? No, this my hand will rather
> The multitudinous seas incarnadine,[9]
> Making the green one red. (II, 2, 56–62)

Lady Macbeth now reenters, calm and self-controlled[10] as before. At the next knocking she says:

> I hear a knocking
> At the south entry:—retire we to our chamber.
> A little water clears us of this deed:
> How easy is it then! (II, 2, 64–67)

Macbeth's main answer to this comes at the sound of more knocking: "Wake Duncan with thy knocking: I would thou couldst!" (II, 2, 73). He had said at the sound of the bell, the signal for the murder: "Hear it not, Duncan . . ."

Altogether overwhelmed, Everyman the spectator flees from damnation; and to further his escape, the knocking is there to lend his flight the wings of panic. In souls that are penetrated by the words of the liturgy, *qui tollis peccata mundi,* "O Thou that takest away the sins of the world," an answer, or a solution, is bound to be generated, in varying degrees of consciousness, by Macbeth's question:

> Will all great Neptune's ocean wash this blood
> Clean from my hand?

The same could be said of Lady Macbeth's sleepwalking utterance: "Here's the smell of the blood still: all the perfumes of Arabia will not sweeten this

---

[9] Macbeth's anguish is so intense that ordinary language will not suffice to express it. This sudden spontaneous coining of two new words which strike us at once as marvellously right—nothing else will do—bear witness to the high degree of Shakespeare's inspiration.

[10] She too, however, had shuddered despite herself at what she had just seen, as we learn somewhat later from the cry she utters in her sleep: "Yet who would have thought the old man to have had so much blood in him!"

little hand" (V, 1, 48–49), and of Macbeth's interrogation of her doctor:

> Canst thou not minister to a mind diseased,
> Pluck from the memory a rooted sorrow,
> Raze out the written troubles of the brain,
> And with some sweet oblivious antidote
> Cleanse the stuff'd bosom of that perilous stuff
> Which weighs upon the heart? (V, 3, 40–45)

With regard to all such questions throughout the play, there is an implicit answer: "No, but something else can," and in that answer there dawns a Purgatory within the murk of Hell. It is beside the point that some members of a modern audience are inclined to agree with Macbeth that:

> Life's but a walking shadow; a poor player,
> That struts and frets his hour upon the stage,
> And then is heard no more: it is a tale
> Told by an idiot, full of sound and fury,
> Signifying nothing. (V, 5, 24–28)

In the England of Shakespeare, such lines would have evoked, in addition to wonder at their beauty, a certain objective pity for the speaker but not a subjective assent. In other words, this speech would be taken as something parallel to the already quoted close of Dante's inscription on the gate of Hell: *Lasciate ogni speranza, voi ch'entrate.*

As to the dimension of Paradise in *Macbeth*, it must be added to what has already been said, that Malcolm, the man who, in life, was to be the husband of St. Margaret, is clearly intended by Shakespeare to represent the ideal of kingship. To repeat an already-made quotation with more of its context:

> Thy royal father
> Was a most sainted king: the queen that bore thee,
> Oft'ner upon her knees than on her feet,
> Died every day she lived. (IV, 3, 108–11)

Moreover, Malcolm is not only the true heir of both his parents; he is also a prolongation of St. Edward, the holy King of England who has given him shelter and who helps him, by force of arms, to regain his rightful heritage from the usurper tyrant. Malcolm's lines in praise of his host are in no sense a digression. Many editors hasten to remark that this speech (IV, 3) must have been written in compliment to King James: but however that may be, it serves to strengthen in advance the effect of the final scene by adding the authority of a known saint and king to that of the relatively unknown Malcolm, who thus becomes still more qualified to personify the ultimate triumph of good over evil.

This leads us to a further consideration of the power of allegory in Shakespeare's plays, a meaning that has been already mentioned but not yet enlarged upon, although we are conscious of it in *Hamlet* and *Measure for Measure,* as well as in *King Lear* and other later plays. We may call it macrocosmic, for it corresponds to the significance of a cathedral not as an image of the human being but as an image of the whole world.

This meaning has more prominence in *Macbeth* than in several of the other great plays, but some may say that like the dogma of original sin it is no longer accessible to most members of a modern audience, because it runs directly counter to their evolutionism and their progressism. It has indeed to be admitted that the two persuasions in question still continue to linger on in many Western minds, considerably affecting the general outlook, despite the facts, first that this century is in itself so powerfully suggestive of the opposite of progress, and second that in its latter half an increasing number of scientists have written devastating refutations[11] of the theory of evolution on purely scientific grounds. But the truth has its rights, and error's scope of influence is limited, for human knowledge has two aspects, mental and existential, which are respectively outward and inward, and it is only the mind that is subject to error. In other words, man was created both to think truth and to live truth; and though he may come to think error, he does not live error. However much a person may have been indoctrinated, from childhood onward, with the theory of evolution, its opposite, the truth of the Fall of man, remains indelibly written in the inner substance of the soul. Consequently, no one can be totally evolutionist: at the most, even today, it is a question of being divided against oneself. But normally the mind also is proof against error: evolutionism and progressism only became possible after religious faiths had weakened beyond a certain degree, and that degree had not nearly been reached by the end of the

---

[11]See, for example, Douglas Dewar, *The Transformist Illusion,* 1957 and Evan Shute, *Flaws in the Theory of Evolution,* 1961, Michael Pitman, *Adam and Evolution,* 1984, and Michael Denton, *Evolution: A Theory in Crisis,* 1986.

sixteenth century. In the world of Shakespeare—"the world of Plato and St. Augustine"—spiritual logic made it inconceivable that primordial man should not have been perfect. So long as men retain "a sense of God," which is very different from a vague, unintelligent, and therefore precarious piety, they knew that this earthly state—especially as regards mankind, its central feature—must have been at its unsurpassable best when it came from the hand of the Creator. The Book of Genesis and the Greco-Roman doctrine of the Golden, Silver, Bronze, and Iron Ages served to fill in certain details of a general conception of the rhythms of time[12] that was already inescapably implicit in the very nature of things, that is, in man as the image of God and, more generally, in earthly things as the shadows of spiritual realities. Beginning with primordial perfection, history was conceived as a record of the repeated backslidings of mankind which at a certain point were always suddenly checked by Divine Intervention—a retribution followed by a restoration of order. Moreover, Shakespeare and his contemporaries naturally expected the rhythm of the past to continue in the future. It still seemed to almost everyone, as it had done throughout the Middle Ages, that things were too bad for the second coming of Christ to be very far off. The words "Something is rotten in the state of Denmark" would have found an echo in every heart. But in any case, when they said: "Thy kingdom come on earth!" they did not look for a gradual upward movement. If the sudden retribution were not immediately at hand, if the worst had not yet happened and if so-and-so were not the Antichrist, then things would have to go on growing worse and worse, as had been predicted, until finally they did reach their lowest point with the real Antichrist. Then, suddenly, the true Christ would come, the guilty would be destroyed, and the remaining few would live on into the Millenium.

They saw how the world goes: a state of harmony, a fatal step of error or sin, growing discord, the passage from bad to worse, more or less sudden retribution, and restoration of harmony. This was the rhythm that they had seen in the miracle plays and that they now saw in *Hamlet* and *King Lear*— to name only two of those mirrors that Shakespeare holds up to the great cycle of time. The cosmic rhythm of *King Lear* is explicitly affirmed when Kent cries out at the terrible events in the last scene: "Is this the promis'd

---

[12] For a fuller treatment of this question, see my *Ancient Beliefs and Modern Superstitions*, chap. 2, Archetype, 2004.

end?" (V, 3, 108–11). And Gloster had already said, with reference to the aged and demented King:

> O ruin'd piece of nature! This great world
> Shall so wear out to naught. (IV, 6, 138–39)

Macbeth is no anomaly as regards its macrocosmic significance. The plot in its main outlines is very similar to the plot of *Hamlet*. A good king is secretly murdered by a kinsman; the murderer succeeds in making himself king; he plunges further and further into guilt; things grow worse and worse; and finally the usurper is killed and the country enters upon another state of harmony under a new king.

In *Macbeth* the reign of King Duncan, like the reign of King Hamlet, corresponds to the Golden Age. The reign of Malcolm, like the reign of Fortinbras, corresponds to the Millennium.

CHAPTER EIGHT

KING LEAR

King Lear has much in common with both *Hamlet* and *Othello*. As regards this last play, it is true that in *King Lear* the love theme concerns parent and child, whereas in *Othello* it concerns husband and wife; but the symbolism is unaffected by the difference. Lear and the Moor represent "Everyman," the human soul, and Cordelia and Desdemona represent the Spirit. In both plays "the pearl of great price" is thrown away; and in *King Lear* this is echoed in the subplot by Gloster's "throwing away" of Edgar.

Of the three higher aspects of a work of art mentioned by Dante, it is the allegorical meaning that asserts itself most immediately in the very dramatic first scene of *King Lear;* and though it subsequently withdraws into the background, we are kept conscious throughout of the presence of the allegory, that is, of the play as an image of the history of mankind. We have already seen, at the close of the last chapter, how the end of that history is indicated. But with regard to its other extremity, Shakespeare is faced with a certain problem in *King Lear* that had not confronted him either in *Hamlet* or *Macbeth*. In both of these tragedies primordial humanity is represented by characters who stand, in a sense, outside the main action of the play, King Hamlet and King Duncan. But Lear on the contrary is the protagonist, King of the present as well as of the past; and in the first scene we find ourselves face to face with a man full of faults and apparently devoid of virtues. On what excellence then are we to focus our attention in looking back beyond the opening of the play to the primordial age, as the allegory demands? Before the play is before the Fall; but all that we know of in that "before" is the bare fact of Lear's long reign. There is no mention of his predecessors, nor are we told anything in his favor that can compare with what Hamlet says of his father or what Macbeth and Macduff say of Duncan. But Shakespeare admirably solves this problem in two different ways.

On the one hand he portrays, in the Earl of Kent, the virtue of fidelity in its very highest sense, that is, not a blind fidelity but one that is exclusively centered on truth and goodness, to which it gives itself without any reservation. Where else in literature can we find a fidelity, a devotion, a homage more perfect, more intense, more profound than that of Kent toward Lear, his liege lord? This homage is to the virtual perfection that Lear, as an anointed king, bears within himself, and not to his as yet unredeemed faults which Kent is the first to criticize, as the faithful guardian of Lear's best and truest self. The relationship between the two men is no doubt of long standing; but there is a timelessness about Kent that makes it easy for us, and even impels us, to look on him as the personification of all devoted fidelity; and as it were by refraction, we tend to think of Lear as an almost proverbial object of homage. In this way, through Kent, the old king acquires a dimension of great venerability that stretches mysteriously far back into the past.

That dimension might well have sufficed in itself as a setting for the outset of the allegory. But its adequacy in this respect is immeasurably strengthened by the symbolism of number. The kingdom of Britain prior to the opening of the play is sanctified by the number three, and it is this harmony of three that can be equated with the great primordial harmony. Cordelia is Lear's third daughter; and his throwing away of that "pearl" represents, allegorically, the Fall. He is not banished from Paradise, which in this play is symbolized by the presence of Cordelia, but he himself banishes Paradise, which amounts to the same. Britain is no longer man's home but his exile. As Kent says: "Freedom lies hence and banishment is here" (I, 1, 182). And this inversion of the natural order of things is repeatedly indicated in various ways during the first scenes of the play, as when Kent exclaims ironically:

Kill thy physician, and the fee bestow
Upon the foul disease. (I, 1, 164–65)

or when the Fool says:

Truth's a dog must to kennel; he must
be whipped out when Lady the brach may stand
by the fire and stink. (I, 4, 121–23)

Like the apex of a triangle, the celestial number three symbolizes the resolution of oppositions (these being represented geometrically by the two lower corners of the triangle) into a transcendent harmony. Lear has banished harmony and left his kingdom at the mercy of discord, represented by Goneril and Regan. By exchanging three for two he has exchanged spiritual wisdom for worldly wisdom, that is, the dual wisdom of the Tree of the Knowledge of Good and Evil. The order of the day is henceforth worldly wisdom. The banishment of Cordelia is inevitably and quickly followed up by the banishment of Kent and Edgar. The good and wise Duke of Albany is not banished, but although he remains present, he is in a sense "absent" in his ignorance of certain facts, an ignorance in which his wife Goneril endeavors to keep him as long as possible. Theatrically speaking it is almost as if he were still in the wings and not yet on the stage; but his hour will come.

Meantime, apart from him, of those characters who may be considered as prolongations of Cordelia in that they stand for spiritual wisdom,[1] only the Fool is allowed to remain. He alone of them can fit into the new order because, although truly wise, he is wisdom masquerading as folly. Kent and Edgar can only return on similar conditions, the one disguised as a humble servant, the other as a lunatic beggar; and Kent is immediately snatched into the domain of folly by the Fool, who makes his first entrance just after Lear has confirmed his agreement to take Kent into his service by giving him his first wage in return for his help against Goneril's insolent steward Oswald. "Let me hire him too: here's my coxcomb!" (I, 4, 104) says the Fool, holding out his fool's cap to Kent; and when Kent asks why, he says:

Why? For taking one's part that's out of favour. Nay, an thou canst not smile as the wind sits, thou'lt catch cold shortly: there take my coxcomb. Why this fellow [indicating Lear] has banished two on's

---

[1] There is a certain hierarchy to be observed among these characters, for in the subplot Edgar is the equivalent of Cordelia, and in the play as a whole, if she represents the transcendence of the Spirit, he may be said to stand for its immanence in this world. As to Albany, his function in this play corresponds, in certain respects, to those of Fortinbras in *Hamlet* and Malcolm in *Macbeth*.

daughters, and did the third a blessing against his will: if thou follow
him thou must needs wear my coxcomb. (I, 4, 108–14)

Then he offers Lear his coxcomb, but says that one is not enough, because
his folly is twofold:

There's mine; beg another of thy daughters

To which Lear responds:

Take heed, sirrah; the whip (I, 4, 118–19)

which prompts the Fool to make his already quoted "Truth's a dog must to
kennel." But he is not afraid, and a few minutes later, when Lear says to him:
"Dost thou call me fool, boy?" he answers: "All thy other titles thou hast given
away; that thou wast born with" (I, 4, 159–61).

If the opening scene stands allegorically for the Fall, it thereby presages
"the promised end," of which the Fall must be considered as the first sign,
despite the ages which have yet to intervene. It is legitimate and even
necessary that sacred art, especially in the compact mode of drama, should
sometimes take a Providential standpoint from which "a thousand years
in Thy sight are but as yesterday." Moreover, if in the play itself the events
which represent the Fall and the end are textually less than a month apart,
on the stage that month is reduced to three hours. It is thus perfectly
acceptable that the end should already be heralded by Gloster in the second scene of the play, as he looks back at the discords of the opening scene,
and as he undergoes the stress of his own domestic tragedy, for his bastard
son Edmund has just convinced him, by dint of forgery and lies, that his
legitimate son Edgar has designs on his life. He speaks of recent eclipses[2]
and relates them implicitly but unmistakably to what the Gospel says about
the signs of Christ's second coming: "The sun shall be darkened and the
moon shall not give her light" (Mark 13:24). He also makes an explicit
reference to the prediction that precedes it, "The brother shall betray the

---

[2] Needless to say, there may be nothing topical here, but in fact, in October 1605, London
witnessed a total eclipse of the sun, preceded by an eclipse of the moon in the previous month.
King Lear is thought to have been written about that time, or perhaps a little before, in which
case the words in question could have been a later addition. All we know for certain is that the
play was performed at Whitehall on St. Stephen's night (December 26th) 1606 in the presence
of James I.

brother to death and the father the son and children shall rise up against their parents" (Mark 13:12).

> These late eclipses in the sun and the moon portend no good to
> us. . . . This villain of mine comes under the prediction; there's son
> against father; the king falls from bias of nature; there's father
> against child. (I, 2, 113–23)

With the end thus in sight as well as the beginning, the period of the play may be said, allegorically, to span the whole cycle of time; and this allegory serves as a vast and universalizing backcloth for the decisive latter days of two individual souls.

The theme of *King Lear*, as far as concerns the King himself, is summed up in his words:

> 'Tis our fast intent
> To shake all cares and business from our age,
> Conferring them on younger strengths, while we
> Unburden'd crawl toward death. (I, 1, 38–41)

These words mark the outset of his journey toward death, a journey that is to be soul-searchingly different from anything that he had imagined. In *The True Chronicle History of King Leir*[3] which must have been, more than anything else, the source of Shakespeare's plot, the King speaks more humbly:

> The world of me, I of the world am weary
> And I would fain resign these earthly cares
> And think upon the welfare of my soul. (IV, 6, 97–98)

Shakespeare's Lear has too good an opinion of himself to express himself quite in these terms. His intention is indeed the same, that is, to be perfectly ready for death when death comes. Of that there can be no doubt, for Lear is deeply conscientious. But he clearly imagines that he has already more or less reached the necessary state. After so good and successful a life—"They flattered me like a dog," he tells us later, looking back to those days with a wisdom that he had not then possessed—what remains to be achieved

---

[3]This play, of anonymous authorship, was published twelve years before Shakespeare's *King Lear* opened. It is based on the legend of a king who reigned in the eighth century B.C.

between now and death? Surely it will be an easy, reposeful, and agreeable passage, in the "kind nursery" of his favorite daughter Cordelia.

The first scene is a demonstration of his extreme unreadiness to die. As in *Henry IV,* the literal and mysterial meanings of *King Lear* are not always altogether distinct, and the lower merges all the more easily into the higher inasmuch as Lear is an anointed King.[4] This means that in respect of the readiness in question he has no right to be anything less than perfect in the sense of that perfection that is the aim and end of the first part of the Mysteries. For the one meaning as for the other, the opening events do not represent the Fall itself but are a reenactment of the Fall. As such they serve as a sharp reminder of the fallenness of fallen man, and as such they mark the first step on the road to wisdom. Their drastic nature might be said to stress the anagogical message, as well as the allegory, at the expense of the literal meaning, in the sense that it is not easy to reconcile Lear's outrageous treatment of Cordelia in the first scene with the character of a man who on the one hand is, as we have seen, an object of profound devotion for a man like Kent, and who on the other hand deliberately and conscientiously undergoes the discipline of having a Fool, for whom he has moreover a great affection, which is amply returned. But the mysterial meaning of the play demands a reaffirmation of what constitutes the need for the Mysteries, that is, the existence of a barrier—willfully erected by the soul between itself and the Spirit. Moreover, the soul's readiness to sacrifice so much of essential importance in order to gratify an upsurge of rebellion against the Spirit shows a lack of sense of proportion that is monstrous and needs to be portrayed as such. Gloster's terse summing up of the first scene, "the king falls from bias of nature" (I, 2, 122), which means literally that he falls away from a father's natural love for his daughter, has to be interpreted allegorically and anagogically, considering what the daughter stands for, as a reference to man's loss of his sensitivity to the upward pull of the Divine attraction, a sensitivity that characterized his first nature. Adam was created biased for the Transcendent and the rebellion that precipitated the Fall was directed against his being subject to that law of celestial gravity. But as regards the literal meaning, we never again see Lear behave anywhere near as badly as he does in the first scene. Shakespeare smoothes away the apparent discrepancy, in this respect,

---

[4]The entry into the Lesser Mysteries was by what the Middle Ages sometimes termed "royal initiation"; as distinct from the "sacerdotal initiation" into the Greater Mysteries (see René Guénon, *Aperçus sur l'Initiation,* 1992, chaps. 39 and 40).

between that scene and what immediately follows it, by making Lear himself look back on it some two weeks later as a partially self-inflicted outrage on his soul brought about by a sudden momentary blindness to the proportion of things. When Goneril begins to show signs of her truly evil nature he says:

> O most small fault,
> How ugly didst thou in Cordelia show!
> Which, like an engine, wrench'd my frame of nature
> From the fix'd place, drew from my heart all love,
> And added to the gall, O Lear, Lear, Lear!
> Beat at this gate, that let thy folly in, [striking his head]
> And thy dear judgement out! (I, 4, 287–93)

Later, but not yet, he comes to see Cordelia's "most small fault" as the virtue that in fact it was. Meantime there is much accumulated rubble to be cleared away, the rubble that constitutes the fallen nature of man and prevents his first primordial nature from manifesting itself.

Lear's ignorance of the true nature of his elder daughters is echoed in the subplot, for Gloster is equally unaware of the nature of his devilish bastard son Edmund. But these two ignorances are scarcely faults. Lear's royal function would have inevitably had an isolating effect, and on the other hand Goneril and Regan are exceedingly cunning. While not taking the trouble to hoodwink their younger sister, they have been most careful not to show themselves to their father as they are, and Goneril is at pains to deceive her husband in the same way. When Albany finally comes, despite her efforts, to see what she is like, he calls her a "self-covered thing," that is, a thing of which the true nature is deliberately covered up. Edmund is no less cunning than Goneril, and his nine-year absence from home has made it all the easier for him, when he returns, to impose himself on both father and brother as being normally affectionate and dutiful, filially and fraternally. Gloster maintains that he loves both his sons equally. Lear does at least prefer Cordelia to her sisters:

> I loved her most, and thought to set my rest
> On her kind nursery. (I, 1, 123–24)

However, considering what Cordelia stands for, the very roots of all Lear's shortcomings may be said to lie in the superficiality of his love for her and his failure to rate her at her true worth. The Moor's love for Desdemona is lacking in light but not in warmth, whereas Lear's love for Cordelia is lacking in both. The light and the warmth are there, buried beneath the aged King's fallen nature, and when he finally discovers them, Shakespeare's conveyance to us of their depth and intensity is one of the most overwhelming achievements of his art; but at the beginning of the play Lear both *sees* too little of Cordelia's inestimable value— "this unprized precious maid" (I, 1, 260) as the King of France describes her—and *feels* too little a wrench in letting her go. Gloster is equally to blame for failing to see how blessed he is in his legitimate son Edgar. *King Lear* is a play of truth and error, seeing and blindness. Very significant in the first scene is Lear's identification, albeit ironical, of Cordelia with truth: "Thy truth then by thy dower!" (I, 1, 108). Here, as also in some other scenes, we are made conscious of the background presence of the words: "And the light shineth in the darkness, and the darkness comprehended it not" (John 1:5).

Good is personified by Cordelia, Edgar, Kent, the Fool, the Duke of Albany, and the King of France. Evil is personified by Goneril, Regan, Edmund, and Cornwall. The devil is not represented by any one of these villains more than another, but his presence is felt in each of them as the root of all evil—a root that is often near to being laid bare. Between the two groups of uncompromising opposites stand the King and Gloster.

In *King Lear* as in *Hamlet* Hell and Purgatory are treated simultaneously which means that the discovery of hidden faults and the transformation of those faults into virtues go side by side. Lear's and Gloster's characters develop throughout the play. The virtues of spiritual poverty, patience, resignation, humility, temperance, fidelity, love, kindness, discernment, and truth are developed against a background of worldly ambition, bitterness, rebellion, pride, anger, treachery, hatred, cruelty, blindness, and untruth.

Of the four vehicles of these vices, Edmund is the most clear cut. When he says:

> Thou, Nature, art my goddess; to thy law
> My services are bound. (I, 2, 1–2)

he means that he is determined to adapt the law of the jungle to human life, and to reject all codes that tradition has established for man insofar as they interfere with that law. Having succeeded, as we have seen, in turning his father against his legitimate half-brother to the point of making Gloster believe that Edgar has designs on his life, he triumphantly comments:

A credulous father and a brother noble,
Whose nature is so far from doing harms
That he suspects none; on whose foolish honesty
My practices ride easy! I see the business.
Let me, if not by birth, have lands by wit:
All with me's meet that I can fashion fit.[5] (I, 2, 199–204)

The three other villains are as self-centered as Edmund, and they fully share his contempt for ordinary goodness as a form of weakness. Goneril explicitly condemns her husband's respect for the old King as "milky gentleness." Like Edmund, she, her sister, and Cornwall follow the jungle law of might is right, and they are all three cruel, more so than Edmund, whose cruelties are always bound up with some seemingly important advantage to be gained for himself. He differs from the other three in that the enormity of his vice is partly due to outward circumstances. His evil tendencies have thriven on his bitterness and rebelliousness at having been born into this world as a bastard and therefore legally, socially, and materially at a considerable disadvantage through no apparent fault of his own. He has a more active intelligence than the others and feels the need to make a kind of philosophy of his ruthlessness and to be unprincipled as it were on principle. The other three simply follow their own unprincipled ruthless natures.

Of the two sisters the elder, Goneril, is the more formidable, with more initiative and more cunning. But Regan makes up for this by following Goneril's lead—or her husband's as the case may be—and going one step further. In the first scene, for example, Goneril tells Lear that he is to her

Dearer than eye-sight, space, and liberty;
Beyond what can be valued rich or rare;
No less than life, with grace, health, beauty, honour . . .
Beyond all manner of so much I love you. (I, 1, 56–61)

Regan says, when her turn comes that she is of the same metal as her sister

Only she comes too short: that[6] I profess
Myself an enemy to all other joys . . .

---

[5] I rule out nothing that I can make serve my turn.
[6] This single word stands here for "in that," in the sense of "in as much as."

And find I am alone felicitate
In your dear highness' love. (I, 1, 72–76)

Similarly, when Cornwall puts Kent in the stocks saying: "There shall he sit till noon," Regan exclaims: "Till noon! Till night, my lord; and all night too" (II, 2, 137–38). Then, when Goneril has told her father that he must dismiss half his 100 knights whom they had promised to house and that she will only accept 50, Regan says she has no room for more than 25, and when Goneril says to her father: "What need you five and twenty, ten or five?" (II, 4, 264) Regan says: "What need one?" (II, 4, 266). And when, on Goneril's initiative, Cornwall has already plucked out one of Gloster's eyes Regan says: "One side will mock the other; the other too!" (III, 7, 74). But here she is not in fact going any further than the others for it is clearly Goneril's intention, as well as Cornwall's, that Gloster should be totally blinded. This episode may be said to show all the villains at their worst, including Edmund who knows very well, when he goes out to escort Goneril home, that in his absence his father will be blinded by Cornwall. He had already excused his betrayal of his father by nature's law: "The younger rises when the old doth fall" (III, 3, 28).

The scene that we have now reached is crucial in more than one respect. Cornwall and Regan have brought some of their own servants with them to Gloster's house; and when Cornwall has plucked out one of Gloster's eyes, and when Regan insists that he shall pluck out the other, one of the servants takes his master by the arm and says:

Hold your hand, my lord.
I have served you ever since I was a child,
But better service have I never done you
Than now to bid you hold. (III, 7, 75–78)

Cornwall draws his sword on the servant, who draws his and seriously wounds his master—mortally in fact as we hear later—whereupon Regan snatches a sword and runs the servant through the back, killing him. Cornwall puts out Gloster's remaining eye, and Gloster cries out for his son Edmund to avenge him, much to the triumph of Regan, who gleefully tells him:

Thou call'st on him that hates thee; it was he
That made the overture of thy treasons to us,
Who is too good to pity thee.

Gloster laments his own inward blindness:

> O my follies! Then Edgar was abused.
> Kind gods, forgive me that, and prosper him!

Thereupon Regan says to one of the servants, indicating Gloster:

> Go thrust him out at gates, and let him smell
> His way to Dover. (III, 7, 91–97)

The servant takes him out, while she herself tends the bleeding Cornwall and helps him to leave the room. The remaining servants comment on the iniquity of their master and mistress, and say they will put Gloster in charge of "the Bedlam," that is, the disguised Edgar.

Gloster's loss of his eyes is a necessary part of his purgatory, a purifying expiation of the sin of having begotten the bastard Edmund. That sin, which he makes light of in the first scene of the play, had intensified in him the inward blindness of fallen man, whence his failure to estimate Edgar at his true value. Thus his outward blindness is a sign of his consciousness of his inward blindness and of his need for a guide. In him eyesight had been the sign of an inward illusion of sight. In his own words: "I stumbled when I saw" (IV, 1, 19) and at the end of the next scene, when the disguised Edgar says to him:

> Give me thy arm:
> Poor Tom shall lead thee (IV, 1, 79–80)

we are suddenly confronted, as they go out together, with a direct image of the very essence of the Lesser Mysteries, the novice, who is by definition blind, guided by the Master, the Seer.

Meantime Cordelia has returned to Britain, and is now in Dover. In her absence, as we have seen, it was only possible for the representatives of good to remain present in disguise, but her return makes it possible once more for virtue and wisdom to manifest themselves as such. The time has thus come for the Duke of Albany to enter at last into the drama. When Goneril, escorted by Edmund, reaches the Albany palace the Duke refrains from going out at once to meet her. He has heard, in her absence, how she and her sister have treated their father, the King. Goneril bids Edmund an amorous farewell, and when he has gone she exclaims:

> O! the difference of man and man.
> To thee a woman's services are due:
> My fool usurps my body. (IV, 2, 26–28)

When Albany finally does come out, and when she complains that previously he had thought her worthy of more consideration, he replies:

> O Goneril!
> You are not worth the dust which the rude wind
> Blows in your face. (IV, 2, 29–31)

After all the evil that the spectators have experienced, spellbound as they are by Shakespeare's art, the impact of these words is immense, the more so in that Albany has until now been something of an enigma. The unexpected spontaneous intervention of Cornwall's servant had already produced a certain relief in the same direction and drawn a powerful assent from the whole auditorium. But the speaker now is not a servant but one of the two most powerful men in all the country. In fact he is virtually King of Britain, since the other man is dead, as we are about to hear. His words may thus be taken as something of a promise. He goes on to condemn the total lack of filial piety in both Goneril and her sister. She tries to stop him: "No more: the text is foolish" (IV, 2, 37). But he is not to be silenced:

> Wisdom and goodness to the vile seem vile;
> Filths savour but themselves. What have you done?
> Tigers, not daughters, what have you perform'd? (IV, 2, 38–40)

A messenger enters with a letter from Regan to Goneril, and he says to Albany:

> O! my good Lord, the Duke of Cornwall's dead;
> Slain by his servant, going to put out
> The other eye of Gloster. (IV, 2, 70–72)

"Gloster's eyes!" exclaims the horrified Albany; and when he asks if Edmund knows that his father has been blinded, the messenger makes it clear that it was Edmund who had informed Cornwall and Regan that his father had disobeyed them by giving shelter to the King:

'Twas he inform'd against him,
And quit the house on purpose that their punishment
Might have the freer course.

Albany says:

Gloster, I live
To thank thee for the love thou show'dst the King,
And to revenge thine eyes. (IV, 2, 92–97)

We have in this scene something of a foretaste of the final harmony in which the play, according to its macrocosmic or allegorical significance, is to end, for Albany wins our total confidence as a man endowed with all the gifts of an ideal king. But for the moment we must look back rather than forward. The stepping stones to the end have yet to be put in place; and something more still remains to be said about the infernal aspect of the Mysteries.

The descent into Hell is here represented in three different ways. First, Lear's discovery of the hitherto unsuspected faults of Goneril and Regan is like a mirror to reflect the discovery of the lower possibilities that lie hidden in his own soul; and in a sense Goneril and Regan are part of him, as Edmund is of Gloster. Lear says to Goneril:

But yet thou art my flesh, my blood, my daughter;
Or rather a disease that's in my flesh,
Which I must needs call mine: thou art a boil,
A plague sore, an embossed carbuncle,
In my corrupted blood. (II, 4, 224–28)

Second, as also in *Hamlet*, the state of the country reflects the soul of Everyman. In virtue of his kingship Lear *is* Britain; and as a supplement to the discovery of vices in Goneril and Regan the following speech of Lear from the storm scene may be quoted:

Let the great gods,
That keep this dreadful pudder o'er our heads
Find out their enemies now. Tremble, thou wretch,
That hast within thee undivulged crimes,
Unwhipp'd of justice; . . .
close pent-up guilts,

113

> Rive your concealing continents and cry
> These dreadful summoners grace. (III, 2, 49–59)

We must also remember that the country now, through Lear's fault, bears the stamp of the number two in its negative aspect of unresolved oppositions, that is discord; and in the background of the drama Shakespeare keeps up a continuous thread of rumor about brewing hostility between the two halves of the kingdom, Albany and Cornwall,

> Although as yet the face of it be cover'd
> With mutual cunning. (III, 1, 20–21)

It never has time to develop, but the rumors of it serve to keep up the impression of discord until it is no longer needed, being completely over-shadowed by the seething mutual hatred that boils up between Goneril and Regan in their passionate desire for Edmund, who is himself attached to neither but bent on using both to serve his own ends. By contrast there is perfect and constant harmony between the representatives of good, even though they do not meet on the stage. The first thing we learn about the Fool, for example, is his great attachment to Cordelia. While still in the house of Goneril, Lear says to one of his knights: "But where's my fool? I have not seen him this two days." The knight replies: "Since my young lady's going into France, sir, the fool hath much pined away." "No more of that," says Lear. "I have noted it well" (I, 4, 78–82). But for the first three acts the mutually attached representatives of good are not representative of Britain, where they are powerless; and as for those who have power, there is a hidden discord even in their shows of concord. "Farewell, dear sister" (III, 7, 14), says Cornwall to Goneril when she leaves Gloster's house. "Farewell, sweet lord and sister" (III, 7, 23), replies Goneril. Yet some two days later, when the news comes to her of Cornwall's death she is clearly delighted to be rid of him and only sorry that his death has left the widowed Regan free to be her rival for the hand of Edmund. As to her own freedom, she has already made up her mind to rid herself of Albany when the right moment comes. So much for the discords of Lear's Britain as a macrocosmic image of the chaotic disorder of the fallen soul. The Mysteries demand total integration into the Way, and there can be no singleness of purpose and unity of soul without order, which presupposes harmony, whereas discord spells division and disorder.

A third and very different way of confronting the protagonists, and through them the spectators, with their lowest possibilities is the work of Edgar by whom Hell itself is as it were churned up on to the stage. When he accuses himself of having been "false of heart, light of ear, bloody of hand, hog in sloth, fox in stealth, wolf in greediness, dog in madness, lion in prey" (III, 4, 97–99) it is not quite the same as when Hamlet says: "I could accuse me of such things that it were better my mother had not borne me" (III, 1, 123–24). In both cases the words are intended to throw light on the hidden evil in the soul of Everyman. But Hamlet's words refer directly to the speaker, whereas Edgar is not really accusing himself but holding out a mirror for Lear to look into. In fact, Edgar may be said to supply the "scenery," the stage setting,[7] for Lear's descent into Hell. His ravings are equivalent to a procession of deadly sins and also a procession of devils, as he traces the human surfaces of evil to their infernal roots. Translated from the language of wildness to that of sobriety, the truth that he preaches without respite in the storm scene is that the state of fallen man is the state of being possessed, in some degree or other, by "the foul fiend, the prince of darkness." In other words, as the Ghost in *Hamlet* put it:

> The serpent that did sting thy father's life
> Now wears his crown. (I, 5, 39–40)

Later Edgar "demonstrates" to his father that it was not merely human initiative but above all the devil that had led him to the top of the cliff and tempted him to commit suicide, and that it was the grace of a divine intervention that had saved him:

> Think that the clearest gods, who make them honours
> Of men's impossibilities, have preserved thee. (IV, 6, 73–74)

It is Edgar's function to dispel the illusion that man is independent and self-sufficient, and to show that his soul is largely a battleground for the forces of Heaven and Hell. We are especially reminded here, by contrast, of Iago's: "Virtue? A fig! 'Tis in ourselves that we are thus or thus" (I, 3, 322–23), a sentiment that Edmund would certainly have endorsed. Edgar is the very opposite of his humanist brother.

Understanding of the nature of evil implies purification from evil, and Edgar is not only a guide for the descent into Hell but also, much more, a

---

[7] In this sense, but in this sense alone, Edgar corresponds to the porter in *Macbeth*.

guide for the ascent of Purgatory. His occupation is, as he says: "To prevent the foul fiend and to kill vermin" (III, 4, 170), that is, to kill those things in the soul that are purely negative and to outwit the devil as regards such psychic substance as can be salvaged and transformed. The inextricable interpenetration of Hell and Purgatory is reflected not only in Edgar but also in the storm, which both voices the anger of Heaven and purifies by the elements.

The deeper Lear descends into the abyss of Hell, the higher he ascends up the mountain of Purgatory. But the ascent is gradual; he is slow to see any parallel between Goneril's and Regan's treatment of him and his treatment of Cordelia. There is one moment, just as he is setting out from Goneril's house, when he starts a sentence, half speaking to himself, with the words "I did her wrong" (I, 5, 4), which would seem to refer to Cordelia. But he evidently stifles any regrets that may have risen up in him, and goes on almost immediately to speak of himself as "so kind a father"; and even so late as the storm scene when, in an already quoted speech, he calls on the Gods to: "find out their enemies now" (III, 2, 49–51) and adds:

> Tremble, thou wretch,
> That hast within thee undivulged crimes

he ends with the words of injured innocence:

> I am a man
> More sinn'd against than sinning. (III, 2, 59–60)

Even so, this scene marks a milestone on his journey. As Kent has said of the world in its worldliness, as represented by the royal court: "Freedom lies hence and banishment is here" (I, 1, 182); and now the world, which itself is banishment, has banished Lear, which means that he is virtually set free from the numerous worldly ties with which his soul was trussed. He had come to be altogether wrapped up in himself. His extreme subjectivity now begins to unfold beneath the humbling and universalizing power of the storm into an outlook that is more objective. When Kent suggests that he take shelter in a nearby hovel—which unknown to them is Edgar's hovel and therefore, symbolically, a palace of wisdom—Lear turns to the rain-drenched and shivering Fool and says:

> Come on, my boy. How dost, my boy? Art cold? . . .

Poor fool and knave, I have one part in my heart
That's sorry yet for thee. (III, 2, 68–73)

And when they reach the hovel and Kent begs him to enter, the King says:

Poor naked wretches, whereso'er you are,
That bide the pelting of this pitiless storm,
How shall your houseless heads and unfed sides,
Your loop'd and window'd raggedness, defend you
From seasons such as these? O! I have ta'en
Too little care of this. (III, 4, 28–33)

But the effect of the storm on Lear is perhaps brought home to us more intimately in a later scene when he recalls how he had been flattered by the court flatterers. We have already quoted the opening words:

They flattered me like a dog, and told me I had white hairs in my
beard ere the black ones were there. To say "ay" and "no" to everything I said! . . . . When the rain came to wet me once and the wind
to make me chatter, when the thunder would not peace at my bid-
ding, there I found 'em, there I smelt 'em out. Go to, they are not
men o' their words: they told me I was everything; 'tis a lie, I am not
ague-proof. (IV, 6, 97–108)

The freedom gained by banishment from the world is personified by Edgar in the extremity of his destitution. As Lear says to him:

Thou owest the worm no silk, the beast no hide, the sheep no wool,
the cat no perfume. Ha! here's three on's are sophisticated; thou are
the thing itself; unaccommodated man is no more but such a poor
bare, forked animal as thou art. Off, off, you lendings! (III, 4, 111–17)

and he begins to tear off his own clothes. Shakespeare cannot quote here "Blessed are the poor in spirit," but this beatitude was no doubt in his mind. Tradition the world over teaches that spiritual poverty, that is detachment from worldly things, was a spontaneous and outstanding attribute of man in his original perfection; and in all mysticisms the regaining of human perfection is conceived as a return to that primordial state. This aspect of human perfection loomed very large on Shakespeare's horizon. He was altogether exempt from that superstitious respect for civilization—"sophistication," as Lear calls it—that has more or less dominated the West since his time and that now dominates almost the entire world. It would not be too much to say that he was haunted by the Golden Age. This comes out partly in his great reverence for virgin nature which is seen explicitly in *As You Like It, Cymbeline,* and *The Tempest* and implicitly in many passages from other plays and in particular from *King Lear;* but it comes out above all in the fact that his ideal is always no less than the primordial ideal. In other words, his hero is, as we have seen, not merely priest and not merely king, but the priest-king who alone is the true and rightful lord of virgin nature. Apart from those characters who personify this ideal from the outset—the banished Duke, for example, in *As You Like It,* Belarius in *Cymbeline,* Prospero in *The Tempest,* and, without the primordial setting, the Duke of Vienna in *Measure for Measure* and Duncan, Malcolm, and the briefly mentioned Edward the Confessor in *Macbeth*—the development that takes place in Hamlet's character along these lines has already been traced. We have also seen that what is needed to make Othello perfect is the addition of a priestly element to his outstanding royalty of nature.

As to *King Lear,* it is clearly the unfolding priesthood of the King that makes him sense the hidden bond between himself and Edgar—his "philosopher" as he calls him; and his "wits begin to turn" as if by spiritual contagion, as if he had "caught" madness from Edgar. His unfolding royalty is expressed in his admission: "O! I have ta'en too little care of this." Lear's madness is exactly parallel to Gloster's blindness and Gloster's remark: "I stumbled when I saw" can be applied to Lear as much as to say that he blundered when he was sane. For just as Gloster's blindness marks the beginning of his spiritual path, so the turning of Lear's wits marks the unlocking of a door that opens onto wisdom. The difference between Edgar's "madness" and Lear's madness only concerns the literal meaning of the play. Symbolically both represent turning one's back on worldly wisdom and embracing spiritual wisdom. The King's attitude toward Edgar is at first that of a novice toward an adept; but in his later mad scene, just before he is discovered by the search party sent out by Cordelia, we are conscious that a certain change has taken place. If he is not yet an adept, he is at least no longer a novice. The change might be said to have come at the already mentioned moment when Gloster asks to kiss his hand and the King replies: "Let me wipe it first; it smells of mortality" (IV, 6, 137).

There are no stage directions, but the words themselves invite the protagonist to take up some elemental and therefore purifying object—a stone, for example—and solemnly wipe his hand with it like a priest performing a rite, a sacrament that may be said to englobe the whole of Purgatory. It does so in virtue of the comprehensive significance of the hand, universally held to be one of the bodily manifestations of the soul in its entirety, whence the age-old traditional science of chiromancy. Lear is now qualified to preach to Gloster:

> Thou must be patient; we came crying hither:
> Thou knows't the first time that we smell the air
> We waul and cry. I will preach to thee: mark ...
> When we are born, we cry that we are come
> To this great stage of fools. (IV, 6, 183–87)

The reentry of Cordelia means a reversion to the normal order of things as we have already seen. So long as she was still present, in the first scene of the play, Lear's lack of wisdom appeared like the folly that it was. Kent had said:

> Be Kent unmannerly
> When Lear is mad ...
> To plainness honour's bound
> When majesty stoops to folly. (I, 1, 145–49)

It is therefore quite consequent that when Lear is once more in Cordelia's presence, his new-found wisdom should show as wisdom, not as folly, and that on being reunited with her he should recover his sanity. But at the moment of change from madness to sanity when Lear opens his eyes and sees Cordelia for the first time since their separation, Shakespeare takes advantage of the King's bewilderment in order to express directly the deeper meaning of this encounter which is no less than a heavenly visitation to a soul in Purgatory. Cordelia is, in virtue of what she symbolizes, definitely not of this world. The King says to her:

> Thou art a soul in bliss; but I am bound
> Upon a wheel of fire, that mine own tears
> Do scald like molten lead ...
> You are a spirit, I know. (IV, 7, 46–49)

Moreover, Lear is echoing here something of what the audience themselves have already felt when they for their part first see Cordelia again after so long and terrible an interval. Her sudden appearance when she enters as Queen of France and sends out soldiers to search the countryside for her father is for us also as though a piece of Heaven had descended to earth. This is a striking example, though not the only example, of Shakespeare's ability to achieve an overwhelming impact without the aid of words. We have not seen Cordelia since the first scene of the play. Meantime the vices of Goneril and Regan have been dug down to their hellish roots, and this has prompted us, if only subconsciously, to go through the opposite process with regard to Cordelia's virtues. As a result the contrast between the two elder sisters and the third sister has become so tremendous that this unexpected and almost unhoped-for return is indescribably moving.

Lear has first of all the Fool for guide; then he is passed on from him to Edgar, and then from Edgar to Cordelia who, when her father's Purgatory is almost at an end, comes to give him a foretaste of paradise and with it a foretaste of human perfection. That perfection, compounded of humility, love and wisdom, with the stress, as regards this last virtue, on discrimination, detachment, and contemplative objectivity, the opposite of Lear's former undiscriminating, undetached, and feverish subjectivity, comes to flower in his speech to Cordelia after they have lost the battle:

> Come, let's away to prison;
> We two alone will sing like birds i' the cage:
> When thou dost ask me blessing, I'll kneel down,
> And ask of thee forgiveness: so we'll live,
> And pray, and sing, and tell old tales, and laugh
> At gilded butterflies, and hear poor rogues
> Talk of court news; and we'll talk with them too,
> Who loses and who wins; who's in, who's out,
> And take upon's the mystery of things,
> As if we were God's spies; and we'll wear out:
> In a wall'd prison, packs and sects of great ones
> That ebb and flow by the moon. (V, 3, 8–19)

It is the fully grown priest-king who then expresses his debt to Cordelia in the words:

> Upon such sacrifices, my Cordelia,
> The gods themselves throw incense. (V, 3, 20–21)

Nor is it possible that Shakespeare has not in mind here, though he has to disguise his thought by the plural "gods," the sacrifice which is, for the Western world, the very archetype of all sacrifice. The parallel is not remote, for in the first scene the King of France had said to Cordelia: "Thou losest here a better where to find" (I, 1, 262), and her sacrifice is that she has left that "better where" for an incomparably "worse where" in order that a man—who stands here for Everyman—might be saved.

In Cordelia the veil of humanity that hides the Spirit is almost transparent. She is not only incorruptible but also undeceivable.

> I know you what you are;
> And like a sister am most loth to call
> Your faults as they are nam'd, (I, 1, 270–72)

she says to her sisters in the first scene. She is also, in a sense, unassailable, like an impregnable fortress. While living in the world she has a hermit's detachment from it. One of her most significant remarks is the one which leads up to Lear's words about sacrifice. She says, when he begs her not to weep:

> For thee oppressed king I am cast down;
> Myself could else outfrown false fortune's frown. (V, 3, 5–6)

The meaning of this second line is: "As far as I myself am concerned, having passed judgment upon this world as the domain of ever-changing, fickle, unreliable fortune, I am always ready to frown on it, for what it is in general, with a frown far more severe than could be merited by any frown it could give me in the form of some particular piece of ill fortune." We are reminded here of Edgar's even more elliptical exclamation when he, having himself suddenly beyond every expectation suffered the loss of all earthly possessions and rights, now sees his newly blinded father approaching, led by an old man:

> My father, poorly led? World, world, O world!
> But that thy strange mutations make us hate thee,
> Life would not yield to age. (IV, 1, 10–12)

This could be paraphrased: "If the unreliable ever-changing world did not make us hate it and thus give us detachment from it, none of us would be able to bear the strain of life and live long enough to die of old age." Both these utterances recall the King's sermon to Gloster: "Thou must be patient;

we came crying hither" (IV, 6, 183). Against the foil of utter worldliness, that is, worldliness inclusive of atheism, the play is penetrated by the ideal of total detachment from this world, total submission to the Will of Heaven, and reliance upon the Gods for everything, an ideal incarnated above all by these two "pearls of great price," thrown away by their respective fathers and then recovered when that recovery had been fully earned.

We are now in the long last scene of the play, and as in the even longer last scene of *Hamlet*, Shakespeare's power to enthrall spectator and reader is exerted to an unsurpassable degree. One aspect of the situation had already been summed up by Edmund in a soliloquy just before the battle:

> To both these sisters have I sworn my love,
> Each jealous[8] of the other as the stung
> Are of the adder. Which of them shall I take?
> Both? one? or neither? Neither can be enjoyed
> If both remain alive: to take the widow
> Exasperates, makes mad her sister Goneril;
> And hardly shall I carry out my side,
> Her husband being alive. Now then, we'll use
> His countenance for the battle; which being done,
> Let her who would be rid of him devise
> His speedy taking off. As for the mercy
> Which he intends to Lear and to Cordelia,
> The battle done, and they within our power,
> Shall never see his pardon. (V, 1, 55–68)

And now, immediately after Lear and Cordelia have been led out to prison, he sends after them a captain with written instructions that we assume to be a death sentence. Later we learn that the sentence, for added weight, bore the signature of Goneril as well as that of Edmund.

On the other hand, quite unknown to either of these, the most recent and most incriminating of Goneril's letters to Edmund has failed to reach its intended destination. Oswald, its bearer, not finding Edmund at home, was told by Regan:

---

[8] In addition to its current meaning this word had also the sense of suspicious, apprehensive, filled with hatred.

It was great ignorance, Gloster's eyes being out,
To let him live; where he arrives he moves
All hearts against us. Edmund, I think, is gone,
In pity of his misery, to dispatch
His nighted life; moreover, to descry
The strength o' the enemy. (IV, 5, 9–14)

Having tried, but in vain, to persuade Oswald to let her read the letter, she tells him that there is a high price on Gloster's head, in case he should come upon him, as in fact he does. Thinking to enrich himself, he tries to kill him, but is himself mortally wounded by the disguised Edgar. With his last breath he tells Edgar to give the letter to Edmund. But Edgar reads it himself; and since it contains the clearest evidence that these two "murderous lechers," as he describes Goneril and his brother, are seeking the death of Albany, he gives the letter to the Duke, who is thus in possession of a proof of their conspiratorial treason. Still disguised, Edgar tells the Duke that if he wins the battle he should, in due course, have a trumpet sounded to summon a champion who will prove, by ordeal of combat, the guilt that the letter avouches.

When Albany enters, after the battle, with Goneril and Regan, we see that he is totally in command. He has already discharged Edmund's soldiers who had all been levied under his own ducal authority. As to Goneril, she has somehow contrived, before or during the battle, to ad-minister to her sister a deadly dose of poison that already shows signs of effect, although Regan does all she can to keep her most inopportune supposed illness at bay. Albany asks Edmund for the captives, meaning in particular the King and Cordelia, and when Edmund suggests they wait till tomorrow, Albany says:

Sir, by your patience
I hold you but a subject of this war,
Not as a brother. (V, 3, 60–62)

This impels Regan to protest that Edmund has every right to consider himself the Duke's brother:

He led our powers,
Bore the commission of my place and person. (V, 3, 64–65)

Then after some altercations with Goneril, Regan says to her:

> Lady, I am not well; else I should answer
> From a full-flowing stomach.

and turning to Edmund, she says:

>   General,
> Take thou my soldiers, prisoners, patrimony;
> Dispose of them, of me; the walls are thine;
> Witness the world, that I create thee here
> My lord and master. (V, 3, 74–79)

Albany remarks to Goneril that she has no power to prevent this: "The let-alone lies not in your good will"; and Edmund, who has remained silent throughout these interchanges, now retorts to Albany:

> Nor in thine, Lord.
>   Half-blooded fellow, yes (V, 3, 80–82)

says Albany; and then:

>   Edmund, I arrest thee
> On capital treason, and, in thine attaint,
> This gilded serpent. [*He indicates Goneril*] (V, 3, 83–85)

He has however decided to follow the suggestion of Edgar and to let the matter, as far as Edmund is concerned, be decided directly by Heaven. He says:

> Thou art arm'd, Gloster; let the trumpet sound:
> If none appear to prove upon thy person
> Thy heinous, manifest and many treasons
> There is my pledge: [*He throws down a gauntlet*].
>   I'll prove it on thy heart,
> Ere I taste bread, thou art in nothing less
> Than I have here proclaim'd thee. (V, 3, 91–96)

Regan is now incapable of intervening; she can only murmur "Sick! O, sick!"

whereas Goneril says, aside: "If not, I'll ne'er trust medicine." Edmund throws down an answering gauntlet:

> There's my exchange: What in the world he is
> That names me traitor, villain-like he lies.
> Call by thy trumpet: he that dares approach,
> On him, on you, who not? I will maintain
> My truth and honour firmly. (V, 3, 98–102)

A herald enters and calls out for "a man of quality" to maintain that Edmund is a manifold traitor. At the third sound of the trumpet Edgar appears, fully armed and therefore still unrecognizable.

Edmund the humanist, for reasons of chivalry, will have had to pay lip service to the acceptance of ordeals, but to himself he will certainly have insisted that in fact it is always a question of strength and skill. It is these that are put to the test, not guilt or innocence; the man who wins, does so not because he is innocent, but because he is a better fighter; and Edmund knows that he himself has both strength and skill to a remarkable degree. But we may assume that he had never before had any direct experience of an ordeal. The same is no doubt true of the vast majority of men. However, from the earliest times, in all parts of the globe, man has been given the means of obtaining exceptionally a response from Heaven where it might seem necessary or desirable, a verdict for example, or an answer to another type of question; and it could perhaps be said that among these superhuman modes of certification, the oracle and the ordeal are the best known. In particular, the right to ordeal by combat was recognized by English law until 1818 when it was abolished.[9]

Whatever the first reactions of Edmund may have been, Albany would have been certain, when he threw down his gauntlet—and the same would apply to Edgar—that for the moment ordinary earthly conditions, as far as concerned the particular issue in question, must necessarily have been suspended by that sacral gesture, to give way to conditions less opaque with regard to the Transcendent and therefore more open and inviting to Divine intervention.

---

[9] In that year a man charged with murder claimed the right to prove his innocence through ordeal by combat, whereupon the law was amended—understandably because the ordeal presupposes, if it is to have a legal function, a high general level of faith throughout the community, which was no longer the case.

Edgar's indictment of Edmund, being based on direct knowledge, is more detailed and therefore more overwhelming than Albany's:

> Draw thy sword,
> That, if my speech offend a noble heart,
> Thy arm may do thee justice....
>   I protest,
> Maugre[10] thy strength, youth, place and eminence,
> Despite thy victor-sword and fire-new fortune,
> Thy valour and thy heart, thou art a traitor,
> False to thy gods, thy brother, and thy father,
> Conspirant 'gainst this high illustrious prince,
> And, from the extremest upward of thy head
> To the descent and dust below thy foot,
> A most toad-spotted traitor. Say thou "No,"
> This sword, this arm, and my best spirits are bent
> To prove upon thy heart, whereto I speak,
> Thou liest. (V, 3, 127–42)

Edmund once more vigorously protests his innocence and calls for the signal to begin: "Trumpets speak." But we have the right to assume, in view of what follows, that at the moment they sound he enters into a world hitherto unknown to him, a world where values are different, where he himself is altogether out of his element, and where nature could in no sense be considered as a goddess. In a word, he now knows what an ordeal is; and knowing that, he sees that the immensity of his guilt makes it altogether impossible for him to prove his innocence by winning the combat. It is not long before Edgar strikes him, mortally wounded, to the ground.

Goneril protests that the fight counts for nothing as an ordeal in as much as Edmund's adversary was unnamed, whereupon Albany says:

> Shut your mouth, dame,
> Or with this paper shall I stop it.

He holds out to her the letter she wrote to Edmund:

> Thou worse than any name, read thine own evil:
> No tearing, lady. I perceive you know it.

---

[10] In spite of.

She retorts:

> Say, if I do, the laws are mine not thine:
> Who can arraign me for't? (V, 3, 155–60)

She goes out, and Albany sends an officer after her: "Go after her: she's desperate; govern her" (V, 3, 162).

Edmund's "philosophy" of life, proved by the ordeal to be false, has faded from his mind. He says to Edgar:

> What you have charged me with, that have I done,
> And more, much more; the time will bring it out:
> 'Tis past, and so am I. But what art thou
> That hast this fortune on me? If thou'rt noble,
> I do forgive thee.

Edgar replies:

> Let's exchange charity,
> I am no less in blood than thou art, Edmund;
> If more, the more thou hast wrong'd me.
> My name is Edgar, and thy father's son.
> The gods are just, and of our pleasant vices
> Make instruments to plague us:
> The dark and vicious place where he thee got
> Cost him his eyes.

Edmund agrees:

> Thou hast spoke right, 'tis true.
> The wheel is come full circle; I am here. (V, 3, 163–75)

It is typical of the "charity" of Edgar—to use his own term—that he refrains from mentioning Edmund himself in the context of Divine retribution, and it is to the credit of Edmund that he at once applies Edgar's words directly to himself. The image of the complete turn of a wheel was commonly used to denote the interval between the wrong committed and the revenge it called down upon itself. The elimination, in Edmund, of his previous outlook has perhaps uncovered memories of better days before it had taken possession of him, days when he still had a natural affection for his father and brother. We may infer this from the fact that when Edgar tells Albany how he kept his blind father company, tended him and begged for him, both of them having been outlawed, it is Edmund who immediately responds:

> This speech of yours hath moved me,
> And shall perchance do good; but speak you on;
> You look as you had something more to say. (V, 3, 200–202)

In his last hour he seems almost to cling to his brother, who goes on to recount how, just after their father's death, Kent had joined him and had himself collapsed almost to the point of death through the accumulated stress of the trials he had suffered. Edgar had left him more or less unconscious beside the body of Gloster.

The news comes that Goneril has stabbed herself to death and that she had confessed to having poisoned Regan. Then Kent enters and says, feeling himself to be very near to death:

> I am come
> To bid my king, and master aye good night,
> Is he not here? (V, 3, 235–37)

"Great thing of us forgot!" exclaims Albany, and his exclamation is echoed throughout the audience because for them also, thanks to the unflagging intensity of all that is set before them on the stage, Lear and Cordelia have for the moment receded into the background. Albany turns to Edmund: "Speak, Edmund, where's the king? and where's Cordelia?" (V, 3, 238). He answers:

> I pant for life; some good I mean to do
> Despite of mine own nature. Quickly send,
> Be brief in it, to the castle; for my writ
> Is on the life of Lear and on Cordelia.
> Nay, send in time.

Edgar asks him for a token of reprieve, and he says:

> Well thought on: take my sword,
> Give it the captain. (V, 3, 235–52)

But no sooner has Edgar gone out with Edmund's sword in his hand, than he comes face to face with the aged King himself.

The entry of Lear, with the dead Cordelia in his arms, wonderfully heralded by Albany's "great thing of us forgot," is an event of cosmic proportions. A true king is, amongst his other aspects, a personification of his kingdom and that confers on him a certain macrocosmic quality that other men lack. As regards Lear, the aspect in question is powerfully brought out in the storm scene. Then, when Gloster encounters the King in his madness, he says:

> O ruin'd piece of nature! This great world
> Shall so wear out to nought. (IV, 6, 138–39)

And now, when it seems that finality itself, in the person of Lear, has entered upon the stage, it is to the world that Kent spontaneously refers rather than to the single man: "Is this the promised end?" (V, 3, 264). He endeavors to explain to the King that it was he who, in disguise, had been his servant, but the King is totally preoccupied with Cordelia, and Albany says:

> He knows not what he says, and vain is it
> That we present us to him. (V, 3, 294–95)

He then goes on to say:

> For us, we will resign,
> During the life of this old majesty,
> To him our absolute power. (V, 3, 299–301)

But he gives us to understand in what follows that he himself will in fact be responsible for governing the country; and when, after the death of the King, he says to Kent and Edgar:

> Friends of my soul, you twain
> Rule in this realm (V, 3, 320–21)

He is clearly inviting them to be his ministers and not, as one Arden editor strangely supposes, abdicating in favor of a dual kingship in Britain. Albany is one of the most truly royal characters throughout the plays, and Shakespeare has contrived to fill his relatively short part with evidence that he has all the qualities that are necessary for perfect kingship. We accept the already quoted reference to him as "this high illustrious prince" with the consciousness that it is eminently deserved; and coming from no less a person than Edgar, these words are indeed a guarantee of excellence.

Why does Shakespeare deliberately make Lear and Cordelia die, whereas Leir and Cordella are left alive at the end of the older play? The deepest reason of all is no doubt what is called "poetic justice," which is partly the theme of a later chapter. Another more obvious reason, also deep yet easier to analyze, is that the old and broken Lear cannot represent the soul in its immortal union with the Spirit. Lear must therefore die into life, and where he is, there must Cordelia be. His reunion with her before the battle is only a foretaste; but in it there is, as we have seen, a hint of the true nature of the union as it will be when it is complete, for at first he thinks that they are both dead and that Cordelia is a blessed spirit; and at the end there is the strongest possible suggestion of the life after death. In a play like *King Lear* the dead cannot be made to speak. The King, when once he is dead, cannot get up and say: "I now know that life is death and death is life." But when he is on the very threshold of death—so near to being across that threshold that we can take what he says as news of the next world rather than of this—he tells us, almost in so many words, that Cordelia is alive. He had already said, before he was quite certain of her death, that if she be alive:

> It is a chance which does redeem all sorrows,
> That ever I have felt. (V, 3, 267–68)

But then he saw for certain, beyond any possible doubt, that she was dead:

> No, no, no life!
> Why should a dog, a horse, a rat have life,
> And thou no breath at all? Thou'lt come no more,
> Never, never, never, never, never. (V, 3, 306–9)

Yet now, with his last breath, he says:

Do you see this? Look on her, look, her lips,
Look there, look there! (V, 3, 311–12)

Bradley took these last words as an indication that Lear's actual death was due to the sudden joy of thinking that Cordelia was alive. I agree with him in being certain that these words can mean nothing other than that Cordelia is alive and that Lear dies in a state of bliss. But all things considered, is it not more likely that the chain of causality is the other way around? It was not because he saw (or thought he saw) that Cordelia was alive that he died; it was because he was dead (or as good as dead) that he saw she was alive—alive not with this life, but with the life after death.

CHAPTER NINE

ANTONY AND CLEOPATRA

In three of his tragedies, *Romeo and Juliet*, *Othello*, and *Antony and Cleopatra*, Shakespeare combines the symbolism of marriage with the symbolism of death. In none of these three plays is the marriage really complete before death. In *Antony and Cleopatra* it is the nuptial bond itself that is lacking. Cleopatra, about to die, addresses the dead Antony with the words:

> Husband, I come:
> Now to that name my courage prove my title.[1] (V, 2, 286–87)

In *Romeo and Juliet*, as in *Othello*, the lovers are in fact husband and wife, but they are allowed no peace and security together this side of the grave. Romeo and Juliet are married in secret and after one night together— a night spent in fear of discovery—they are separated. The rebirth and fulfillment of marriage after death are suggested by Romeo's dream of which he tells us just before the news comes to him of Juliet's death:

> I dreamt my lady came and found me dead;—

---

[1] Let my courage, in dying for your sake, prove that I have a right to call you husband.

> Strange dream, that gives a dead man leave to think—
> And breath'd such life with kisses in my lips
> That I reviv'd, and was an emperor. (V, 1, 6–9)

The union is further suggested by their being buried together in one tomb, as are Antony and Cleopatra.

One of the differences between *Othello* and the other two tragedies is implicit in the singleness of the title. We have here the story of the Moor, not of his wife. He as Everyman represents the soul and she, perfect from the outset and having to undergo no process of development, represents the Spirit. There can be no question here of reversing the symbolism, whereas in *Antony and Cleopatra*, as we shall see on examining the text in more detail, each of the lovers has a double aspect, according to whether the play be considered as the story of Antony or the story of Cleopatra. If Cleopatra be taken as the more central figure, then it is she who represents the soul, while Antony, apotheosized after his death, symbolizes the Spirit, whereas for Antony as Everyman, the Spirit is symbolized by the Queen of Egypt.

But can the same be said, analogously, of *Romeo and Juliet?* The following quotation may help us to an answer, and it is less of a digression than it might at first seem:

> The marriage of sulphur and quicksilver, sun and moon, king and queen, is alchemy's central symbol, and in the light of its meaning we can clearly distinguish between alchemy and mysticism. . . . The starting point of mysticism is that the soul has alienated itself from God through turning itself toward the world and that it must be re united with Him. . . . Alchemy on the other hand takes the stand-point that through the loss of his primordial "Adamic" state, man is rent with inward discord, and can only regain his full being when the two powers whose strife has robbed him of his strength have been reconciled with each other. Human nature's inward divided-ness, which has become as it were organic, is moreover a result of its having fallen away from God, inasmuch as it was the Fall that first made Adam and Eve aware of their opposition and thrust them out into the vicious circle of generation and death. Conversely man's winning back of his full nature, which alchemy expresses through the image of the male-female Hermaphrodite, is a necessary prelude to union with God though it may also be considered from another point of view as the fruit of that union. . . .

The marriage of the soul's masculine and feminine forces ultimately opens out onto the marriage of Spirit and soul . . . which is none other than the mystical marriage. Thus the two states overlap: the realization of psychic plenitude leads to the soul's giving itself to the Spirit, and the alchemical symbols have, correspondingly, more than one meaning: the sun and the moon can denote the two powers of the soul which are termed sulphur and quicksilver; at the same time they are images of the Spirit and the soul. . . .

Closely connected with the symbolism of marriage is the symbolism of death: according to some representations of the "chemical marriage" the king and queen are killed at their wedding and buried together, thence to rise up rejuvenated.[2]

If *Romeo and Juliet* were the only play of Shakespeare's that had come down to us, and if in the light of the above quotation we were called upon to answer the question: "Is the symbolism of *Romeo and Juliet* mystical or alchemical?", there would be a strong case for replying that it is alchemical, the more so in that the two lovers are as it were transmuted into gold after their deaths, for Romeo's father says: "I will raise her statue in pure gold" (V, 3, 298), and Juliet's father replies: "As rich shall Romeo by his lady lie" (V, 3, 302). Moreover, the strife between the two powers of the soul would seem to be adequately represented by the enmity between the houses of Montague and Capulet, an enmity that is at the end transformed into friendship. On the other hand there can be no doubt that the symbolism of the maturer plays is mystical, love having here a higher significance expressive of the relationship between soul and Spirit; and apart from what has already been said about *Othello* and *King Lear,* a clear indication of this higher symbolism is to be found in the presence of Juno and Ceres, representing Heaven and earth, that is, Spirit and soul, at the betrothal of Ferdinand and Miranda in *The Tempest.* Needless to say, Shakespeare could have changed his perspective in the approximately ten-year interval between *Romeo and Juliet* and *Othello.* But a closer examination of the text shows that his ultimate outlook was already, to say the least, well on its way to being formed when he wrote the earlier play, and the metal gold is here without doubt a symbol of the Spirit which each of the lovers represents for the other, as in *Antony and Cleopatra,* and which each, through death, has now actually become.

---

[2] Titus Burckhardt, *Alchemy,* Stuart & Watkins, 1967, pp. 149, 155–56.

There is nothing strange or forced in this reversible relationship between the two lovers. Symbolism is not arbitrary, but is based on the very nature of things, on the make-up of the universe. According to all cosmological and metaphysical doctrines, whether Eastern or Western, earthly phenomena are nothing other than the shadows or reflections of spiritual realities. The symbolism of a thing is its power to recall its higher reality, in the same way that a reflection or shadow can give us a fleeting glimpse of the object that casts it; and the best symbols—the only ones worthy to be used in sacred art—are those things that are most perfect of their kind, for they are the clearest reflections, the sharpest shadows, of the higher reality which is their archetype. One of the chief applications of this doctrine to mysticism is that every object of love is a symbol of the Divine Beauty of the Spirit and therefore has power to recall something of that Beauty. This explains why in all love worthy of the name there is always an element of worship. Love has always a double aspect: the beloved is loved for himself or herself and, beyond that, for the sake of the Reality in whose image man was created.

For Romeo "Juliet is the sun," at their first encounter her hand is a "holy shrine," she is a "saint" and he a "pilgrim," and at the end the presence of her body transforms the burial vault to a "lantern," that part of a cathedral which according to Masonic symbolism corresponds to Heaven and the Spirit. For Juliet, Romeo is the "god" of her "idolatry."

The last words are tantamount to her saying of him, as he says of her, that he "is the Sun." If the symbolism were "alchemical" in the narrower sense, he would be irreversibly the sun and she the moon, which is not the case. However, the alchemical marriage cannot be altogether excluded here, for whether it entered into Shakespeare's direct and immediate intention or not, he was fully aware that a symbol cannot be limited to one level only. Marriage is a symbol of all the complementary pairs that lie above it, whether the two terms of the pair are on the same level as in the case of the "alchemical marriage," or one above the other as in the case of the mystical marriage of Spirit and soul; and although Shakespeare has this "vertical" symbolism directly in mind, he would have known that when an artist uses a symbol it is as if he had set free a bird to fly in a certain direction without his being able to limit the extent of its flight, and that independently of his intention marriage necessarily symbolizes also, below its mystical significance, the perfect union of the active and passive aspects of the soul; and he would have known that above all, beyond the union of soul and Spirit, marriage is a symbol of the inseparable union of two complementary Qualities or Aspects of the Divinity Itself, for the Divine Beatitude, which is nothing other than God's Love for Himself, is the Supreme Archetype of all the complementary pairs in existence, just as each single thing has its Supreme Archetype in a single Divine Quality. In other words, a symbol is fraught with repercussions for the soul of man, and on the "wings" of these repercussions the intuition may rise up through a series of higher realities in the direction of Absolute Reality, and it is precisely because symbols are the language of sacred art that a work of this art has different meanings at different levels.

In addition to its general symbolism, and despite the great outward differences, *Romeo and Juliet* has also some important details in common with *Antony and Cleopatra.* Each of the four lovers is called upon eventually to face the fact that the beloved can only be reached through the "narrow gate" of death. The difficulty of placing all four in this same situation is overcome by the device of the false news which Romeo receives of Juliet's death and which Antony receives of Cleopatra's; and like the Moor of Venice, each of the four souls dies a self-inflicted death for the sake of being united with the beloved in the next world.

But is there no inconsistency between the conception of suicide in *Hamlet* and *King Lear* as a deadly sin, and the representation of the suicides of Romeo, Juliet, Othello, Antony, and Cleopatra as noble acts? As regards the last three characters, the answer is undoubtedly "No." In *Hamlet* and *King Lear* suicide is considered in a purely literal sense. But where death is symbolic of the "narrow gate" that leads to life, then of all manners of deaths suicide is one of the most powerfully symbolic, for it expresses most clearly the fact that the aspiring soul seeks its own death; and as regards *Antony and Cleopatra,* we must remember that suicide in certain circumstances was not only legitimate but even highly meritorious according to the more ancient religious perspectives. As to *Othello,* although the Moor is a Christian, he stands at the very fringe of Christendom. Consequently, it is not difficult for us to accept his suicide as an objective act of justice against himself in accordance with some law unknown to us. Moreover, if we recall the words of Edgar, "ripeness is all," Shakespeare makes us feel that Othello, like Antony and Cleopatra, is "ripe" for death, that he has fully completed the course of his little earthly cycle, whereas when Hamlet thinks about suicide he is not "ripe," neither is Gloster when he actually attempts it. In their case suicide would have been a revolt against destiny, but in the case of Othello we know that it is, on the contrary, an acceptance of destiny, the inescapability of which makes him cry out: "Who can control his fate?" (V, 2, 263). There is nothing here, just as there is nothing in *Antony and Cleopatra,* to mar the effectiveness of suicide as a perfect symbol of the mystic's fully intentioned "dying into life." But in the earliest of these three plays has Shakespeare fully succeeded in convincing us that either Romeo or Juliet is "ripe" for death? Their tragedy is moreover set in the very heart of Christendom where it is not easy to forget that suicide is among the most deadly of sins.

It is to be suspected that Shakespeare was one of his own severest critics, and he must have been well aware of this shortcoming, at any rate in his later years. However that may be, and whether or not *Romeo and Juliet* was actually present in his mind when he wrote *Antony and Cleopatra,* it cannot be denied that he is at some pains in the later play to avoid what is perhaps the fault of the earlier one, and he certainly succeeds.

But in all justice, it must be admitted that if we had to sacrifice one of these two plays, the choice would not be obvious. Nor would our hesitation be due to any inferiority or mediocrity in *Antony and Cleopatra* but rather to the overwhelming beauty of *Romeo and Juliet* as an expression of love. The perfecting of the Moor's love for Desdemona is the theme of *Othello* just as the perfecting of the love of Antony and Cleopatra for each other is the theme of the play we are now considering. But in *Romeo and Juliet* there is no comparable development of soul, and the play is largely centered on the tragic contrast between the extreme perfection of a love and the extreme imperfection of the circumstances it is set in. Consequently, Shakespeare is able to dwell throughout this earlier play on a perfection that is only reached at the end of the other two, with the result that if we simply compare the three as regards the element "love," it is no doubt the love between Romeo and Juliet which has, as symbol, the strongest wings for the highest flights.

A striking feature of *Antony and Cleopatra* that we do not find in any other play of Shakespeare is that the outer or macrocosmic meaning runs contrary to the inner one. Normally the two meanings are parallel: Hamlet, for example, while representing the soul that seeks to restore the lost harmony of the inner world represents at the same time a man who seeks to restore the lost harmony of the outer world. But in *Antony and Cleopatra* according to the outer meaning it is Octavius Caesar who is in the right, so to speak, from the beginning of the play, and it is he who finally restores order in the capacity of "sole sire of the world" as Cleopatra calls him. This outer meaning becomes reconciled with the inner meaning at the very end of the play when Caesar pays a certain tribute of admiration to Antony and Cleopatra after their deaths. But throughout the course of the play the hero and heroine are both very much in the wrong according to the outer meaning, and they are mercilessly presented as being so from the start. The opening speech, which is all the more derogatory for being spoken by Philo who is one of Antony's friends, rings with scorn at Antony's besotted doting on a "gypsy" who has made him completely forget his duty as Triumvir, one of the three rulers of "the world." Philo expresses here the general unhesitating and sweeping censure of Antony's conduct; and yet according to the play's deeper meaning—a meaning that is felt in some degree or other by every member of the audience—Antony's love for Cleopatra is the richest jewel of virtue in his soul. This opposition between the outer and inner meanings is itself symbolic, for it reflects the truth that the Mysteries can only be understood by a few, or more generally, for those who know nothing of the Mysteries, the truth that the majority are by no means always right and that the ways of Heaven are sometimes inscrutable.

Let us quote here a short passage starting from line 10 of the play, at the entry of Antony and Cleopatra:

> PHILO. [*to Dercetas*] Look where they come:
>   Take but good note, and you shall see in him
>   The triple pillar of the world transform'd
>   Into a strumpet's fool: behold and see.
> CLEOPATRA. If it be love indeed, tell me how much.
> ANTONY.   There's beggary in the love that can be reckon'd.
> CLEOPATRA. I'll set a bourn how far to be beloved.
> ANTONY.   Then thou must needs find out new heaven,
>   new earth.
> ATTENDANT. [*entering*] News, my good lord, from Rome.
> ANTONY.   Grates me: the sum.[3] (I, 1, 10–18)

And in the end Antony does not even listen to "the sum" of the news, but goes off with Cleopatra.

In a sense the whole play is contained in these eight lines, at any rate that aspect of it according to which the soul is represented by Antony. Let us consider this aspect of the play first. Outwardly Rome stands for duty, sobriety and morality in general; it also stands for reason, and the dialogue abounds in powerful arguments why Antony should leave Egypt altogether—Egypt which spells neglect of duty, lack of sobriety, lack of moral principles,

---

[3] It annoys me: give me a brief summary of it and no more.

and also the vanity of unreason. But this outer meaning does not constitute in any sense a morality play; it is like the thinnest of veils, which hides the truth from no one, although needless to say the truth is for the most part felt rather than analyzed. What are the means by which, beneath this most transparent outside, Shakespeare contrives to weight the scales so heavily in favor of Egypt? One of the first things that comes to mind is the symbolism of East and West which correspond to Heaven and earth; and it is certainly not Rome that stands at the celestial point of the compass. Rome is this world, and nothing but this world—a down-to-earth well-being, social stability, and material security. And as Antony says, in the first scene of the play:

> Kingdoms are clay: our dungy earth alike
> Feeds beast as man: the nobleness of life
> Is to do thus, when such a mutual pair
> And such a twain can do't. (I, 1, 35–38)

In other words the Roman Empire is a mere stretch of land. All that Rome stands for is that aspect of man wherein he merely has the virtue of being an animal rather than a vegetable or a mineral. But the noblest aspect of life is the love that is felt between two perfectly matched lovers.

In the light of what the East stands for, Roman "virtues" are no more than human limitations: Roman rationality is human intelligence deprived of its supra-rational, superhuman dimension; Roman morality is a system of ethics made to fit the shortcomings of that intelligence; Roman sobriety is a dismal lack of spiritual intoxication. Conversely, the "vices" of Egypt amount to a breaking down of the barriers of human limitations. In Shakespeare's other representations of "the pearl of great price," the divine Qualities of the Spirit are symbolized by outstanding human virtues. But in this play the stress is on the Spirit's incomparability, the lack of any common measure between this world and the next; and as a symbol of the celestial, it is the function of Egypt to convey to us something of the next world's elusive mysteriousness that passes human comprehension, its infinite riches, its marvelous variety, and its boundless freedom. Everything that Egypt stands for is personified by Cleopatra. Moreover, as Queen of Egypt she is virtually divine and we are told that it was her practice to give audience "In the habiliments of the goddess Isis" (III, 6, 17). From the point of view we are taking here it is only a glib and superficial judgment that will attribute faults to her. There is an elusive infallibility about her, a mysterious overall "rightness" that transcends human rightness and defies criticism. Antony expresses this when he says:

> Fie, wrangling queen!
> Whom everything becomes, to chide, to laugh,
> To weep. (I, 1, 48–50)

And when it seems that Antony, newly betrothed to Octavia, has finished with Cleopatra, and when Maecenas says: "Now Antony must leave her utterly," Enobarbus replies:

> Never, he will not:
> Age cannot wither her, not custom stale
> Her infinite variety: other women cloy
> The appetites they feed: but she makes hungry
> Where most she satisfies; for vilest things
> Become themselves in her, that the holy priests
> Bless her when she is riggish. (II, 2, 233–40)

There is also a cosmic, "collective" quality about Cleopatra that bursts out beyond the bounds that limit the sphere of an ordinary single human individual, so that she is in some respects more a macrocosm than a microcosm. This is true in a sense of all monarchs, but what is more or less virtual in other kings and queens is actualized in Cleopatra to an outstanding degree. With her it is not merely a question of function. We are made to feel that her very psychic substance is macrocosmic. As Enobarbus says of her: "We cannot call her winds and waters sighs and tears; they are greater storms and tempests than almanacs can report" (I, 2, 144–46). Rich in implication also is Cleopatra's own remark when she is chided for unjustly striking the messenger who brings her the news of Antony's marriage: "Some innocents scape not the thunderbolt" (II, 5, 77).

Another aspect of this same quality is to be seen in the grandeur of her lavishness—which Rome would call extravagance—as when, on being asked why she sends so many messengers to Antony she replies:

> Who's born that day
> When I forget to send to Antony
> Shall die a beggar. Ink and paper, Charmian ... (I, 5, 63–65)

> He shall have every day a several greeting,
> Or I'll unpeople Egypt. (I, 5, 77–78)

These illustrations of aspects of the "supernatural" in Cleopatra's nature are not all taken from the earliest scenes of the play. But the very concentrated first scene of all is quite enough to give us our orientation—in the literal sense of the word. Consequently, no member of the audience is misled when in the second scene Antony says:

> These strong Egyptian fetters I must break,
> Or lose myself in dotage . . .
> I must from this enchanting queen break off:
> Ten thousand harms, more than the ills I know,
> My idleness doth hatch. (I, 2, 112–27)

We know that despite his logic Antony is here "in the wrong" and that he is expressing a kind of worldly escapism from his higher destiny. As far as he is concerned the basic theme of this play, his Purgatory,[4] is the perfecting of his devotion to Cleopatra. For this love to become wholehearted he needs to extricate his soul from worldly ties and to purge it from the dross of "Roman thoughts." Apart from this his spiritual path cannot be traced by any marked psychic development but simply by his gradual worldly ruin. Perhaps the most significant milestone in this development is when, for no logically justifiable cause, he suddenly follows Cleopatra in flight from the Battle of Actium; the event is described by Scarus, one of Antony's more devoted followers:

> The greatest cantle of the world is lost
> With very ignorance; we have kiss'd away
> Kingdoms and provinces . . .
> I never saw an action of such shame;
> Experience, manhood, honour, ne'er before
> Did violate so itself. (III, 10, 6–24)

There is symbolically an analogy between Lear's madness and Antony's blundering; if we can say of Lear "the madder the wiser," we can say of Antony "the

---

[4] In this play the descent into Hell is merely implicit in the ascent through Purgatory.

more he fails the more he succeeds" or "the weaker the stronger" or "the poorer the richer"; and this Antony himself confirms when he says, after the battle, that one of Cleopatra's tears alone is worth all that he has lost.

Antony's being purged of "Roman thoughts" proceeds to the outward accompaniment of his being deserted by Roman after Roman—Canidius, Enobarbus, and others. This spiritual death—being stripped of all worldly powers and posssessions—is not without its death agonies; as Charmian says:

> The soul and body rive not more in parting
> Than greatness going off. (IV, 13, 5–6)

In the most violent of these agonies Antony cries out:

> The shirt of Nessus[5] is upon me; teach me,
> Alcides, thou mine ancestor, thy rage:
> Let me lodge Lichas on the horns of the moon;
> And with those hands, that grasp'd the heaviest club,
> Subdue my worthiest self. The witch shall die:
> To the young Roman boy she has sold me, and I fall
> Under this plot; she dies for't. (IV, 12, 43–49)

---

[5] The centaur Nessus sent Hercules (Alcides), Antony's ancestor, a poisoned shirt. Hercules, dying in agony, hurled Lichas, who had brought the shirt, up to the sky, and then put an end to his own life. Although outwardly the cause is quite different, Hamlet's outburst against Laertes at the burial of Ophelia (see p. 48), his last show of weakness, is also a kind of death agony, and corresponds exactly to this outburst of Antony in that it marks the same point upon the spiritual path. Hamlet, like Antony, realizes that he has been utterly stripped of this world; and both outbursts have much in common as regards what might be called the magnificent extravagance of their imagery. Hamlet "rants" (to use his own word):

> I loved Ophelia; forty thousand brothers
> Could not, with all their quantity of love,
> Make up my sum.—What wilt thou do for her? . . .
> Woo't weep? woo't fight? woo't fast? woo't tear thyself?
> Woo't drink up eisel? eat a crocodile?
> I'll do't—Dost thou come here to whine?
> To outface me with leaping in her grave?
> Be buried quick with her, and so will I:
> And, if thou prate of mountains, let them throw
> Millions of acres on us, till our ground,
> Singeing his pate against the burning zone,
> Make Ossa like a wart! (V, 1, 291–305)

It is natural that the dying soul should have its reaction against that which is killing it. The "witch" in question, Cleopatra, is in fact the cause of Antony's worldly failure. However, his particular accusation is unjust, for there can be no doubt that she has not betrayed him. This brings us to another aspect of Antony's shortcoming: one of the flaws in his devotion to Cleopatra is that like Othello he does not love wisely enough. He does not know Cleopatra as well as he should. "Not know me yet?" (III, 13, 157) she complains when, not for the last time, he loses faith in her and accuses her of betraying him. He can be excused for not knowing her as well as she knows him, because she has about her an enigmatic inscrutability that together with her extreme acuteness of perception is part of her "transcendence." But his liability to lose faith in her—he does so twice toward the end of the play—is symbolically as inexcusable as the weakness of losing faith in religion which can also be inscrutable.

When his final rage subsides, it leaves him at the extreme limit of poverty, that is, at the very verge of extinction and nothingness:

> ANTONY. Eros, thou yet behold'st me?
> EROS.   Ay, noble Lord.
> ANTONY. Sometime we see a cloud that's dragonish,
>   A vapour sometime like a bear or lion,
>   A tower'd citadel, a pendent rock,
>   A forked mountain, or blue promontory
>   With trees upon't, that nod unto the world
>   And mock our eyes with air: thou hast seen these signs;
>   they are black vesper's pageants.
> EROS.   Ay, my Lord.
> ANTONY. That which is now a horse, even with a thought,
>   The rack dislimns, and makes it indistinct,
>   As water is in water,
> EROS.   It does, my Lord.
> ANTONY. My good knave Eros, now thy captain is
>   Even such a body: here I am Antony;
>   Yet cannot hold this visible shape, my knave. (IV, 14, 1–14)

The "false" news that then comes of Cleopatra's death is really a truth in disguise, and it is so in a double sense: it teaches Antony the truth that she belongs to the next world, not this, and that he can only be united with her by himself passing through death; and it also "proves" to him beyond any doubt that she is altogether faithful to him, so that when he deals himself the wound he is to die of, his love is no longer lacking in wisdom. His situation at this moment is very similar in almost every respect to that of the Moor at the close of *Othello*.

At the moment where the story of Antony ends, the story of the pilgrimage of Cleopatra comes into the foreground. The spiritual aspect of Antony has been present in the background throughout, and has come once or twice into the foreground, especially in the scene where Alexas brings a pearl from him to Cleopatra who says:

> How much unlike thou art Mark Antony!
> Yet, coming from him, that great medicine[6] hath
> With his tinct gilded thee. (I, 5, 35–37)

We may quote also from the same scene:

> CLEOPATRA. What, was he sad or merry?
> ALEXAS.　　Like to the time o' the year between the extremes
> 　　　　　Of hot and cold, he was nor sad nor merry.
> CLEOPATRA. O well-divided disposition! Note him …
> 　　　　　He was not sad, for he would shine on those
> 　　　　　Who make their looks by his; he was not merry,
> 　　　　　Which seem'd to tell them his remembrance lay
> 　　　　　In Egypt with his joy; but between both:
> 　　　　　O heavenly mingle! Be'est thou sad or merry,
> 　　　　　The violence of either thee becomes,
> 　　　　　So does it no man else. (I, 5, 50–61)

This scene prepares us for the conversation between Cleopatra and Dolabella in the last scene of the play, that is, after Antony's death.

> CLEOPATRA. I dreamt there was an Emperor Antony:
> 　　　　　O such another sleep, that I might see
> 　　　　　But such another man! …
> 　　　　　His face was as the heavens; and therein stuck

---

[6] The Philosopher's Stone which, having power to transmute baser metal into gold, is an image of the Divine Spirit.

> A sun and moon, which kept their course, and lighted
> The little O, the earth . . .
> His legs bestrid the ocean: his rear'd arm
> Crested the world: his voice was propertied
> As all the tuned spheres, and that to friends;
> But when he meant to quail and shake the orb
> He was as rattling thunder. For his bounty,
> There was no winter in't; an autumn 'twas
> That grew the more by reaping . . .
> Think you there was, or might be, such a man
> As this I dreamt of?
> DOLABELLA. Gentle madam, no.
> CLEOPATRA. You lie, up to the hearing of the gods. (V, 2, 76–95)

The alternative that faced Antony throughout the whole play, the choice between Heaven and earth, the celestial East and the worldly West, and that is finally forced on him by the "false" news of Cleopatra's death, is also brought home to Cleopatra by Antony's death. But for her the symbol vanishes into the reality; the choice is not between Egypt and Rome but quite literally between Heaven and earth. It now faces her for the first time; until then, as she says,

> It were for me
> To throw my sceptre at the injurious gods;
> To tell them that this world did equal theirs
> Till they had stol'n our jewel. All's but naught;
> Patience is sottish and impatience does
> Become a dog that's mad. (IV, 15, 75–80)

The word "injurious" does not make Cleopatra's remark comparable to Gloster's

> As flies to wanton boys are we to the gods:
> They kill us for their sport. (IV, 15, 67–68)

She does not need Edgar to tell her that "impatience does become a dog that's mad." Her attitude is as much intellectual as sentimental. Now that Antony, a brief loan from Heaven to earth that she never really possessed, has been snatched back, she sees this world as utter vanity.

And there is nothing left remarkable
Beneath the visiting moon. (IV, 15, 67–68)

Both patience and impatience are equally pointless. The situation is for her
as a Divine summons to the next world.

In the following scene, the last of the play, she continues in the same vein:

My desolation does begin to make
A better life. 'Tis paltry to be Caesar;
Not being Fortune, he's but Fortune's knave,
A minister of her will: and it is great
To do that thing that ends all other deeds;
Which shackles accidents and bolts up change;
Which sleeps, and never palates more the dung,
The beggar's nurse and Caesar's. (V, 2, 1–8)

In the first scene of the play Antony had already said:

Our dungy earth alike
Feeds beast as man. (I, 1, 35–36)

But, to kill herself is, for Cleopatra, the most difficult thing in the world—
as difficult as it is for Isabella to forego her revenge on Angelo. There is
nothing at all of the European romantic about Cleopatra. She has a deep-
rooted Oriental practicality and no one needs less to be taught the old adage
that warns us against putting all our eggs into one basket. Earlier on, when
Caesar's messenger suggested to her that her attitude to Antony was one of
fear rather than of love, she agreed with him for no other reason, apparently,
than because she could not bear to throw away a possible advantage. Might
it not be very useful to her in the future that Caesar should have such ideas
in his head about her relationship with Antony? It was not for nothing that in
a previous scene Antony had said of her: "She is cunning past man's thought"
(I, 2, 142). And now, when she is overflowing with contempt for this world
and when she has already decided, so it seems, to put an end to her life, she
is nonetheless prepared to go to some lengths in order to prevent Caesar
from laying hands on the bulk of her treasure. Her treasurer's betrayal of her
perhaps helps her to make up her mind altogether and overcome her last lin-
gering weaknesses. In view of these weaknesses, in view of the fact that to kill

herself is, for her, the most difficult thing in the world, suicide is in her case doubly symbolic: it means both killing "the dragon" and passing through the "narrow gate," and as such it is equivalent both to Hamlet's killing Claudius and to his dying himself.

When singleness of purpose finally crystallizes in her, she says:

> Show me, my women, like a queen: go fetch
> My best attires: I am again for Cydnus,
> To meet Mark Antony. (V, 2, 226–28)

and then:

> Give me my robe, put on my crown; I have
> Immortal longings in me: now no more
> The juice of Egypt's grape shall moist this lip ...
>   Husband, I come:
> Now to that name my courage prove my title!
> I am fire and air; my other elements
> I give to baser life. (V, 2, 279–89)

Previously Antony had said, in just the same situation:

> I come, my queen:
> stay for me
> Where souls do couch on flowers we'll hand in hand,
> And with our sprightly port make the ghosts gaze ...
> I will be
> A bridegroom in my death, and run into't
> As to a lover's bed. (IV, 14, 50–101)

CHAPTER TEN

CYMBELINE

In *The Divine Comedy,* shortly before he reaches the top of the Mountain of Purgatory, Dante is made to pass through the fire, fire that harms not a hair of his head yet that is so fierce to the senses that—to use his own image—if there had been a vat of molten glass at hand he would have plunged into it to cool himself. After this there remains no further obstacle between him and the top of the mountain on which is the Garden of Eden. But the night has fallen, and so, unable to go any further, he lies down to sleep; and in that sleep he dreams of the Earthly Paradise which he is to enter the next day.

In all the plays we have considered so far except *Macbeth,* Shakespeare takes his heroes and heroines up the Mountain of Purgatory and through the final fire to that sleep, and sometimes to that dream of Paradise; but he takes them no further. Even at the end of *Measure for Measure* we are, as it were, only upon the threshold. As to the other great plays of his so-called "middle" period, they are in any case all tragedies and as such could at the most only imply or herald what lies beyond Purgatory, without directly representing it on the stage. But in the latest of these, *Antony and Cleopatra,* Shakespeare's treatment of his theme comes near to bursting the tragic form and to overflowing across the threshold of Paradise. It is therefore not surprising that for his last plays, *Pericles, Cymbeline, The Winter's Tale,* and *The Tempest,* he should have abandoned that form for one that would allow him to express directly not merely Purgatory itself, but also something of what Purgatory leads to.

The opening situation of *Cymbeline* reminds us, in different ways, both of *Hamlet* and of *Othello*. Daughter and father in *Cymbeline* correspond to son and mother in *Hamlet*. Cymbeline himself, like Gertrude, represents the passive aspect of the human soul in its state of fallenness, and Imogen, like the Prince of Denmark, represents the active aspect of the soul, its conscience and its intelligence. The soul's state of corruption is indicated by Cymbeline's second marriage, his being dominated by his "wicked queen" as he calls her at the end, just as in *Hamlet* it is indicated by Gertrude's marriage to Claudius. For the rest, the same truths are expressed in each play, but by means of different symbols. In *Hamlet* the Fall is marked by the murder of Gertrude's first husband, which brought about the soul's separation from the Spirit. In *Cymbeline* it is not represented by the death of the King's first wife, which is not mentioned, but by the loss of his "immortality," that is, by the loss of his two sons, the result of his misguided rupture with his wise counselor Belarius. Unlike Cordelia, Imogen is not enhanced as a symbol through being the King's third child. It is only at the very end of the play that the number three comes into its own when Cymbeline, having regained all his children, speaks of himself as being "A mother to the birth of three" (V, 5, 369). Until then it is the number two, in its positive aspect, that takes precedence. The King's two elder children represent here the two natures, heavenly and earthly, of primordial man. Fallen man, by comparison, is single, with a singleness of nature that is at the same time fragmentary, inasmuch as the remaining earthly nature is no longer perfect as it was before; and Cymbeline is reduced to that fragmentary singleness by being left with only a daughter, that is, with something less good, from the point of view of succession, than a single son would have been. The two sons are "the two worlds," Heaven and earth, which Imogen (including her father) regains at the end of the play. She says: "I have got two worlds by't" (V, 5, 351–52), that is, by the return of her two brothers. Their presence at her final union with Posthumus is thus exactly equivalent to the presence of Juno and Ceres at the betrothal of Miranda and Ferdinand; and although the symbolism of *The Winter's Tale* is not strengthened by any such presence, it is significant that Leontes at least mentions the two worlds in question when he says, of the newly betrothed Perdita and Florizel:

> I lost a couple, that 'twixt heaven and earth
> Might thus have stood, begetting wonder as
> You, gracious couple, do. (V, 1, 132–34)

The significance of Cymbeline's two sons is thus the same as that of Castor and Pollux,[1] and it seems almost certain that Shakespeare had the heavenly twins in mind here, for he makes Belarius say of the two princes:

> They are worthy
> To inlay the heaven with stars. (V, 5, 351–52)

and at the end Cymbeline prays that they may continue to "reign" in their "orbs." They are also, like Antony, the Philosopher's Stone, for like "that great medicine"[2] they too have power to turn baser metals into gold, inasmuch as they are spoken of as having "gilded pale looks" in the battle. Relatively speaking both the brothers, and not merely one, may be called "heavenly" because the earth that the second brother signifies is not the earth as it is but as it was primordially, a Paradise altogether penetrated with celestial influences.

The symbolism of the two brothers calls for no less than the perfection which in fact they have; and this brings us to a point that concerns Shakespeare's last plays in general. These plays are less naturalistic and more medieval not only in virtue of the presence of Divine Powers albeit necessarily in "pagan" disguise—Diana in *Pericles,* Jupiter in *Cymbeline,* Apollo in *The Winter's Tale,* and Juno, Iris, and Ceres in *The Tempest*—but also through the relative absence of psychological detail in the characters, an absence that is made up for by detail of another kind. It is to be noticed, for example, that in the three latest plays, those persons who represent the lost spiritual wisdom are not only perfect in character, like Desdemona and Cordelia, but also perfect in the circumstances of their lives: the two sons of Cymbeline have been brought up amid entirely natural surroundings, far away from all contact with corrupt civilization; Perdita has been brought up by shepherds

---

[1] The heavenly twins were born from an egg that was laid by Leda, having been engendered by Jupiter in the form of a swan. Réne Guénon in *The Great Triad,* Quinta Essentia, 1991, p. 40 remarks that in Hinduism, to which the ancient Greek tradition is related, the creation of the universe is represented by the hatching of a swan's egg out of the two halves of which come Heaven and earth. The swan is here the symbol of the Spirit of God which "breathed upon the face of the waters": and the "dividing of the waters" in Genesis is equivalent to the dividing of the "egg of the Universe" in Hinduism.

[2] See above, p. 142, note.

whose way of life has always been associated with purity and innocence; and Miranda has been brought up on the enchanted island.

What the openings of *Cymbeline* and *Othello* have in common is that in both plots the powers of darkness had been scheming to bring the soul of Everyman still further under their domination. Iago had been doing his utmost to have himself appointed as the Moor's lieutenant; and in *Cymbeline* the wicked stepmother had been doing her utmost to marry Imogen to her son Cloten. In both cases the devil has failed to increase his hold upon his victim; and what is more, a sudden and secret marriage between soul and Spirit has taken him altogether by surprise.

Posthumus is an eagle—

> I chose an eagle,
> And did avoid a puttock.[3] (I, 1, 139–40)

says Imogen   and he is also Leonatus, the "the lion's whelp," the eagle and the lion being the bird and beast of the sun which is the great symbol of the Spirit. There is no common measure, from this point of view, between Leonatus and Imogen, since he, as she says,

> overbuys me
> Almost the sum he pays. (I, 1, 146–47)

and since Iachimo in the hour of repentance describes Posthumus as being

> The best of all
> Amongst the rarest of good ones. (V, 5, 159–60)

we may quote him also as sincere in his earlier remark: "He sits 'mongst men like a descended god" (I, 6, 169). But in *Cymbeline*, as in *Othello*, the marriage is only virtual. It has not yet been consummated, and does not become fully actualized until the very end. Posthumus is immediately banished; and by banishing him, the king in a sense re-enacts the Fall, reiterating the loss of his two sons. The complete reversal of the situation at the end is indicated by Cymbeline's taking a lesson from Posthumus, who has just pronounced his forgiveness of Iachimo. Cymbeline says:

---

[3] Kite.

Nobly doomed!
We'll learn our freeness of a son-in-law;
Pardon's the word to all. (V, 5, 420–22)

And Posthumus' symbolic identity with the King's two sons is confirmed by their joyful acceptance of him as a brother.

Although, as we have seen, the relationship between Imogen and her father corresponds globally to the relationship between Hamlet and his mother, there is a considerable difference of detail. In *Hamlet* both the Prince and the Queen share the imperfection of fallen man and both have to develop and be purified. In *Cymbeline* all the faults are concentrated in the King, who remains entirely static, his only development being his repentance. Imogen personifies fallen man's better nature struggling to free itself. Unlike Hamlet she is represented as being perfect from the start, her only imperfection being that she is not yet free. The spiritual path is her escape from the court and her journey to Milford Haven in order to make good her marriage. This journey is a perfect image of the "straightened way which leadeth unto life"; and it is so fraught with destitution and desolation that she may be said to have passed through the narrow gate of death. It is significant that when she is finally found by the Roman Lucius she replies, in answer to his question who she is:

I am nothing: or if not,
Nothing to be were better.[4] (IV, 2, 367–68)

But on the journey she has been given a foretaste of Paradise in her fleeting reunion with her two lost brothers. Here again the symbolic identity between them and Posthumus is brought out, for they take as it were his place in Imogen's eyes, and although she does not know who they are, she momentarily transfers her allegiance from him to them, since he has forsaken her.

Pardon me, gods!
I'd change my sex to be companion with them,
Since Leonatus false. (III, 6, 86–88)

---

[4] It would be better to be nothing than what I am.

Meantime other effects of her spiritual striving are to be seen, not in herself where there is no room for development, but in that part of the soul which is directly dominated by the powers of darkness. These powers are gradually being forced to loosen their hold upon Cymbeline himself. The lesser of them, Cloten, is drawn onward in pursuit of Imogen until he trespasses upon the very outskirts of Paradise, where he is killed outright by the Spirit; and his mother dies as a result of the Spirit's return to Cymbeline's palace. Thus the whole soul is finally set free from its bonds.

So far we have only considered the play from one angle, according to which Everyman is represented by the synthesis of Imogen and her father. But like *Antony and Cleopatra, Cymbeline* has a reversible symbolism: it is also the story of Posthumus Leonatus, and from this point of view it is he who stands for the soul and Imogen, the princess, who represents the Spirit. Imogen's transcendence is stressed throughout the play, by various characters in various ways. For Posthumus she is "a gift of the gods"; for one of the courtiers she is "divine Imogen" just as for Cassio Othello's wife is "divine Desdemona"; for Pisanio she is "more goddess like than wife like," but perhaps the most significant of all, considering the wisdom of the speaker, is Belarius' exclamation when he first sees her (she is at that time disguised as a boy):

> By Jupiter, an angel! or, if not,
> An earthly paragon! Behold divineness
> No elder than a boy! (III, 6, 42–44)

The path of Posthumus Leonatus is a descent into Hell followed by an ascent of Purgatory. The sin of spiritual pride—manifested by his public boasting about Imogen—is brought to light, and brings with it its own retribution, a too easy loss of faith in Imogen, which breeds the sins of raging anger, treachery and, by intention, murder, for he treacherously seeks to lure Imogen to her death. It is only when the false news of her death comes to him that light dawns and his Purgatory begins. The change from the descent to the ascent is marked by his deciding to change sides in the battle and fight for Britain instead of Rome.

> I'll fight
> Against the part I come with; so I'll die
> For thee, O Imogen, even for whom my life
> Is, every breath, a death. (V, 1, 24–27)

He helps Belarius and the two princes to rescue Cymbeline in the battle and to put the Romans to flight. Then, in despair at not having died, he gives himself up to the Britons as a Roman prisoner, hoping to find death that way, and is led off to prison. His eloquent prayer for Divine Mercy—a passage too little known on account of the language difficulties caused by its elliptical concentration—recalls Hamlet's "the readiness is all" and Edgar's "ripeness is all." In Posthumus' case, "ripeness" takes the form of having paid all debts, that is, of having expiated all sins or, in other words, of having passed through Purgatory in this life. He is altogether confident that the act of death will work the final purifying touch and win him the fullness of Divine Mercy, thus opening for him the door from the prison of Purgatory to the freedom of Paradise. His certainty is confirmed by the vision which he then has of blessed spirits from Elysium interceding with Jupiter on his behalf. It is in virtue of this that he can so flatly contradict the gaoler at the end of the same scene. The gist of their argument might be expressed as follows. The gaoler insists that death is a closed door and that no one knows for certain what lies on the other side of it. Posthumus maintains that death is an open door through which anyone who is prepared to open his eyes can see what lies beyond. "I tell thee, fellow, there are none want eyes to direct them the way I am going, but such as wink and will not use them" (V, 4, 191–93). The meaning already given to these words is the literal one in answer to the gaoler. But in the case of Posthumus this meaning coincides with a deeper one, for "the way I am going" is the path of the Mysteries, "the straitened way that leadeth unto life," and "few are they that find it" because although it lies in front of everyone as the obvious course to take, most people turn a blind eye to it. The "narrow gate" itself, however, is not reached by Posthumus until the final scene when, still thinking that he has killed Imogen, he learns that she is entirely innocent, and cries out:

> O, give me cord, or knife, or poison,
> Some upright justicer! Thou, king, send out
> For torturers ingenious: it is I
> That all the abhorred things o' the earth amend
> By being worse than they. (V, 5, 213–17)

It is by virtue of his being "absolute for death," like Claudio and Angelo in *Measure for Measure,* that he may be said to have "died into life" just as much as those of Shakespeare's heroes and heroines who literally do die.

In *Antony and Cleopatra* the symbolism of Egypt and Rome is not reversible. For Cleopatra as well as for Antony Rome is this world, and at the end the choice for Cleopatra is between this world, represented by Rome and Caesar, and the next world represented by the dead Antony.[5] But in *Cymbeline* Britain and Rome have each a positive and a negative significance. Where Everyman is represented by Imogen and her father, the court of Britain represents this world just as it does in *King Lear*, and Kent's words "Freedom lies hence, and banishment is here" (I, 1, 182) might just as well be applied to Cymbeline's palace as to Lear's. One aspect of Cymbeline's corruption is that he has refused to pay tribute to Caesar; and there is also a special connection between Rome and Jupiter in virtue of his bird, the Roman eagle. Moreover Caesar's ambassador Lucius, Rome's chief representative in this play, is extremely venerable. When advising Imogen to seek service with him, Pisanio says of him:

> He's honourable,
> And, doubling that, most holy. (III, 4, 179–80)

Considering the play from this point of view there is a certain identity between Rome and Belarius' cave inasmuch as both are spiritual centers with regard to which Cymbeline is at fault; and it is to be noted that Cloten, who is actually killed for his sacrilege of trespassing upon the precincts of the cave, has previously expressed his readiness to commit sacrilege with regard to the other sanctuary. In preparing to follow Imogen he says:

> I will pursue her
> Even to Augustus' throne. (III, 5, 101–2)

It is to be noted also that although the speeches expressing Britain's defiance

---

[5] It is true, however, that the presence of Antony in the next world, "a Roman by a Roman/ valiantly vanquisht" (IV, 15, 57–58), adds as it were a certain "prestige" to Rome; and although in the last scene Cleopatra says: " 'Tis paltry to be Caesar" (V, 2, 2) and although her own death and the deaths of her attendants are hastened on through the imperative need to escape being taken to Rome, of which she conjures up the most sordid pictures, she has nonetheless already said over Antony's dead body:
> We'll bury him, and then, what's brave, what's noble,
> We'll do it after the high Roman fashion,
> And make death proud to take us; (IV, 15, 86–88)
and the play ends on a note of grandeur and magnanimity from Caesar.

of Rome have a patriotic ring about them and might seem in themselves to be positive, they are for the most part put by Shakespeare into the mouths of no more reputable characters than the Queen and her degenerate son.

On the other hand, from the point of view of the banished Posthumus, Britain, the abode of Imogen, is a Paradise. From this standpoint the faults of Cymbeline are not relevant. The soul, represented by Posthumus, is not yet worthy to be united with the Spirit, and has been justly banished. The celestial aspect of Britain is brought out strongly when the devilish Iachimo, who is a Roman, says that he feels the very air to be taking revenge upon him:

> The heaviness and guilt within my bosom
> Takes off my manhood. I have belied a lady,
> The princess of this country, and the air on't
> Revengingly enfeebles me. (V, 2, 1–4)

As we have seen, it is a milestone in Posthumus' spiritual journey when he discards his Italian clothes for the garb of a British peasant and decides to fight for Britain against Rome.

The two opposite points of view are reconciled at the end and merged into one standpoint from which both Britain and Rome are celestial. Cymbeline says:

> Although the victor, we submit to Caesar
> And to the Roman empire,[6] promising
> To pay our wonted tribute, from the which
> We were dissuaded by our wicked queen;
> Whom heavens in justice on both her and hers
> Have laid most heavy hand. (V, 5, 460–65)

This reconciliation is the meaning of the soothsayer's vision:

> The Roman eagle,
> From south to west on wing soaring aloft,

---

[6] To digress for the moment from Shakespeare's deepest meaning, and also from the literal meaning, is it possible to read into Cymbeline's somewhat unexpected submission a plea to the son of Mary Stuart to find some way of mending once more the breach between Britain and Rome?

Lessen'd herself and in the beams o' the sun
So vanish'd: which foreshow'd our princely eagle,
The imperial Caesar, should again unite
His favour with the radiant Cymbeline
Which shines here in the west. (V, 5, 470–76)

As regards the cause of this harmony and of the restoration of other harmonies, the literal meaning stands in need of help from what lies above it. Esoterically, everything is to be explained by the fact that from the outset of this scene the two sons of Cymbeline are once more with their father. At first their identity is unknown, but their miraculous presence has already, against all expectations, won the battle for Britain, no earthly forces being able to stand up against them. This same presence makes it impossible for the powers of evil, concentrated in the person of the wicked Queen, to maintain their hold over the King; the Queen is smitten with a mortal sickness, and her dying soul disintegrates, spilling all its evil secrets. It is therefore to be expected, in virtue of what the two sons signify, that when Belarius at last reveals their identity to Cymbeline, their full restoration to him will precipitate still further blessings.

As for ourselves, a comprehensive result of the radiance of their presence is our consciousness, without our being able to say exactly how or when, that the drama itself has been snatched up to a higher plane. The transition from earth to Heaven is not so clear-cut as at the end of *The Winter's Tale,* but the celestial effect is no less overwhelmingly conveyed by the altogether unearthly piling up of happiness upon happiness—the sudden blissful perfect recovery of so much that had seemed to be irretrievably lost, the simultaneous realization of all the fullness of conjugal, filial, and fraternal love. This celestial wealth of felicity finds perhaps above all its expression in Cymbeline's words:

> See,
> Posthumous anchors upon Imogen;
> And she, like harmless lightning, throws her eye
> On him, her brothers, me, her master,[7] hitting
> Each object with a joy: the counterchange

---

[7] The Roman Lucius, whom she had served as page.

Is severally in all. Let's quit this ground,
And smoke the temple with our sacrifices.
[*To Belarius*] Thou art my brother, so we'll hold thee ever. (V, 5, 392–99)

We learn from Shakespeare that the opposite of tragedy, as well as tragedy itself, can have power to produce catharsis; and we may wonder whether that opposite has ever been expressed with such plenitude in dramatic art as it has in this play and, we might add, in its sister plays which we are about to consider. Each of these three has also its more particular powers; but of all the plays it is perhaps *Cymbeline* that comes nearest to being an expression of that "perennial" truth which Christ revealed to St. Julian of Norwich: All shall be well . . . all manner of thing shall be well.

CHAPTER ELEVEN

THE WINTER'S TALE

Of all Shakespeare's plays the nearest parallel to *The Divine Comedy* is perhaps *The Winter's Tale*, though needless to say, even this cannot take us as far as Dante's epic does. Like the epic, however, it falls into three distinct parts. For Leontes, as for Othello, Angelo, and Posthumus, Hell and Purgatory are represented separately. The first part of *The Winter's Tale* deals with the discovery of the evil that until then had lurked hidden in the soul of Leontes. His behavior in his first scene has something in common with Posthumus' boasting about Imogen. Both men are in possession of a secret treasure that in a sense they profane. Leontes' great fault is that he exploits the forces of the Spirit, represented by Hermione, for a purely trivial purpose. There is no reason why Polixenes should stay any longer in Sicilia and there are many reasons, so he tells us, why he should return to Bohemia. But Leontes squanders Hermione's irresistible power to make Polixenes change his mind, and then even forgets himself so far as to say:

> Hermione, my dearest, thou never spok'st
> To better purpose. (I, 2, 88–89)

She takes him up on this point, and he admits that she had spoken to better purpose once before, namely when she had consented to marry him. But his admission cannot atone for the enormity of so monstrous a loss of sense of proportion. It is in fact no less than sacrilege, considering what his marriage means, although in his case as in the other cases we have seen, the union of soul and Spirit is as yet only virtual, the marriage signifying initiation rather than realization, for he has not yet learnt to rate Hermione at her true worth. No sooner has she persuaded Polixenes to prolong his visit than Leontes begins to suspect her of an adulterous relationship with their royal guest. He orders his faithful counselor Camillo to poison Polixenes; and Camillo, having tried in vain to persuade Leontes that the Queen and their guest are totally innocent, warns Polixenes of the danger he is in and organizes his escape from Sicilia back to his own kingdom of Bohemia whither he accompanies him as an exile.

To say, as is so often said, that the jealousy of Leontes is less convincing than that of Othello serves merely to confuse the issue. As we have already seen, it is impossible to represent all the different aspects of the truth in one play. Iago is a wonderful portrayal of the devil in all his hellishness; but at the price of such a portrait Shakespeare is scarcely able, in *Othello*, to convey the fact that the devil is inside the soul of fallen man as well as outside it. Leontes is Othello with Iago inside him. There is no outward personification of the devil in *The Winter's Tale,* or indeed of any evil, except for the knavery of Autolycus which has no direct bearing on the plot. The other characters stand around like guardian angels while Leontes plunges deeper and deeper into Hell. They know that he is not himself. What has already been said about Angelo in connection with Mariana's line: "They say best men are moulded out of faults" (V, 1, 437) applies equally well to Leontes. The lost psychic substance has first of all to be rediscovered and then purified and reintegrated, and there is or can be a dangerous moment between the discovery and the purification. Leontes has woken up dormant elements in his soul that have leapt upon him and overpowered him before he could subdue them. He is, as Camillo puts it, "in rebellion with himself." But he has saved himself in advance by submitting the whole issue to the judgment of Apollo:

> Yet, for a greater confirmation,
> (For in an act of this importance, 'twere
> Most piteous to be wild), I have dispatch'd in post
> To sacred Delphos, to Apollo's temple,
> Cleomenes and Dion . . .
>   now from the oracle

> They will bring all; whose spiritual counsel had,
> Shall stop or spur me. (II, 1, 180–87)

Later we learn that Cleomenes and Dion have returned from Delphos with almost miraculous speed; and we are given a brief glimpse of them as they land in Sicilia, quite overwhelmed by the blessedness of Apollo's temple, the solemn reverence of the priests, the unearthliness of the sacrifice, and the voice of the oracle that reduced the hearers to a feeling of nothingness. Shakespeare is clearly determined that God shall preside over his play, despite puritanical laws to the contrary!

Having disowned his newborn daughter and sent her out of Sicily to be left in some desert place where she is more likely to die than to live, Leontes puts his wife Hermione on trial for adultery and treason. The descent into Hell goes on, without any question of Purgatory, until finally Hermione appeals to Apollo for justice. Cleomenes and Dion are called into court and the statement of the oracle is read:

> Hermione is chaster; Polixenes blameless; Camillo a true subject; Leontes
> a jealous tyrant; his innocent babe truly begotten; and the king shall
> live without an heir, if that which is lost be not found. (III, 2, 132–36)

The oracle precipitates Leontes to the nethermost depth of Hell and he cries out:

> There is no truth at all i' th' oracle:
> The session shall proceed: this is mere falsehood. (III, 2, 140–41)

thus bringing to light the greatest of all evils, impiety against Heaven. Immediate retribution follows: unknown to any of those present, the King's son is dead and the King is in fact "without an heir" except for "that which is lost," the baby daughter whom he has cast out. No sooner has Leontes uttered his blasphemy than a servant enters, announcing the death of the Prince. This one terrible blow shatters in an instant all the rebellion in Leontes' soul. We have seen that in *Othello*, when Emilia suddenly proves beyond doubt Desdemona's innocence and Iago's guilt, the whole of the Moor's dark descent into Hell is immediately lit up in retrospect. Symbolically, that moment is the exact equivalent of the *Fiat lux* brought about by the oracle in *The Winter's Tale*. At the news of his son's death, the scales fall from Leontes' eyes, and seeing exactly what has happened, he is all repentance. Meantime his wife has fainted and is carried off; and then the news is brought that she, too, is dead.

The Purgatory of Leontes takes place in the interval of the sixteen years that elapse between this act and the next. But although it is not represented on the stage, Shakespeare gives us a wonderful glimpse, at its outset, of the immensity of the task in all its apparent hopelessness, and of the soul's contrition which makes all things possible. Paulina says to Leontes:

> A thousand knees
> Ten thousand years together, naked, fasting,
> Upon a barren mountain, and still winter
> In storm perpetual, could not move the gods
> To look that way thou wert.

Leontes replies:

> Go on, go on;
> Thou canst not speak too much; I have deserv'd
> All tongues to talk their bitterest. (III, 2, 210–16)

After he has said at the end of the scene

> Come and lead me
> To these sorrows, (III, 2, 242–43)

we do not see him again until the sixteen years have passed.

This undisguised miracle play is intensified in its effect upon us by the symbolism of death and birth combined with that of winter and spring. It is Leontes' son, the young Prince Mamillius, who dies; and it is he who tells the winter's tale, the story of Hell and Purgatory. When asked by Hermione to tell her a "merry" tale he says: "A sad tale's best for winter" (II, 1, 25). He then puts his mouth close to his mother's ear to whisper to her his "tale about the man who dwelt by a churchyard," and just at that moment the raging Leontes rushes in and sets in motion the train of sorrowful events. The last of these is that when Perdita, the newborn daughter of Leontes, has been left in a desert place in Bohemia, Antigonus who left her there is killed by a bear and the crew of his boat are shipwrecked. These deaths are witnessed by the son of a shepherd; meantime Perdita has been found by the shepherd himself, who says to his son: "thou mettest with things dying, I with things new-born" (III, 3, 111–12). This brings a new note into the play, and identifies Perdita with birth, just as her brother was identified with death; and when next we see her, after sixteen years, she is dressed as Flora, the Goddess of Spring.

In virtue of her name, given her by Apollo in the words of the oracle "That which is lost" and confirmed, in its feminine form, by her mother to Antigonus in a vision, Perdita must be identified with what man lost at the Fall, his state of primordial perfection; and we have already seen that her upbringing among shepherds has a significance parallel to that of the upbringing, in virgin nature, of Cymbeline's two sons, who likewise personify man's original state. Also significant is the way in which Florizel, the son of Polixenes, had first made contact with her. We are told that he had been one day out hawking and that his falcon, bird of Apollo, had flown over the shepherd's land, thus causing him to meet the man's "daughter." The Prince and she are now deeply in love with each other; and King Polixenes, noticing his son's frequent absences from court, has him traced, and then goes together with Camillo, both disguised, to see for himself what he is about.

It is the sheep-shearing festival, and this scene, like the whole of the second half of the play, takes place in late summer, which is the season that Leontes has now reached in life. But Shakespeare overstamps this season with the seal of spring, personified by the two lovers; and it is thus that Perdita, robed as the Goddess of Spring, distributes flowers to the guests.

Polixenes and Camillo are exceedingly impressed by the nobility of her deportment; and there is a striking dialogue between her and the King which, side by side with the pastoral innocence of her upbringing, likewise affirms her primordial significance. It begins with her excuse for not being able to give him any of the fairest flowers of that time of year, namely streaked gillyflowers. She says she does not like to have them in her garden because they are hybrids, the result of artful human interference with nature, "nature's bastards" as they are sometimes called. The King defends the art of grafting on the grounds that it is derived from nature and that it is in the nature of things, otherwise the art would fail. As to the metaphor, we have already seen an example of its use by Hamlet[1] with reference to the need for the old stock of corrupt latter-day human heredity to be inoculated with the new stock before it can be effectually overcome, that is, to the point

---

[1] See pp. 20–21.

that we no longer stink of it. He is referring to initiation into the Mysteries which is precisely the inoculation of the old stock of subhuman fallen nature with a new graft of primordial human nature. This graft comes from the spiritual chain that constitutes as it were the backbone of every mystical order, the chain of Saints going back from the living master to the founder of the religious form in question and it is thus that the novice acquires by initiation a second birth with a new ancestry. But Polixenes is speaking unawares at cross purposes with Perdita: to him it seems that by her avoidance of gillyflowers she is acting directly against her own interests, for she herself, as a perfect example of wild stock, a bark of baser kind, would have everything to gain by being married to a man of nobler birth, a "gentler scion." She admits without reservation his general argument about the natural origin of the art in question, but when he replies: "Then make your garden rich in gillivors" (IV, 4, 98) her refusal to do so has something adamantine about it, as if to express an intuitive consciousness that she belongs to the primordial age, and that all the developments he speaks of are "after" her time and cannot be any concern of hers. In the age she belongs to there is not yet any "wild stock" in existence such as might need an "inoculation."

The fact that Polixenes pleads here for the principle of marrying "A gentler scion to the wildest stock" (IV, 4, 93) suggests that he is on his way to being won over by the innate nobility of her nature and that it is not impossible that he might consent to allow his son to marry her, even before he knows that she is not the shepherd's daughter. But when the shepherd announces her marriage to Doricles, that is, Florizel, the disguised King asks his son if he has a father, and if so, has he been told of the marriage, and if not, as the prince admits, why not. Moreover, despite his unknown questioner's reiterated pleas, supported by the plea of the shepherd, that he should tell his father, Florizel insists that he will on no account do so. Then Polixenes throws off his disguise and goes out in great anger, having ordered his son to follow him to the court and never again to come to the cottage, on pain of death for Perdita and of being himself barred from succession to the throne. The shepherd also goes out in great distress a few moments later, and the young couple are left alone with Camillo.

Florizel is not to be moved from his determination to marry Perdita, and he tells Camillo that he has a boat ready to take them away, but that so far he has no plans of where to go. Camillo advises him to go to Sicilia and, once there, to send word to King Leontes that he and his bride have come to visit him, bearing a message for him from his father King Polixenes of Bohemia.

Any needs they may have can be supplied from Camillo's own fortunes which are still there. Florizel agrees and Camillo bids them embark without delay.

Meantime the shepherd's son persuades his father that the time has now come to inform the King, so as to avoid incurring further anger from him, that Perdita is only an adopted child, no blood relation of theirs, and to tell him how she was found, showing him the bundle of rich objects that lay beside her. But Autolycus the rogue, having been at one time a servant to the Prince, still feels a certain loyalty toward him; and fearing that the shepherd may tell the King of his son's flight, he prevents him from going to the palace on the grounds that the King is about to set sail. He then offers to show the shepherd and his son where the King's boat is, but in fact he brings them to the Prince's boat, which they board and which takes them to Sicilia with Florizel and Perdita.

As to Camillo, when he has given the lovers time to escape, he tells Polixenes where they have gone, and persuades him to take him with him, in pursuit of them, to the court of Leontes.

It is significant, as we have seen, that the latter part of this play should be set in late summer, because that is the season that Leontes has now reached in life. But the two lovers personify the youth of the year; and now that they have decided to elope to Sicilia, we have reason to think that the winter's tale will end for Leontes and a tale of spring will begin. This is confirmed by the opening speech of the next scene, which has already been quoted in an earlier chapter. We are once more with Leontes in Sicilia, and Cleomenes says to him:

> Sir, you have done enough, and have perform'd
> A saint-like sorrow: no fault could you make,
> Which you have not redeem'd; indeed, paid down
> More penitence than done trespass: at the last,
> Do as the heavens have done, forget your evil;
> With them, forgive yourself. (V, 1, 1–6)

These words tell us that we are now at the point beyond which the plays of the middle period do not go.

A gentleman comes in to announce the arrival of Florizel, Prince of Bohemia, accompanied by his princess, of whom it is said:

> Women will love her, that she is a woman
> More worth than any man; men, that she is

The rarest of all women. (V, 1, 110–12)

Paulina says:

> Had our prince,
> Jewel of children, seen this hour, he had pair'd
> Well with this lord: there was not full a month
> Between their births. (V, 1, 115–18)

This indicates that Florizel is to replace the dead Prince Mamillius. He and Perdita together, like Cymbeline's two sons, represent the "immortality" of primordial man which was lost and has now been found again.

Leontes is thus on the very threshold of the Earthly Paradise; and the sight of Florizel and Perdita is as a direct vision of that Paradise. The entry of the Prince and Princess can be quite overwhelming, provided that those who play their parts are adequate, and provided that there is the right kind of music (we will come back to this question later), continuing long enough, after their entry, to enable them to "beget wonder" in Leontes and his court, and also in the audience, before Leontes says to them:

> I lost a couple, that 'twixt heaven and earth
> Might thus have stood, begetting wonder, as
> You, gracious couple, do; (V, 1, 132–34)

and later:

> Welcome hither,
> As is the spring to th' earth. (V, 1, 150–51)

The words "twixt heaven and earth," which are quite unnecessary as regards the literal meaning, help to underline the spiritual degree that Leontes has reached with the return of "that which was lost," for they are a reminder that the function of primordial man is to be, precisely, mediator between Heaven and earth. The fact that Leontes does not yet know that the Princess is his lost daughter is altogether outweighed, as regards the mysterial significance of their meeting and the impact it makes on us, by the fact that the audience themselves know who she is and are certain that he must be on the point of knowing. Moreover he himself has equated the couple with his lost son and daughter. At the same time Shakespeare takes advantage of his ignorance that Perdita is indeed the second of these to show us a little more of the remarkable changes that Purgatory has effected in his soul. It has already been made clear earlier in this scene, from remarks we have not quoted, that his willful stubbornness, his opinionated self-confidence, and his pride have been eliminated; but the lines we are now considering show us that a rigid egocentrism has been replaced by the spontaneous altruism of true magnanimity. We see a man who is still sorrowing for losses that are among the greatest that one can suffer but who even so is able to rejoice wholeheartedly in the happiness of others and to delight objectively in the youthful beauty and bliss of a couple who are, as he thinks, quite unrelated to himself.

The vision of Paradise fades for a moment with the entry of a lord who bears a message from the newly arrived Polixenes asking Leontes to place Florizel under arrest. Florizel begs Leontes to plead with his father on behalf of himself and Perdita, and he seems disposed to do so. But meantime Polixenes and Camillo have come upon the shepherd and his son who assure them that Perdita is a foundling of unknown parentage.

Perdita's looks already remind Leontes of her mother; and those of the audience who do not know the play are now expecting, consciously or subconsciously, a scene in which her true identity is made known to him. But the economy of the master dramatist will not allow it. Another recovery of loss lies in the offing; and the emotional receptivity of the spectators must not be over-squandered on the paternal-filial reunion, but must rather be kept in reserve for a still greater blessing about which, unless they already know the play, they are as ignorant as Leontes himself. So it is off-stage that Leontes and Polixenes and Camillo take the shepherd and his son with them to the palace, the shepherd carrying the bundle of objects that he had found beside the babe Perdita and that he has been treasuring ever since. The bundle is opened in the presence of Leontes, and it includes a mantle belonging to Hermione together with one of her jewels, as well as a piece of writing in the recognizable hand of Antigonus by which it is known that the babe's name is Perdita.

We witness nothing of this, but it is recounted to us by attendant gentlemen. Then Paulina's steward describes the effect of the discovery on those concerned. With regard to Leontes, he says:

> Our King, being ready to leap out of himself for joy of his found
> daughter, as if that joy were now become a loss, cries "O, thy mother, thy
> mother!", then asks Bohemia forgiveness; then embraces his son-in-law;

then again worries he his daughter with clipping[2] her; now he thanks the
old shepherd. . . . I never heard of such another encounter. (V, 2, 50–58)

The regaining of "that which is lost" marks the end of the Lesser Mysteries; and they, being incomplete in themselves, necessarily open out onto the
Greater Mysteries which transcend what leads up to them in a way that can
be symbolically described as a change from the horizontal to the vertical.
We have seen that *Cymbeline* ends with the attainment of that opening. The
threshold between the two Mysteries has not been crossed, but the vertical
dimension is already implicit enough to wing the intuition of spectator or
reader for flight beyond the limitations of the horizontal domain of mortality. We now find ourselves, in *The Winter's Tale,* upon the same threshold,
that of the Hereafter; but the play has not yet come to a close. This in itself
prepares us for a change of level, a transposal further implied by the sacred
setting of the final scene, which takes place in a chapel, and still further by
the exalted position allotted to Hermione herself within that sanctuary.
Moreover these suggestive outward indications correspond perfectly to our
own inward predispositions; for although according to the literal meaning of *The Winter's Tale* Hermione never really died at all, but has remained
hidden for sixteen years, the audience, for once, have not been taken into
the secret. They, like Leontes, are sure that she is dead and in Heaven. Her
appearance in the last scene has therefore the implicit effect of raising that
scene to a celestial plane. There is yet another factor that, on the basis of all
the others, has an overwhelming impact toward the same end, and that is
the music, played in accompaniment to Hermione's slow descent from her
high-raised pedestal. Nor can there be much doubt, such was the author's
recognition of the power of music, that he would prolong it, if only on
muted strings, until the end of the play, as a mysterious undercurrent of
transcendence.

Of high significance in this scene is the graduality of Leontes' reunion with
Hermione. It is by degrees that he comes to realize that she is truly alive; and
these stages are suggestive of stations of certitude, one above the other, in
the hierarchy of the degrees of spiritual realization. The play thus ends in
happiness that would be supreme but for the prospect of greater happiness to
come, not only at the same level but also by the transcending of one level for
another; and it must be remembered that ultimately immortality is bound to

---

[2] Embracing.

open onto Eternity. To resort once more to an already used image, when an artist sets before us a symbol, in this case a marriage, he has as it were liberated a bird from a cage, but he cannot control the extent of its flight. Nor indeed would he wish to do so, for it is in the essential nature of sacred art to open up a vista that will satisfy the needs of even the most farsighted of visionaries.

This question of illimitation leads us to that other passage through the Mysteries which is the secondary theme of *The Winter's Tale*. In the last speech of the play Leontes presents Florizel to Hermione as having been directed by Heaven toward his betrothal to their daughter; and insofar as it is a quest, the pastime of hawking is indeed susceptive of a mysterial significance, the more so in that it sets in motion the powers of the Spirit symbolized by the bird of Apollo. In the hawking that brought the Prince to the shepherd's farm the "prey" was "that which is lost." Nor is it without meaning that when we first see Perdita she is arrayed like a goddess; and it is in accordance with the simplicity of the play that on analogy with Leontes and Hermione, Florizel stands for the soul and Perdita for the Spirit. There is no call for the relationships to be considered reversible as they are in *Cymbeline* and, as we shall see, in *The Tempest*. The spiritual path is the Prince's unswerving devotion, most eloquently and movingly expressed, to "That which is lost," and his ultimate gaining complete possession of that treasure. Nor, once again, is there any need for us to seek to estimate its value, and thus to close what should be left open.

CHAPTER TWELVE

THE TEMPEST

The Tempest is by general consent Shakespeare's last complete play. We have already seen something of how it is anticipated by both *A Midsummer Night's Dream* and *Measure for Measure*. But the most immediately obvious parallel to *The Tempest* is *As You Like It*. In both the reigning duke is driven out of his duchy by a usurping brother; the plot of each turns around the love story of the rightful duke's daughter who has also been exiled; in each the usurping brother finally yields and the rightful duke gains once more possession of his duchy: and the most striking resemblance of all is that each takes place in a setting which is beyond—and above—the confines of civilization.

The forest of Arden represents the Golden Age. The banished duke and his followers are said to "fleet the time carelessly, as they did in the golden world" (I, 1, 112–13). We are transported back to an age when man still lived as it were in the neighborhood of the lost Paradise.

> Here feel we but the penalty of Adam,
> The season's difference . . .
> And this our life exempt from public haunts
> Finds tongues in trees, books in the running brooks,
> Sermons in stones, and good in everything. (II, 1, 5–17)

says the Duke. The enchanted island of *The Tempest* also transcends the rest of the world. Like the forest of the earlier play it is near to Heaven and therefore the ideal setting for the love that symbolizes the reunion of the celestial with the terrestrial. At the end of *As You Like It*, Rosalind is led on by Hymen who says:

> Good Duke receive thy daughter:
> Hymen from heaven brought her. (V, 4, 109–10)

And in *The Tempest*, as we have seen, the "marriage" of Heaven and earth actually takes place in the persons of Juno and Ceres, who are brought together by Iris, the celestial rainbow messenger, to attend the betrothal of Miranda and Ferdinand.

In addition to the already mentioned resemblance between *The Tempest* and *Measure for Measure*, it may be noted that if Prospero is banished from Milan, the Duke is also banished—self-banished—from Vienna; and if the Duke secretly remains in Vienna to observe what happens in his supposed absence, Prospero keeps Milan under his observation by transporting it, together with Naples from which it is symbolically inseparable, to his island. Naples and Milan, like Vienna, are this world. In a sense the whole world is on board the boat; and at the center of that world stands Alonso, the King of Naples, with his son Ferdinand. After appearing briefly in the scene of the shipwreck that opens the play, they retire below and we do not see them again on deck, though we are made to feel their presence. Gonzalo says:

> The king and prince at prayers! Let's assist them,
> For our case is as theirs. (I, 1, 55–56)

This remark is more significant than it might appear, for it is calculated to find an echo in the souls of the audience. They likewise are on board the boat of this world, which the tempest has revealed in its true light as the highly precarious and dangerous place that in fact it is. We may also note that the speaker of these words is defined in the *dramatics personae* as "An honest old Counsellor," and throughout the play he is something of a prolongation of Prospero himself. The actor who plays his part would be justified in addressing this speech to everyone, off stage as well as on, for the best of the audience, whether they know it or not, have come to the theater to identify themselves with two men who are "at prayers," and of whom anyone with a true sense of reality can and must say:

> Let's assist them,
> For our case is as theirs.

The King and Prince in this play, like the King and Princess in *Cymbeline,* together represent the human soul that is on its way through purification to sanctification. Hell is not portrayed, except in retrospect; the powers of evil are present, but they are already under control. Prospero's treacherous brother Antonio, the usurping Duke of Milan, has much in common with Claudius in *Hamlet.* It was Antonio who had contrived to bring about the exile of the Spirit by seducing the soul, in the person of the King of Naples, into an unholy alliance.

The greater part of Purgatory is concentrated in the tempest at the opening of the play. The enchanted island itself is no less than a setting for the sacred precinct of Prospero's cell, which may be said to transcend Purgatory. By extension the rest of the island is also a sanctuary; even Caliban is aware of its blessedness:

> Be not afear'd; the isle is full of noises,
> Sounds and sweet airs, that give delight and hurt not.
> Sometimes a thousand twangling instruments
> Will hum about mine ears; and sometimes voices,
> That, if I then had waked after long sleep,
> Will make me sleep again; and then, in dreaming,
> The clouds methought would open, and show riches
> Ready to drop upon me; that, when I waked,
> I cried to dream again. (III, 2,144–52)

Alonso and Ferdinand reach the island separately. It must be remembered that in the King-Prince Everyman of this play, as in the pair Cymbeline-Imogen, it is the parent who personifies the old and fallen soul, and the child who is virtually the new perfect soul that is waiting to be delivered.[1] That moment has now come, inasmuch as the son is certain his father is dead. Despite the considerable difference of details between the Prince of *The Tempest* and the Prince of *Henry IV* Ferdinand is now in a situation that recalls the scene where Prince Henry places the crown on his own head, believing himself to be already King. The parallel is all the stronger in that

---

[1] See p. 152.

both Princes are at the outskirts of Paradise, for Prince Henry crowns himself at the threshold of the Jerusalem Chamber.[2] Symbolically, the belief of each that he is King may be said to be equivalent to the actuality of kingship; and true kingship signifies, as we have seen,[3] man's primal state, fallen man being a usurper to the throne of earth. But in *The Tempest*, unlike the earlier play, the regenerated perfection of the Prince is made more clearly implicit at this point not only by Ariel's confirmation of the King's death and burial "full fathom five," but also and above all by the use of Hermetic symbolism.

The boat, apparently on fire when Ferdinand left it—"all afire with me," as Ariel says—is the funeral pyre, the Athanor of the alchemists. One might at first be surprised that Shakespeare does not pursue this fiery theme exclusively, and that he should speak of the sacrificial vessel not as a pyre but as "wreck," and of the alchemical transmutations themselves not as a fire-change but as a "sea-change." However, quite apart from the fact that fire is not, throughout this play, the dominant element in the consciousness of the audience, water is here a technical necessity, for it represents the first of the two terms of the great formula *solve et coagula*, and it is none other than the Quicksilver that has to be penetrated by the fire of Sulphur. "Through the union of opposites the soul becomes 'fluid fire' and 'fiery water.'"[4] The tempest itself, after which the play is named, is the alchemical "work," and Ariel assures Prospero that it was effectively an interpenetration of fire and water:

> the fire and cracks
> Of sulphurous roaring the most mighty Neptune
> Seem to besiege, and make his bold waves tremble. (I, 2, 203–5)

Prospero is here the master Alchemist, and the result of his "work" is the Prince himself, who later speaks of his future father-in-law as being the one "of whom I have received a second life" (V, 1, 194–95). Ferdinand may thus be considered as the newborn Phoenix that rises from the flames and from the waves.

It is as such that he now enters upon us, his natural beauty enhanced by the beauty of the music and of his wonderment at it, as well as by the beauty

---

[2] See p. 18.
[3] See pp. 16–17.
[4] Titus Burckhardt, *Alchemy*, p. 74.

of the words he speaks, and of the words that Ariel then sings:

> Where should this music be? i' th'air or th' earth?
> It sounds no more: and, sure, it waits upon
> Some god o'th'island. Sitting on a bank,
> Weeping again the king my father's wreck,
> This music crept by me upon the waters,
> Allaying both their fury and my passion[5]
> With its sweet air: thence I have follow'd it,
> Or it hath drawn me rather. But 'tis gone.
> No, it begins again. (I, 2, 387–95)

Ariel sings:

> Full fathom five thy father lies
> Of his bones are coral made;
> Those are pearls which were his eyes:
> Nothing of him that doth fade,
> But doth suffer a sea-change
> Into something rich and strange. (I, 2, 396–401)

Wonderment is an essential characteristic of primordial man inasmuch as wondrousness is an essential quality of Paradise which is his home. The heroine of this play has not been named at random; and when Ferdinand first sees her, thinking she must be a goddess in whose service the music is played, he addresses her, even before he knows her name: "O you wonder!" (I, 2, 426); and later he is to say, this time with reference to Prospero:

> Let me live here ever;
> So rare a wonder'd[6] father and a wise
> Makes this place Paradise. (IV, 1, 122–24)

Miranda, the Marvelous, is also necessarily the marveling. When Ferdinand enters she is asleep, but she gradually awakens during Ariel's

---

[5] Suffering.
[6] Possessed of wonders, able to work wonders.

song, which may be said to prepare her for a vision of "something rich and strange."[7] The song itself is directly concerned with King Alonso, but it also points to the Prince. To affirm the death of the old soul is to herald the birth of the new perfect soul; and it is Ferdinand himself who, as we have seen, embodies the result of the "sea-change" that is Ariel's theme. Shortly after the music ends, or perhaps[8] while the "burthen" or undersong still continues as a soft accompaniment to the spoken word, her father bids her open her eyes, to see what she can see; and it is as with the wonderment of Eve at her first sight of Adam that she sets eyes on the Prince, never before having seen a man other than her father:

> I might call him
> A thing divine; for nothing natural
> I ever saw so noble. (I, 2, 417–19)

"Rich and strange": these two epithets strike the key-note of this scene, and indeed of the play as a whole. Both reoccur at the climax, when Prospero gives Miranda to Ferdinand and says, with regard to the ordeal that he has imposed upon him:

> All thy vexations
> Were but my trials of thy love, and thou
> Hast strangely[9] stood the test: here, afore Heaven,
> I ratify this my rich gift. O Ferdinand,
> Do not smile at me that I boast her off,
> For thou shalt find she will outstrip all praise,
> And make it half behind her. (IV, 1, 5–11)

If we draw a comparison between Shakespeare's first great drama of love and this his last, it goes without saying that the essential in both is the factor of love itself, the mutual human attraction at its highest degree in virtue of each consort being the other's lost and longed-for half.[10] But in *Romeo and Juliet* the magnitude of the love is stressed by being measured out against the formidable strength of the adverse circumstances over

---

[7] This word is much nearer to "wonderful" in Shakespeare's use of it than in ours.
[8] According to the production.
[9] Wonderfully.
[10] See p. 59.

which, unshakable and invincible, it triumphs. In *The Tempest* on the other hand the circumstances are altogether favorable: unlike their less fortunate predecessors, Ferdinand and Miranda have the stars on their side. Their union is expressly blessed, not only by Heaven, Juno, but also by Earth, Ceres. There is every outward or secondary reason why they should be married, whereas the love of Romeo and Juliet is in sharp conflict with its earthly setting. The union of these star-crossed lovers of old Verona is a metacosmic or celestial necessity in tragic collision with a cosmic impossibility. The ultimate triumph of Heaven is marked by their burial side-by-side and their statues of pure gold. The union of Ferdinand and Miranda is likewise a marriage that has been made in Heaven, while being at the same time a cosmic necessity, so much so that they are betrothed within three hours of meeting. In the final scene when father and son are suddenly reunited, each having thought that the other was dead, the King takes immediate note of the intimacy between Ferdinand and Miranda and asks his son who she is, adding, with some surprise, that he cannot have known her for as long as three hours, whereupon he is obliged to confess that she is nonetheless already his betrothed. Their wedding will be, moreover, the wedding of two "worlds," Milan and Naples; nor is this its only macrocosmic significance, for there is also one of a deeper and a more universal order: the irresistibility of each lover for the other takes on an added vastness from the fact that Ferdinand is for Miranda quite literally the one and only man, whereas she is for him, as he tells her expressly, the sum of feminine virtue.

These remarks are not intended to exalt their love over that of Romeo and Juliet, which is clearly unsurpassable—to the point of being almost proverbial. As such, it stands in no danger of being underestimated. But the love of Ferdinand and Miranda must also be allowed its own unique and unsurpassable quality—a quality that is in a sense the measure of the greatness of the masterpiece to which it belongs. To praise *The Tempest* is to praise its love scenes, which are essential to it; and the following exclamation of Prospero, whole-heartedly echoed by the audience, may be said to sum up the play:

Fair encounter
Of two most rare affections! (III, 1, 74–75)

If it be asked which of the lovers represents the Spirit and which the soul, the answer is clearly that the symbolism is reversible, as in *Romeo and Juliet*,

Antony and Cleopatra, and other plays. Miranda is Prospero's daughter; and the significance of the place of her upbringing, far from the corruption of the world, has already been mentioned in this very context.[11] We must not forget, however, that at the first meeting of these lovers, each thinks that the other is divine; and Miranda's attitude of worship is altogether in line with the way in which, by Prospero's contriving, she has her first "vision" of the Prince. Moreover, once her father has entrusted her to him, this future King will take, insofar as she is concerned, the place of Prospero. On the one hand, then, it may be said that Prospero stands for the Spirit-Intellect, and that Miranda is an extension of him, just as Perdita is an extension of Hermione, who, like Desdemona and Cordelia, is the "pearl of great price" that was wantonly thrown away. On the other hand Miranda is Prospero's disciple who, from her earliest years, has followed the path of his guidance, a path of which the ultimate goal is the illustrious marriage that he has planned for her. From this point of view, which takes into consideration also the symbolism of rank, it is the future King of Naples who represents the Spirit and Miranda the soul.

We will return to this second relationship later. But as regards King Alonso, it is the first that is relevant, for to repeat in other terms what has already been said, he represents the "lead" of the soul, the base metal in which Ferdinand is the potential "gold."

> According to the famous Muslim mystic Muhyi'd-Din ibn 'Arabi, gold corresponds to the sound and original condition of the soul which freely and without distortion reflects the Divine Spirit in its essence, whereas lead corresponds to its "sick," distorted, and "dead" condition, which no longer reflects the Spirit. The true essence of lead is gold. Each base metal represents a break in the equilibrium which gold alone exhibits. In order to free the soul from its coagulation and paralysis, its essential form and its *materia*[12] must be dissolved out of their crude and one-sided combination. It is as if spirit[13] and soul had

---

[11] See p. 151.

[12] Its "condition of base metal, especially lead which in its obscurity and heaviness resembles crude mass" (Titus Burckhardt, *Alchemy,* p. 72).

[13] Spelled without a capital, spirit here means the essential "gold" in the soul in virtue of which it is a prolongation or reflection of the Spirit in the strict sense. In other words, that is, in the terms of the persons of this play, if "spirit and soul:" as used above, are respectively Ferdinand and Alonso, the soul in its full and normal significance must be named Ferdinand-Alonso, with Prospero-Miranda as Spirit.

to be separated from one another, in order, after their "divorce," to become "married" again. The amorphous *materia* is burnt, dissolved, and purified, in order finally to be "coagulated" anew.[14]

The King and the Prince, like Cymbeline and Imogen, represent precisely the "crude and one-sided combination" that is mentioned here—one-sided because in both cases it is the base metal that has the sovereign power; and the above passage shows that the temporary separation of Ferdinand and Alonso is alchemically necessary. Highly significant in this respect is the question that, at his first sight of Miranda, the father puts to his son:

> Is she the goddess that hath sever'd us,
> And brought us thus together? (V, 1, 187–88)

Miranda is here a prolongation of the master Alchemist, upon whom Alonso, like Ferdinand, depends entirely for his spiritual regeneration. In passing through the Athanor of the tempest, he dies the death of believing that his son is dead; and the end of his Purgatory is marked by his complete repentance, after Ariel, at Prospero's command, has caused him to be penetrated through and through by a sense of his guilt. Alonso says:

> O, it is monstrous, monstrous!
> Methought the billows spoke and told me of it;
> The winds did sing it to me; and the thunder,
> That deep and dreadful organ-pipe, pronounced
> The name of Prosper: it did bass my trespass.
> Therefore my son i'th'ooze is bedded; and
> I'll seek him deeper than e'er plummet sounded,
> And with him there lie mudded. (III, 3, 95–102)

Later, when he meets Prospero, still thinking that his son is dead and thinking also that Prospero has lost his daughter, his complete sincerity is not to be doubted when he says:

> O heavens, that they were living both in Naples,
> The king and queen there! that they were, I wish

---

[14] Titus Burckhardt, *Alchemy,* pp. 72–73.

Myself were mudded in that oozy bed
Where my son lies. (V, I, 149–52)

It is only when Alonso's repentance is assured that Ferdinand, for his part, comes to the end of his ordeal of carrying logs, and Prospero consents to his marriage with Miranda. When Prospero finally reveals the betrothed couple to Alonso, this King may be said to have reached exactly the same point that is reached by the repentant and purified King in *The Winter's Tale* when Perdita and Florizel come to his court.

There is no character in *The Tempest* to correspond to Hermione. Instead, a stress is laid on the difference between betrothal and marriage. The Earthly Paradise is not the complete union of the soul and Spirit but the leaning down as it were of Spirit to soul, of Heaven to earth. In the Earthly Paradise, symbolized here by the betrothal of Ferdinand and Miranda, Everyman has reached the fullness of earthly possibility. It is therefore at this point that Prospero prepares Ferdinand and Miranda for the Greater Mysteries of the Celestial Paradise by telling them that all the glories of earthly life are nothing more than a dream:

Our revels now are ended. These our actors,
As I foretold you, were all spirits, and
Are melted into air, into thin air:
And like the baseless fabric of this vision,
The cloud-capp'd towers, the gorgeous palaces,
The solemn temples, the great globe itself,
Yea, all which it inherit, shall dissolve,
And, like this insubstantial pageant faded,
Leave not a wrack behind. We are such stuff
As dreams are made on; and our little life
Is rounded with a sleep. (IV, 1, 148–58)

The Celestial paradise is not represented in *The Tempest*, as it is in *The Winter's Tale*, but the whole play reciprocates its leaning down by reaching up toward it, that is, toward the final marriage of the lovers.

As in *Cymbeline*, the hierarchic precedence of places is reversible as well as that of the lovers. The enchanted island, like the cave of Belarius, transcends the corrupt world of civilization; but that world will no longer be the same now that its inhabitants, and in particular its rulers, have been purified. At the end of *The Tempest* Milan and Naples take on a purely positive significance as things that were lost and are regained. The two points of view, as regards place and person, are intertwined in the last scene. For King Alonso, as for his son, Miranda is divine; for her, on the other hand, her future kingdom, personified by the Neopolitan visitors to the island, is the object to be marvelled at:

> O, wonder!
> How many goodly creatures are there here!
> How beauteous mankind is! O brave new world,
> That has such people in't! (V, 1, 181–84)

Gonzalo has already been quoted as saying in the first scene:

> The king and prince at prayers! let's assist them,
> For our case is as theirs.

Equally characteristic of his function in the play is his final summing up in the last scene, for here also he spreads wide the "net" as if to include as many persons as possible in the blessing of the alchemical work:

> Was Milan thrust from Milan, that his issue
> Should become kings of Naples? O, rejoice
> Beyond a common joy! and set it down
> With gold on lasting pillars: in one voyage
> Did Claribel her husband find at Tunis,
> And Ferdinand, her brother, found a wife
> Where he himself was lost, Prospero his dukedom
> In a poor isle, and all of us ourselves
> When no man was his own. (V, 1, 205–13)

The transcendent significance of the play and its final issue is here doubly affirmed by the two imperatives "Rejoice beyond a common joy" and "Set it down with gold." The latter is also clearly an alchemical reference; and in connection with the closing words of this speech we may repeat the already quoted dictum, "The true essence of lead is gold," in the sense that only primordial man knows and is his true self, fallen man having "lost" his first nature, beneath the rubble of "second nature" symbolized by lead.

"Let me know myself, Lord, and I shall know thee," said St. Augustine; and it may be recalled here that the Duke in *Measure for Measure*—a character very relevant to *The Tempest*—is defined as "One that, above all other strifes, contended especially to know himself"[15] (III, 2, 22–27). To find and know one's true self is the end of the Lesser Mysteries; but as the above saying of St. Augustine teaches us, this is a stage on the way to a higher knowledge. What Gonzalo says may thus be taken as pointing also, implicitly and in aspiration, to knowledge of the Real Self in whose image the human self is made; nor would this be out of keeping with the play as a whole that reaches up toward these Greater Mysteries, that is, toward the marriage beyond the betrothal.

The play may also be said to reach up toward them in another sense. Again and again in his plays Shakespeare has likened this life either to the part played by an actor on the stage, or to a shadow, or to a dream. Now to speak of a play or any kind of fiction necessarily means that as a term of comparison one has in mind something that may be called "real life"; to be continually likening things to shadows suggests a longing for the substance; and to dismiss everything that we experience and possess as a mere dream betrays a nostalgia for the state of being awake. But in order to reach that state of waking, that is, the Paradise of seeing "face to face" and not "as in a glass darkly," it is necessary to pass through that sleep that is the surrounding wall of the dream-world in which we live; and it is clearly in view of that sleep as a gate—for in itself it is not worth meditating on—that Shakespeare, about to give up his art and retire to Stratford, makes Prospero say, when about to give up *his* art and retire to Milan: "Every third thought shall be my grave" (V, 1, 311).

These words are usually taken as a reminder to be ready for death, a precept by way of example, but that is only a part of their meaning. Prospero is set before us from the start as a supreme spiritual master, and as such he must already have died, before his death, that greater death that is implicit in the Lesser Mysteries. The traditions of both East and West are in agreement that it is possible to pass during one's earthly life through both the Mysteries to the Supreme State of Union, the state that Christianity terms *deificatio*. The life of the deified man, the Master in the fullest sense, is bound

---

[15] III, 2. Both these quotations are given by Whitall Perry in the section on "Know Thyself" (pp. 859–68) of his momumental *Treasury of Traditional Wisdom*, Quinta Essentia, 1991, and the reader will find there a wealth of other formulations of this universal rule, many of them being from Hermetic, Pythagorean, Platonic, Christian, and other sources within the orbit of Shakespeare.

to be purposeful, for the presence of holiness here below is always providential; and the Oneness of Union will providentially release its hold on the human nature of the Saint so that he may fulfill his earthly function. His soul will thereby be conscious of a certain separation[16] albeit within the framework of Union; and since he knows that he has tasks to accomplish, he is bound to give them some thought. Secondly, he is bound to be always reiterating thoughts of gratitude for the great blessings of his spiritual state as it is. But thirdly—and three is a celestial number—he has the right to give "every third thought" to the eventual death of his human nature and its final reabsorption into the Spirit, a transubstantiation that will close forever the gaps of seeming exile.

---

[16]That apparent separation is, for the mystics of all traditions, one of their most recurrent poetical themes, and I have dwelt at some length on this question in my chapter "Mystical Poetry" in *The New Cambridge History of Arabic Literature,* vol. II, pp. 235–64. This second volume is entitled *Abbasid Belles Lettres.* See also my annotated translations in the anthology *Sufi Poems,* Islamic Texts Society, 2004.

CHAPTER THIRTEEN

Notes on Performance and Production

How can actors and directors best do justice to the deeper meaning of Shakespeare's plays? A general answer to this question is: by being as faithful as possible to the literal meaning. Take care of that, and the deeper meaning will take care of itself. But to be true to the letter is less easy and more exacting than it may sound, for Shakespeare's maturer plays, even as regards their literal meaning, center around human perfection, if not already achieved at any rate in the making—a perfection that is absolute and unsurpassable:

> A combination and a form indeed
> Where every god did seem to set his seal
> To give the world assurance of a man. (*Hamlet*, III, 4, 60–62)

Shakespeare has in view a universal norm, a coin that would remain current even as far East as feudal Japan, and as far West as the Red Indians of North America—a complex but not complicated psychic substance made up of marvelously rich elements that are closely woven into a total effect of unity, simplicity, and unfathomable depth; and this ideal spells great danger to an actor, for it cannot fail to measure out his capacities to their very fullest extent.

In *Hamlet*, for example, the actor may be said to have failed in his part if in the last scene the audience does not assent whole-heartedly to Horatio's admiring exclamation: "Why, what a king is this!" (V, 2, 62) and to the last words of Fortinbras over the Prince's dead body:

> He was likely, had he been put on,
> To have proved most royally. (V, 2, 408–9)

Similarly, to take another example, the actor of the part of Antony cannot afford to forget during his performance that at the end, when Antony's men find him dying, they are to say:

> The star is fallen.
> And time is at his period.[1] (IV, 14, 106–7)

and that Cleopatra is to say, when he actually dies:

> There is nothing left remarkable
> Beneath the visiting moon. (IV, 15, 67–68)

But if, as a loophole of escape, from a greatness hard to portray, the actor seizes on the word "dotage" so often applied to Antony by Cleopatra's enemies, and if he sets out to portray a man who, however great he may have been, is now psychically dilapidated, then the whole significance of the play will be seriously impaired. No actor would, however, admit, even to himself, that for fear of putting on a garment that was too big for him, he was cutting down the garment to fit his own size. The conscious motive for sidetracking is usually the desire to be thought original or "up-to-date." However that may be, an actor may well stand in fear of a central Shakespearean part; and whatever the motive, it happens all too often that the main issue, which is one of sincerity and depth, is avoided, and as a miserable "compensation" all sorts of psychological subtleties, quite unwarranted by the text, are invented.

To revert to *Hamlet*, there is not a trace of evidence in Shakespeare's text that the Prince's attitude toward his mother is not altogether normal. His

---

[1] Time has realized its final phase.

deep distress at her having fallen away from her own better nature is com-mensurate with the depth of his love for both his parents, in virtue of which he is a model of filial piety. It is inexcusable to deface this aspect of Hamlet's charac-ter by the totally unwarranted fabrication of an "Oedipus complex."

To illustrate still further the importance of fidelity to the text, let us take an example from a play that so far has been mentioned no more than by name; and since the plays written before *Hamlet* have scarcely come within the scope of this book except incidentally, it must be admitted here and now, while leaving the all-important question of total effect to be considered in the next chapter, that if we were to choose out from Shakespeare what we might call his greatest single moments, not a few of these would be found to come from the earlier plays. One such moment is in *Twelfth Night.* But if the part of Olivia be made comic through affectation—as it sometimes is—this moment will be sadly diminished, if not reduced to nothing. As regards her love for Cesario, that is, for the disguised Viola—who, it must be remembered, is consciously imitating her twin brother Sebastian—it is essential that it should be portrayed with all the depth and sincerity that an actress can muster. It must be intense enough to compel the audience to echo in thought Viola's "alas!" when she says:

> As I am a woman,—now, alas the day!—
> What thriftless sighs shall poor Olivia breathe!
> O Time, thou must untangle this, not I;
> It is too hard a knot for me to untie. (II, 2, 39–42)

It is clear that Shakespeare intended the audience to share this sentiment, for only if their feelings are properly roused can the "knot's" sudden and blissful "untanglement" make its full impact, when Olivia comes running out of the house to protect her beloved Cesario—as she thinks—from her uncle, and finds herself face-to-face with Sebastian for the first time. Several factors contribute to the strength of that impact, and not the least of these is its unexpectedness. So well contrived is it that however often we have seen the play before, it tends to come as something of a shock, partly because our attention is absorbed by the comic effect of the mistaken identity on Sir Toby and Sir Andrew and we are expecting more comic effects rather than a profoundly serious one. But by far the chief factor is the audience's deep concern for Olivia's happiness, and this can only be assured if they take her and her love altogether seriously. Shakespeare has already paved the way for them to do this by making the Duke say, in the first scene, in reference to her long mourning for her dead brother:

O, she that hath a heart of that fine frame
To pay this debt of love but to a brother,
How will she love, when the rich golden shaft
Hath kill'd the flock of all affections else
That live in her! (I, 1, 32–36)

Sebastian is no less than the lost half, the perfect complement, which Olivia has always, albeit unconsciously, been yearning to recover. She is therefore not so very much mistaken when she falls in love with the disguised Viola, for in view of the irresistible mutual attraction that has always existed virtually between herself and Sebastian it is not unnatural that for want of ever having seen him she should feel a foretaste of that love on seeing his disguised twin sister, enough even to prefer her to all the world. From the abnormality of this strange and somewhat puzzling situation Shakespeare snatches something of the abnormality of miracle. Viola has already become for the audience, as far as Olivia is concerned, a symbol of all that the soul most deeply desires. Sebastian is therefore something more than a symbol. In him the shadow has given place to the substance. It is as if he had dropped straight from Heaven; and it is in the "opening of Heaven" that there lies the secret of this moment's extraordinary power.

The effect of this first meeting between Olivia and Sebastian can be immeasurably deepened by the accompaniment of music.[2] This brings us from the question of acting to that of production, though the two things necessarily overlap, since in most modern productions the director is mainly responsible for the interpretation of the parts.

Despite what some may say, it is very conceivable that Shakespeare would have welcomed many of the facilities of the modern theater, at any rate in principle. He might well have been glad to exploit some of the scenic effects which can be obtained now and could not then. He would almost certainly have preferred not to have his medieval kings and queens all dressed as Elizabethans as they were in his own productions. But the

---

[2] This can he achieved most successfully—and most naturally—if Olivia's musicians are playing indoors, and the music suddenly becomes louder when she runs out.

wider range of possibilities has also its drawbacks, for it opens the door to many blunders that would have been out of the question in Shakespeare's own day. There might seem to be a certain logic in the argument that since Shakespeare produced his plays in the sort of clothes that were worn by his audience why should we not do the same? Might it not make the audience feel more "at home"? But apart from the fact that the audience do not go to Shakespeare in order to be made to feel "at home"—or rather they go in order to be made to feel at home in quite a different way—Shakespeare in modern dress does not make them feel at home in any sense at all. The utter disparity between Shakespearean verse and twentieth-century fashion is bound to create a feeling of uneasiness even in the least critical members of an audience. Whatever the limitations of early Jacobean and late Elizabethan dress may be, it at least belongs to the tail end of a tradition that was based on the conception of man as the representative of God on earth. In those days garments were still conceived of as a means of enhancing the dignity and beauty of man's body just as verse and poetic imagery are a means of enhancing the dignity and beauty of man's speech. But modern dress, which to say the least has no such pretensions, cannot possibly join forces with the splendors of Shakespeare's language.[3] It can only fight against that splendor, fatally diminishing its impact upon us.

Moreover, as regards this chapter's initial question, it will inhibit the opening out of the literal meaning onto higher meanings. Modern Western dress is a triumph of humanism. There is something implacably horizontal about it that makes all transcendent realities seem improbable. To see this, let us remember that there are medieval paintings that depict blessed Spirits dancing in Paradise, dressed without the least incongruity in such clothes as the artist and his contemporaries might have worn on festive occasions. And let us now imagine a modern painting on the same theme with the haloed Saints in modern dress! It is significant also that the more "correctly" they were dressed, the more shattering would be the effect.

From a slightly different angle, but in this same context, to seek to give

---

[3] Neither can nineteenth-century dress, for the same reason. Nor, for different reasons, can eighteenth-century dress, for though the age of white wigs would certainly have claimed that its dress enhanced the dignity of man's body, the artificiality and effeteness of its style is so alien to the spirit of Shakespeare that here again we should have the weakness of discord rather than the strength of concord.

the plays a modern slant amounts to a lack of fidelity to the text. To resort once again to the simile of a stone thrown into water, the imposition, on the literal meaning, of another meaning at the same level as itself, will arrest the natural flow of the ripples in the direction of transcendence. If Shakespeare "was not of an age but for all time" this does not mean that his plays can be twisted into line with the particular limitations of each successive age, least of all our own age which on the surface is so very remote from his ideals. If he was "for all time" and therefore of our age also, this is because he was an intellectual in the ancient sense of the word, with his eye on the universal, and because the universal is by definition always present, however little it may be in evidence. It was in virtue of his intellectuality that Shakespeare, unlike his contemporary dramatists, was able to escape from the prison of his own age into the universal world of Plato and St. Augustine. What therefore can be more perverse than to seek to imprison him in the particular limitations of our own age? Besides, a Shakespeare audience is composed of people who have chosen to come of their own free will, and who could have gone, if they had wanted, to a modern play instead. They are certainly not present because they are men and women of the twentieth century but because they are men and women; and it would not perhaps be far wrong to say that even if for the most part they are not fully conscious of it, they are present because they are men and women who have in them something that is in danger of being starved to death by the twentieth century.

Admittedly, even after the most modernist productions, many of the audience will leave the theater without any thought that they have wasted their time and their money—such is the excellence of Shakespeare the dramatist in the technical sense of this term. But the fact remains that if the production had been adequate, they would have left the theater overwhelmed, conscious of having had a great experience. What then is the ideal that a director should aim at? Is it not, beyond any doubt, that Shakespeare's text, followed with scrupulous fidelity, should make as strong an impact as possible upon the audience? This is what the audience wants above all, and it will of course depend mainly on the actors. Nonetheless, the director can help the actors immensely just as he can also—and today frequently does—hang millstones around their necks. A strong impact presupposes that what we see harmonizes perfectly with what we hear, for there can be no strength without unity. But to this obvious truth, which used to be the generally recognized guiding principle, a blind eye now tends to be turned more often than not. The cause is what might be called the "originality mania"[4] that has dominated Western art since the end of the First World War and that, for the last fifty years, has been overflowing into the theater.[5] As a result, the average director today—there are some exceptions—would much rather have his production reviewed as "an interesting experiment" than as being "somewhat unoriginal yet nonetheless deeply satisfying."

For the sake of unity and therefore of strength of impact, not only the dresses but also the setting must be in harmony with the spoken words. The medieval plays invite us to exploit the beauty of the Middle Ages, and within this framework there is endless scope for variety. The framework for *Antony and Cleopatra* is obvious, as also for *Julius Caesar*. *King Lear* and *Cymbeline* are set in pre-Christian Britain, but since the plays are chivalric in spirit, certain compromises and even anachronisms are arguably legitimate. Much the same applies to *A Midsummer Night's Dream* and *The Winter's Tale* which can be set in classical antiquity or at a somewhat later period.

To take one example, the part of Cordelia is very short in the first scene of *King Lear*, and almost the whole play has elapsed before we see her again. That second appearance is potentially a wonderful moment. For it to be so in the theater, however, the audience must have no doubts, when the curtain goes upon her, as to who this relative stranger is. But at least they know that Cordelia is Queen of France; and in a memorable performance of many years ago, she was immediately recognizable as such by the gold fleurs-de-lys with which her majestic blue cloak was brocaded—a most unjarring anachronism that one could only applaud.

---

[4] This malady is based on a monstrous perversion of the word originality. Rightly used, it signifies a going back to the original source of an earthly object, that is, to its spiritual archetype, its "idea" in the Platonic sense. True originality is thus inseparable from inspiration, both of which trace the same path from Heaven to earth by a vertical descent that is independent of horizontal borrowings, whence a marvelous freshness that is often likened to the purity of uncontaminated water drawn directly from a mountain spring. This virtue clearly confers a certain difference but not in the sense of divergence; today however the divergent or even the grotesque is hailed as "original"; and ironically, as a result of this perversion, any true originality that might now come into being would be unlikely to receive recognition as such, not being different enough from what has gone before. However that may be, the concern of actors and directors must surely be to allow the true originality of Shakespeare to manifest itself as clearly as possible and to avoid blurring it with "originalities" of their own devising.

[5] Until recently the opera house had escaped this overflow, but is now also in danger.

There is yet another element, already touched on briefly, that can be immeasurably enriching to a presentation of Shakespeare. Every director has at his disposal, or can have, that great treasury of music that Shakespeare himself knew and loved and that seems to have inspired much of his poetry. Nor can we do better, in this respect, than conform to the practice of the Elizabethan theater, even to the point of accompanying the plays with just the same music now as then.[7] This concerns not merely the songs but also the incidental music for broken consorts of recorders, viols, lutes, and drum. Shakespeare knew well that some of the most powerful effects of the theater are gained with the help of music, and he wrote on the understanding that he would be supported when necessary by a marvelous undercurrent of sound. The affinity between Shakespeare's plays and the music of his day is remarkably strong, for whatever features of ancient Greece and Rome the Renaissance may have discovered, it could not bring to a "rebirth" their music. Consequently, for want of a classical model on which to be re-molded, this was of all arts the least affected by the Renaissance; and so, like Shakespeare himself, the music of his day tended to be "behind the times." At any rate it is possible to choose out from it any number of pieces that lean back toward the Middle Ages as he did. In particular, he also seems to have had a special love for "old music."

For most of the plays the dance music, carefully chosen, is ideal, but in addition to the stately pavane, the basse dances and the gayer though no less profound galliards, a wide range of possibilities is offered by the instrumental fantasias or *ricercari,* enough to suit any occasion. In a word, the music that the poet may be supposed to have had in his head, if only in the back of his mind, when writing the plays is able, almost uniquely,[8] to enter into

---

[7] For the modern theater the music would no doubt have to be somewhat less in quantity. Clearly it must not be allowed to seem obtrusive, and in a play of such prolonged dramatic intensity as *King Lear,* for example, music can scarcely serve any purpose after the first scene, except for the occasional fanfare, until the end of Act IV where it plays a part of great importance when Lear is waking out of madness into sanity and into reunion with Cordelia.

[8] Not that it would be altogether impossible for some later composition to do the same or almost the same, but a far greater sensitivity would be needed to choose it. In this context it is perhaps not irrelevant to say that outside the theater it is always a pleasure to hear the best-known *Midsummer Night's Dream* music, for it is a work of genius. But in the theater it tends to limit the play, quite unable to do for it what Elizabethan music can do. To experience both the possibilities in question and to compare them is to realize amongst other things that the seventeen-year-old Mendelssohn's conception of fairies was much less transcendent than Shakespeare's.

them and blend with them—to melt into them, we might say—and to become an integral part of them, adding the impact of its own beauty to theirs, deepening them and being deepened by them, inspiring the actors to excel themselves, and making the audience doubly responsive. Moreover there is a great and growing interest in such music today,[9] no doubt far more than there has been for the last three centuries. How is it then that we so rarely have the pleasure of being overwhelmed in the theater by these "sounds and sweet airs that give delight and hurt not," and that we are almost invariably given instead some quite mediocre sounds especially composed for the occasion?[10]

Why so much about music, the reader may ask. Because in considering the different elements that go to make the impact of Shakespeare's plays upon the audience, this particular element, so persistently neglected today, is of an importance that can scarcely be overestimated.

> Therefore the poet
> Did feign that Orpheus drew trees, stones and floods,
> Since nought so stockish, hard, and full of rage,
> But music for the time doth change his nature. (*The Merchant of Venice*, V, 1, 79–82)

These last words anticipate our final chapter, for they reflect an acute consciousness, already in the young Shakespeare, of the original and traditional function of music, and therefore, implicitly, of art in its other forms. The true poet is able, through the impact of his plays, to exert such an effect on spectator and reader as "for the time doth change his nature"; and by repetition, with the help of other means, the temporary may become permanent.

---

[9] For what may serve as accompaniment to the plays, one obvious source is Atteignant's early sixteenth-century collection of dances. Another rich source, somewhat later, is the *Fitzwilliam Virginal Book*, but we should not hesitate to transcribe its contents for consorts, since most of this music is greatly enhanced by a certain interplay of instruments which it seems to call for, nor was it exclusively composed for the keyboard.

[10] A part answer to this question was given us by one of our leading theatrical directors, who writes: "I think that most people would prefer to have the music of Shakespeare's time... What happens is that when one asks someone to *arrange* the music, he begs so hard to be allowed to *compose* it that one usually takes the line of least resistance, and gives way."

CHAPTER FOURTEEN

The Mystery of Things

The Western world has been for so long under the spell of humanism, which Edmund (until he finally renounces it) personifies, that in some ways the bastard is better understood today than his legitimate elder brother Edgar, who personifies an outlook that is now remote. When modern man is faced with a typical medieval reaction he is sometimes rather at a loss. In *King Lear* the Duke of Albany, hearing that Cornwall has died of a wound he received from a servant when he was putting out Gloster's eyes, says:

> This shows you are above,
> You justicers, that these our nether crimes
> So speedily can venge! (IV, 2, 78–80)

and at the end, when he hears of the death of Goneril and Regan, he says:

> This judgement of the heavens, that makes us tremble,
> Touches us not with pity. (V, 3, 232–33)

A few moments previously Edgar, referring to his father's sin of adultery, has said to Edmund:

> The gods are just, and of our pleasant vices
> Make instruments to plague us:
> The dark and vicious place where thee he got
> Cost him his eyes.

Edmund endorses his brother's remark and adds, in connection with his own sins that their inevitable just punishment has come:

> Thou hast spoken right, 'tis true.
> The wheel is come full circle; I am here. (V, 3, 171–75)

At a cursory reading of the play these speeches are almost embarrassing to some of us. Our reaction is spontaneously rationalistic. We ask ourselves what is the meaning of these reiterated assertions that the gods are just. Can Shakespeare have forgotten for the moment that the world is full of injustice? Or is he simply making Edgar and Albany express a rather primitive and unintelligent point of view which he does not hold himself? The answer to both questions is certainly "No." Our medieval ancestors did not believe in chance. When a worldly event seemed just, they immediately recognized the workings of Providence. But their faith remained quite unruffled in the face of triumphant and prosperous wickedness, for they knew that any apparent injustices in this world would be made good in the next. The remarks of Albany and Edgar are simply spontaneous comments on events, equivalent to some ejaculation such as "Praise be to God." If they jar on the humanist, it is because he wrongly suspects an attempt to justify the ways of God to man. In other words he attributes to Albany and to Edgar something of a modern psychology, a sort of primitive rationalism, cruder and less fully developed than his own. He fails to realize how little store was set in the Middle Ages, despite all their dialectic, by logical proof.

Shakespeare, unlike Milton, had no illusions about his scope of reason. He knew that since reason is limited to this world it is powerless to "justify the ways of God." Milton may have known this in theory, but in practice he was very much a son of the Renaissance, very deeply under the spell of humanism. *Paradise Lost* cannot be called an intellectual poem. Milton portrays the next world by sheer force of human imagination. His God the Father, like Michelangelo's, is fabricated in the image of man; and the purely logical arguments that he puts into the mouth of God to justify His ways inevitably fail to convince us. Now Shakespeare also seeks to justify the ways of God to man. That is, beyond doubt, the essence of his purpose in writing. But his justification is on an intellectual plane, where alone it is possible; and this brings us back to the theme of his plays, for the intellect is none other than the lost faculty of vision that is symbolized by the Holy Grail and by the Elixir of Life.

In considering how Shakespeare conveys his message to us we must remember that the true function of art is not didactic. A great drama or epic may contain little or much teaching of a didactic kind, but it does not rely on that teaching in order to gain its ultimate effect. Its function is not so much to define spiritual wisdom as to give us a taste of that wisdom, each according to his capacity. We may quote in this connection a profound remark that has been made about sacred art in Christianity: "It sets up against the sermon which insists on what must be done by one who would become holy, a vision of the cosmos which is holy through its beauty; it makes men participate naturally and almost involuntarily in the world of holiness."[1] In its original context it is the great Norman and Gothic Cathedrals, the sanctuaries in which the sermon is preached, which immediately spring to mind as examples of art that reveals a vision of the cosmos. But drama can also yield such a vision; and to reveal the beauty and thereby the harmony of the universe is to justify the ways of God.

The first spectators of Shakespeare were probably more receptive than we are. We tend to take art less seriously than they did. For modern man the supreme distinction is between "fiction" and "truth," as we say, between art on the one hand and "reality" on the other. Now naturally our medieval ancestors made the same distinction, but for them it was not so sharp. They were not in the habit of speaking and thinking of life as "truth." By truth, by reality, they meant something different; for them the supreme distinction was not between life and art, but between the next world, that is, Truth, and this world, which is the shadow of Truth. The sharpness of that distinction took the edge off all other distinctions. Moreover, art for them was not merely a copy of life, that is, it was not merely the shadow of a shadow; it was also by inspiration, partly—and in some supreme cases even almost wholly— a direct copy or shadow of the "substance" itself. The distinction between art and life is therefore not so much between a shadow and a reality as between two shadows. This sounds exaggerated, and no doubt the divergence in outlook between then and now was far slighter for the vast major-

---

[1] Titus Burckhardt, *Sacred Art in East and West,* p. 46.

ity than might appear from what has just been said. But it went certainly further than a mere verbal quibble over the meaning of the word "reality," and it would have been enough to make an appreciable difference to the attitude of an audience toward a play. By attributing a less absolute reality to life they attributed more reality to art. They no doubt entered into it more wholeheartedly. But the difference is relative. We also can enter in. Let us consider what actually happens.

In life we have no view of the whole: we see only bits and pieces here and there, and our view is quite distorted. What is near to us we look at with feverish subjectivity; what is not near we look at with more or less cold objectivity. Above all we fail to see the pattern. It is as if life were a great piece of tapestry and as if we looked at it from the wrong side, where the pattern is obscured by a maze of threads, most of which seem to have no purpose. Now a play of Shakespeare's is like a much smaller piece of tapestry, partly copied from the other but also, in virtue of an aspect of what we call his secret, copied from the transcendent Original of the other, that Divine Harmony of which the temporal and spatial cosmos is a reflection, but of which it is merely a reflection, whence the superficial discords which, for fallen man, give the lie to the profound beauty of the image as a whole—a totality that he cannot see, being, by definition, cut off from the vision of it. The remarkable intensity of Shakespeare's copy is redoubled by the corresponding intensity of those who hear it and see it. The dramatist is highly privileged with a privilege that he shares with no other artist, except the composer of music, namely the extreme passivity of his audience. It is in the nature of things that people go to a play in the hope that they will be spellbound. Shakespeare holds out this smaller piece of tapestry to us in the theater, between ourselves and him. He is on the right side of it and we are again on the wrong side just as, unlike him, we are on the wrong side of the great tapestry of life. To begin with we look at the rather chaotic maze of threads with the same cold objectivity with which we view the threads of our neighbors' lives. But little by little, as the play goes on, we are drawn into it and become more and more bound up with its threads. Our cold objectivity vanishes and we feel the warmth of subjectivity. So it is with any dramatic piece, one may say. That is true; but with most drama what is the benefit to be gained? It is simply a question of exchanging one's ordinary subjectivity for another one that is no better and that may be worse. But when a drama is created as an image of the whole universe, and when the hero represents a great soul that is being purified of all its faults, and being developed toward the limits of human possibility, then it is no light thing to be drawn into the web of the tapestry and to become identified with its central figure. But that is not all: the purification of the hero is in view of an end. By the close of the play we have become objective once more, but with a higher objectivity that is completely different from the initial one; for Shakespeare has drawn us right through the tapestry and out at the other side, so that we now see it as it really is, a unity in which all the parts fit marvelously together to make up a perfect whole. Having been given a taste of the hero's purification we are now given one of the spiritual wisdoms to which it leads: and just as Shakespeare's small tapestry merges mysteriously with the great tapestry of life, so our view of the harmony and beauty of one is also, in a sense, a view of the harmony and beauty of the other. We "participate naturally and almost involuntarily in the world of holiness." It is only a momentary glimpse, and it does not last. But it does make an imprint upon the soul, which may not be easily effaced.

Shakespeare's being from the outset on the right side of the small tapestry he holds out to us in the theater is part of his secret as an artist; his being on the right side of the great tapestry of life is part of his secret as a man. This higher objectivity is directly mentioned by King Lear at the beginning of the last scene of the play. He is now almost at the end of the quest, and he imagines what it would mean to be altogether united with Cordelia who, according to the deeper meaning of the play, is herself a personification of the same objectivity that can, to use her own words, "outfrown false fortune's frown" (V, 3, 6). In an already quoted speech, the King says that they will live together in prison:

> And pray, and sing, and tell old tales, and laugh
> At gilded butterflies, and hear poor rogues
> Talk of court news; and we'll talk with them too,
> Who loses and who wins; who's in, who's out;
> And take upon's the mystery of things
> As if we were God's spies. (V, 3, 12–17)

Alone the eye of the intellect, the eye of the angels who are "God's spies," can perceive the justice of the workings of Providence. It is clearly from the standpoint of this higher objectivity that the maturer plays were written; and when at the end, having passed through the tapestry, we stand side by side with Shakespeare himself, we also for the moment have in a sense taken upon ourselves "the mystery of things."

Let us consider this in a slightly different way. The fall of man is represented traditionally as the acquisition of the knowledge of good and evil. The intellectual knowledge of Absolute Good is lost and is replaced by a purely mental knowledge that is only capable of grasping a relative good, that good which is the opposite of evil. We have thus the illusion that the devil is the opposite of God, whereas in reality nothing at all can stand in the scales against Divine Providence. In the course of *Othello,* for example, as also in the course of *King Lear,* Shakespeare has shown us the extremities of relative good and evil; but by the end it is as if for the moment he has taken out of our mouths the taste of the fruit of the Forbidden Tree. The knowledge of good and evil is there, but it no longer blinds us to the Absolute Good. We no longer ask ourselves that most difficult of all questions "Why does God allow evil?" for we have mysteriously felt the answer to it, where alone the answer lies, upon the plane of the intellect. We accept everything with serenity and would change nothing. We feel in an inexplicable way that all is well, not according to human justice which in any case is fragmentary, being largely based on ignorance, but according to "poetic justice," which is none other than Divine Justice. But it is not only sorrow that can work this wonder in us: just as we accept the endings of *Othello* and *King Lear,* so also we accept the endings of *Cymbeline* and *The Winter's Tale.* It is not the same with the happy endings of *Twelfth Night* and *As You Like It,* for example. Nor is the total effect of *Romeo and Juliet* comparable to that of the great tragedies. The best of the pre-*Hamlet* plays, *Romeo and Juliet* and *A Midsummer Night's Dream* included, have a total effect of undeniably exalting and peace-giving harmony, but this is something less transcendent than the harmony of the Universe itself, nor can it come near to making us forget "the knowledge of good and evil" or to justifying the ways of God.

But once he has succeeded in justifying those ways, Shakespeare does so not only once but again and again, which suggests that his own life was patterned upon the pattern of his plays, and that he was writing about what he himself knew. There is nothing really extravagant in such a claim, for according to the traditional conception of poetry, a poet should be no less than a seer, *vates*; and the Garden of Helicon, the abode of Apollo and the Muses, the only source of true poetic inspiration, is as Dante tells us none other than the Garden of Eden, where grows the Tree of Life whose fruit is the only antidote to the poison of the knowledge of good and evil.

Always allowing that there are many different degrees of being inspired, the explanation of what Shakespeare is able to do to us can only lie in his inspiration or, if one prefers it, in his intellectuality, which according to the true sense of the word really amounts to the same. It is certainly not a mere question of the power of language, neither is it merely a question of the feelings of pity and terror, as might be concluded from Aristotle's all too inexplicit references to catharsis. The verse of Webster's *Duchess of Malfi* is fine enough, like that of Shelley's *Cenci;* nor are the elements of pity and terror lacking, to say the least. Yet these two plays leave us rather with feelings of horror than with visionary acceptance and serenity. The key to what Aristotle meant by catharsis lies above all in the example he gives, and it is clear from this that the "purification" in question is no less than what has been described here in other terms, for the effect upon us of Sophocles' *Oedipus* is in fact essentially the same as that of *King Lear.*

Many secondary features of Shakespeare's plays suggest that the poet had power to draw upon the transcendent. Characters like Hamlet and Cleopatra for example are not so much fabrications as "creations." There is something almost miraculously alive about them as if they had been brought down ready-made from above. An analogous remark could be made about his coining of words.[2] Created also rather than fabricated are the worlds in which the plays are set: each is like a unique sphere of existence with its own atmosphere that makes it quite distinct from all the other Shakespearean macrocosms. But contact with a transcendent source is above all suggested by the constant repetition of a transcendent total effect. That contact is a secret, for it belongs to the domain of the Mysteries; but the true and original purpose of art—the primal reason for its existence—is precisely to communicate secrets, not by blurting them out but by offering them as it were with half-open hand, by bringing them near and inviting us to approach.

It is generally agreed that in *The Tempest,* Prospero's magic, aside from its other meanings, is intended to represent Shakespeare's own powers as an artist; and truly inspired art is indeed a kind of white magic that casts a spell over us and momentarily changes us doing as it were the impossible and making us quite literally excel ourselves, as if we were God's spies.

---

[2]See p. 96, note 9.

BIBLIOGRAPHY

Al-Farid, Umar ibn. "al-Khamriyyah." In *Sufi Poems*, by Martin Lings. Cambridge: Islamic Texts Society, 2004.

Alighieri, Dante. *Dante's Il Convivio*. Translated by Richard H. Lansing. London: Taylor & Francis, 1990.

Arnold, Paul. "Esotérisme de Shakespeare." *Mercure de France* (1955): 130–39 and 60–61.

Burckhardt, Titus. *Alchemy: science of the cosmos, science of the soul*. Translated by William Stoddart. London: Stuart & Watkins, 1967.

———. *Chartres: And the Birth of the Cathedral*. Indiana: World Wisdom, 1995.

———. *Sacred Art in East and West: Its Principles and Methods*. Kentucky: Fons Vitae, 1992.

Denton, Michael. *Evolution: A Theory in Crisis*. Bethesda, Maryland: Adler & Adler, 1986.

Dewar, Douglas. *The Transformist Illusion*. Tennessee: Dehoff Publications, 1957.

Guénon, René. *Aperçus sur l'Initiation*. France: Editions traditionnelles, 1992.

———. *L'Esotérisme de Dante*. Paris: Gallimard, 1957.

————. *The Great Triad.* Louisville, Kentucky: Quinta Essentia, 1991.

Lings, Martin. *Ancient Beliefs and Modern Superstitions.* London: Archtype, 2004.

————. *The Eleventh Hour: The Spiritual Crisis of the Modern World in the Light of Tradition and Prophesy.* London: Archetype, 2002.

Paris, Jean. *Shakespeare.* France: Seuil, 1981.

Perry, Whitall. *A Treasury and Traditional Wisdom.* Louisville, Kentucky: Quinta Essentia, 1991.

Pitman, Michael. *Adam and Evolution: A Scientific Critique of Neo-Darwinism.* London: Rider, 1984.

Ruysbroek, Jan Van. *The Adornment of the Spiritual Marriage: The Sparkling Stone & The Book of Supreme Truth.* Translated by C. A. Wynschenk Dom. Paris: Ibis Press, 2005.

Schuon, Frithjof. *Esoterism as Principle and as Way.* New York: Harper Perennial, 1982.

————. *The Essential Writings of Frithjof Schuon.* Edited by Seyyed Hossein Nasr. Australia: Element Books, 1991.

————. *The Transcendent Unity of Religions.* New York: Harper and Row, 1984.

Shute, Evan. *Flaws in the Theory of Evolution.* London: Temside Press, 1961.

Wilson, Dover. *The Fortunes of Falstaff.* Cambridge: Cambridge University Press, 1964.

INDEX

ABOUT THE AUTHOR

Martin Lings was born in 1909 in Burnage, Lancashire, England. As he grew, he studied English at a public school in that area as well as in the United States, where his father often traveled and worked. Lings attended Clifton College in Bristol, becoming Head Boy before studying English literature at Magdalen College of Oxford University, where he became student and then close friend to famous author and scholar, C. S. Lewis.

Lings taught in several universities in Europe before becoming a lecturer on Anglo-Saxon and Middle English. He traveled to Egypt in 1939 to visit a friend and decided to stay. Also at that time, he completed the conversions that he had been undergoing from Protestant to Atheist and finally to Islam.

In Egypt, he became an English professor at the University of Cairo, where he had an annual production of a Shakespeare play, which quickly became the highlight of his year. His love of Shakespeare inspired those around him to read and study Shakespeare's work. In 1952, funding was cut for the British University staff in Egypt, and Lings was forced to move back to London.

Back in London, Lings received various degrees for his work in Arabic and African studies, leading to his writing of *A Sufi Saint of the Twentieth*

Century, published in 1961. He joined the British Museum in 1955, where he was made assistant keeper of oriental printed books and manuscripts. He was promoted to keeper in 1970, and that same year, he also began performing those tasks at the British Library. In 1966, he published *Shakespeare in the Light of Sacred Art*, the first edition of the now titled *Shakespeare's Window into the Soul*.

From that time on, he wrote constantly and published books on a variety of topics, including his internationally acclaimed biography of Muhammad (1983) and his book *Symbol and Archetype: A Study of the Meaning of Existence* (1991), which shows symbolism to be present in all things, such as numbers, colors, senses and elements. After writing and publishing eighteen books, Martin Lings died on May 12, 2005, at his home in Westerham, Kent County, England, at the age of 96.

BOOKS OF RELATED INTEREST

Muhammad
His Life Based on the Earliest Sources
by Martin Lings

Shakespeare and the Ideal of Love
by Jill Line

Meditations on the Soul
Selected Letters of Marsilio Ficino
Edited by Clement Salaman

A Mystical Key to the English Language
by Robert M. Hoffstein

Harmonies of Heaven and Earth
Mysticism in Music from Antiquity to the Avant-Garde
by Joscelyn Godwin

The Hermetic Tradition
Symbols and Teachings of the Royal Art
by Julius Evola

The Biology of Transcendence
A Blueprint of the Human Spirit
by Joseph Chilton Pearce

Radical Knowing
Understanding Consciousness through Relationship
by Christian de Quincey

Inner Traditions • Bear & Company
P.O. Box 388
Rochester, VT 05767
1-800-246-8648
www.InnerTraditions.com

Or contact your local bookseller